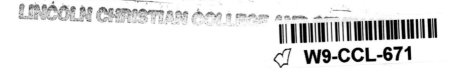
The Unauthorized Guide
to Choosing a Church

The Unauthorized Guide to Choosing a Church

Carmen Renee Berry

Brazos Press
A Division of Baker Book House Co
Grand Rapids, Michigan 49516

Published by Brazos Press
a division of Baker Book House Company
P.O. Box 6287, Grand Rapids, MI 49516-6287
www.brazospress.com

Printed in the United States of America

Published in association with the literary agency of Alive Communications, Inc., 7680 Goddard Street, Suite 200, Colorado Springs, Colorado 80920.

Library of Congress Cataloging-in-Publication Data
Berry, Carmen Renee
   The unauthorized guide to choosing a church . Carmen Renee Berry.
       p.   cm.
   Includes bibliographical references and index.
   ISBN 1-58743-036-3 (pbk.)
   1. Christian sects. I Title.
BR157 .B47 2003
280—dc21   2002154568

To the memory of my grandfather,
Reverend Earl Powell,
whose devotion to God and passion for books
shaped my life beyond measure.

Contents

Part 3 A Few Items to Help Make More Sense of It All

Acknowledgments

"I started going to church," I said to my agent, Kathy Helmers one day on the phone. After a moment of stunned silence, Kathy exclaimed, "You should write a book on that!" So I did. As a consequence, Kathy is first in line for my gratitude—for proposing a great idea and for finding the perfect publisher for the project. Kathy, you're the bestest.

Second, I want to thank the Souled Out ministry team—Perry, Jennifer and Katerina Moore, Joel, Priscilla and John Geddes, Chris Adams, Glenn Ness, Craig and Linda Bunch, Roy Dyche, Charmaigne Reed, Steve Travato, Bill Pierson, Jeff and Lori McVay, and JP Ellmore. The prayer team holds a special place in my heart—Deborah, Tammy, and Pierson. In addition, I want to express my admiration and appreciate to those who survived the PazNaz bruhaha—Jim and Lynnie Martindale, Mike and Wendy Schoonover, Sam and Kristi Fowler, Howie, Dianne, and Faye Briggs, Wayne and Glenda Blacklock, Curt and Kathy Gibson, Mark and Darlene Sanford, Dick Pritchard, Anne and Warren Rood, Eleana Smith, and Brenda Zimmerman. You guys restored my faith in "church." I'm in much better shape spiritually than before I met you all.

Special thanks goes to Rev. Michael Platter, Rev. Mark Sanford, and Daniel Psaute for giving freely of their ideas, many of which shaped the structure of this book. I am grateful to Mike and Dan, who went beyond the call of duty by reviewing portions of the manuscript and letting me steal their best ideas.

A big thank you goes to Rev. Jeff McVay and Lori McVay who put in hours researching information and confirming details in the manuscript. Plus, they usually brought in dinner so I didn't waste away while obsessing on the project, and they always made me laugh. Thanks, you two, I couldn't have done this without you.

Another indispensable person to this project, and to my very survival, is Marianne Croonquist, my assistant. Not only did she make thousands of phone calls to denominational headquarters to track down data, she made sure my cats were fed, my phone calls returned, and my mail retrieved. She makes my life work.

My mother, Mary Ellen Berry, deserves all the gratitude I can muster for being such a great mom. She's savvy, insightful, encouraging, and amazingly funny. If you ever meet her, you'll understand why I am the way I am. (Mom, I mean that as a compliment . . . really.)

I am grateful to all my friends—at least those who continued to be my friends even though I disappeared for nearly six months while working on this project—Bob Myers, Cathy Smith, Bob Parsons, Joel Miller, Pat Luehrs, Rene Chansler, Cynthia Bell, Lynn Barrington, Gail Walker, JoAnne Montana, Sandee Foster, Kristin Decker, Renee Lonner, Roger Marum, Irene Flores, Kathleen Fitzgerald, Carolyn Rafferty, Ruth Porter, Joe and Sheila Palacios, Colleen Sutton, Marsha McCarville, and the entire Police clan—Alice, Robin, Peter, Jeanne, Tom, Wren, Will, Lou, and Carol. Thanks to my support group—Carolyn Thacker, Cindy McRoskey, Amanda Kennedy, Donna Goodman, and Suzanne Baker—for being a sounding board and source of encouragement. And, of course, I'm thankful for Roy M. Carlisle, my friend, fan, and a source of endless ideas.

An enthusiastic exclamation of gratitude goes to the deserving Brazos team: Rodney Clapp, editorial director, Rebecca Cooper, managing editor and Brian Brunsting, designer. This book is the most complicated and challenging I've ever worked on—in content and layout. Trust me when I say that Rodney, Rebecca, and Brian should be nominated for sainthood for their patience alone. (I've been told I'm a bit demanding . . .) Thank you for your diligence, creativity, and perseverance.

Appreciation for providing current data goes to:

American Baptist Convention—Dr. Ivan George, Department of Professional Registry and Rev. Valentine Royal, Office of Women in Ministry

American Methodist Episcopal Zion Church—Beth Shalken

Assemblies of God—Sherri Doty, Statistician

Christian Church (Disciples of Christ)—Curtis Miller, Executive Director of Communication Ministries

Church of the Nazarene—Laura Lance, Research Center

Episcopal Church—Charles P. Clark, Manager of Parochial Report Systems and Sally Sedgewick, Acting Coordinator for Women's Ministry

Evangelical Lutheran Church in America—David Alderfer, Director for Roster and Statistics

Greek Orthodox Church in America—Bishop Savas of Troas and Father Seraphim

International Church of the Foursquare Gospel—Dr. Ronald Williams, Communications Officer

Lutheran Church, Missouri Synod—Scott Kostencki, Business Analyst

Mennonite Church, USA—James Horsch, Editor

National Association of Free Will Baptists—Jack Williams, Executive Assistant

Presbyterian Church USA—Kris Valcrius, Manager for OGA Reports

Roman Catholic Church—Nancy Patterson, Archives Records Management Specialist

The Salvation Army—Lt. Col. Tom Jones, National Community Relations and Development Secretary

Southern Baptist—John Revell, Conventions Relations

United Church of Christ—Ronald Buford, Manager of Marketing and Public Relations

United Methodist Church—Miss Gray, UMC Information Services Consultant

VineyardUSA—Cyndie Norwood, Receptionist

Part 1

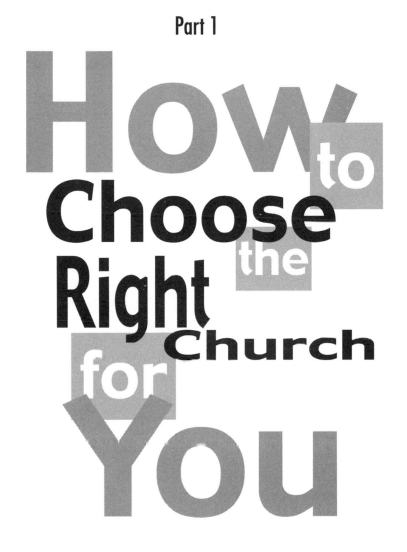

How to
Choose
the
Right
Church
for
You

one

What Does Church Have to Do with Spirituality?

I'm one of the fortunate ones.

Sure, I was raised in a very strict Christian home with mandatory church attendance (Sunday mornings, Sunday nights, Tuesday night Bible study, Wednesday night prayer meeting, vacation Bible school, choir practice, and all special events). And yes, as an adolescent I grew weary of the foibles of my denomination, having plenty of opportunity to observe the inconsistencies of a lot of flawed people who never quite lived up to their stated beliefs. But my parents made a distinction between having a faith in God and doing the church thing. As I questioned what I believed and how I wanted to practice my faith, I didn't feel compelled to throw out the baby (God) with the bathwater (the church). I envisioned my faith in God as a different issue from my church affiliation. As a young adult,

I kept God (or God kept me), but I had nothing much to do with or much good to say about the church.

I wasn't the only one to view spirituality—personally held beliefs about how the universe works and about how we fit into the grand design—as a private affair. Resistance to opening up our treasured convictions to outside criticism or instruction may motivate some to steer clear of organized spiritual gatherings altogether. And who isn't aware of the misconduct, even injustice, perpetrated over the ages by organized religion? The Crusades, the Spanish Inquisition, burning heretics at the stake, to say nothing of how TV evangelists can make one's skin crawl—who would want to be a part of that?

I set out on my own spiritual path, unwilling to belong to a group of Christians. Over the years, I met a variety of "believers"—incense burners and Bible thumpers; charismatic hand wavers, twelve-steppers, and genuflecters; priests, pastors, and prayer warriors; militant social justice demonstrators and right-wing activists; and lots of theologians who were straight, gay, male, female, fighting for purity, and fed up with the status quo—a varied spectrum of people all living under the umbrella of the "church." I've listened to, and argued with, them all.

What have I discovered? God is still God, and people are as flawed as ever. Nothing much has changed there except my interpretation of these truths. Where human frailty once served as a reason for me to withdraw from the church, with its unruly and divergent congregants, this is now what compels me back to spiritual community. I had overlooked one essential factor—that I am as finite and flawed as everyone else.

Granted, we've complicated the church thing over the years, creating elaborately tiered, contentious institutions that require enormous effort to maintain. But that's not what participating in a Christian spiritual community, in the purest sense, is about. Jesus said, "where two or three come together in my name, there am I with them" (Matt.

18:20). This spiritual truth extends beyond how God relates to each of us individually or how misguided we can be once we get organized.

The fact remains that spirituality is nurtured and expanded when we meet in a group. Philip Yancey writes in *Church: Why Bother?* "Whenever I abandon church for a time, I find that I am the one who suffers. My faith fades, and the crusty shell of lovelessness grows over me again. I grow colder rather than hotter. And so my journeys away from the church have always circled back inside." We need each other.

Anne Lamott tells this story in her book, *Traveling Mercies*:

. . . There would be different pastors along the way, none of them exactly right for us until a few years ago when a tall African-American woman named Veronica came to lead us. She has huge gentle doctor hands, with dimples where the knuckles should be, like baby's fists. She stepped into us, the wonderful old worn pair of pants that is St. Andrew, and they fit. She sings to us sometimes from the pulpit and tells us stories of when she was a child. She told us this story just the other day: When she was about seven, her best friend got lost one day. The little girl ran up and down the streets of the big town where they lived, but she couldn't find a single landmark. She was very frightened. Finally a policeman stopped to help her. He put her in the passenger seat of his car, and they drove around until she finally saw her church. She pointed it out to the policeman, and then she told him firmly, "You could let me out now. This is my church, and I can always find my way home from here."

And that is why I have stayed so close to mine—because no matter how bad I am feeling, how lost or lonely or frightened, when I see the faces of the people at my church, and hear their tawny voices, I can always find my way home.

I continue to experience my faith in God as a personal relationship between the two of us. However, having admitted my commonality with the human race, I find that my faith does not flourish in isolation. As much as I hate to admit it, my faith is enhanced and enlarged when in relationship to other less-than-perfect human beings. Even though at times other Christians can be quite annoying, I feel very fortunate to have found my way back to a spiritual community that puts up with me even when I'm a bit annoying myself.

My reasons for belonging to a spiritual community will not necessarily be your reasons, but this book will help you figure out why you'd

> **"** Doing **church** is simply getting together with one or more other **people** to share the journey of faith. **"**

want to go to church in the first place, and then help you find a congregation best suited to your needs. Or you may have already found a church home but are curious about other approaches to worship. Maybe you're fed up with organized denominations and want to find a local community church that suits your needs. Perhaps you've been invited to attend a wedding or christening or other ceremony at a friend's church and you want to be clear on what to expect and how to behave yourself. No matter why you may enter into a worship service for the first time, you'll find here tips on how to dress, the terms that will be used, and what various religious symbols mean. You'll also learn how to deal with the limitations of a group of people, albeit well meaning, who are nevertheless flawed and prone to making mistakes. But then, that's the point of church, isn't it? We're all in need of God's grace and the support of each other.

Doing church is simply getting together with one or more other people to share the journey of faith. This shared journey meets different needs. Some look to churches for moral guidance—especially important to parents raising their children in our world of uncertain change and moral ambiguity. Others find church a unique opportunity to be of service and to share collective resources unavailable to a single individual. Emotional support and social contacts motivate some, while others are intrigued by studying the Scriptures and exploring doctrine and theology. Sharing the sacraments as an encounter with

How Do **Christians** Multiply?
By Dividing.

God draws thousands to corporate worship on a regular basis, while songs of praise accompanied by a guitar or two attract others. Some resonate with traditions that have withstood the test of time, feeling a part of a long line of believers. And there are those who enjoy being on the cutting edge of spiritual transformation and growth, impassioned by a vision of a changing, more responsive church. Perhaps there are as many reasons to do church as there are people in pews.

Here are at least ten reasons you might want to get involved in a church:

❶ Expressing your love for God through worship
❷ Being grounded in tradition
❸ Having a sense of belonging and receiving support in times of crisis
❹ Being obedient to God by honoring the Lord's Day
❺ Having a basis for moral behavior
❻ Learning about God and spirituality
❼ Being involved with music, drama, and worship
❽ Contributing to others through ministry and service

9 Finding peers and social contacts for yourself and your children

10 Having somewhere to share your doubts, triumphs, and day-to-day experiences

ₐDenomination
By Any Other Name Would **Smell** As Sweet

Not all of the churches described here like to be called denominations. Technically, a denomination is a single legal and administrative body overseeing a number of local congregations, so those that don't fit in this category take exception to the term.

For example, the Roman Catholic and Orthodox Churches don't see themselves as denominations—they each see themselves as **the** church. Another group that resists the denominational label are churches associated together as "conventions." Mostly comprised of Baptist churches, conventions do not have administrative authority over the local churches. The autonomy of the individual congregation is highly valued and part of their treasured history.

Perhaps the most unwilling churches to be referred to as denominations would be those who openly identify themselves as "nondenominational." (How much more explicit could that be?) Nondenominational churches, whether they meet in large auditoriums or private homes, are adamant about not being lumped in with denominational churches. Often, as nondenominational churches grow in experience, they band together in loose associations.

Having acknowledged all these nuances and admitting that some are very significant, I will be using the term "denomination" in a generic, nontechnical sense—as a group of churches affiliated with one another in some way. It's just easier that way.

If any of these reasons strike a chord with you, you might want to check them. In addition, jot down other reasons you're interested in becoming a part of a spiritual community:

_____

_____

So Many Denominations, So Little Time

In my phone book, there are fifty-two denominations, associations, and conventions listed, and under each are dozens of local congregations. With approximately 235 churches in my area, it would take me five years of Sundays to visit each one only once. If I narrowed the list down to churches I could walk to, I'd still have eight to choose from. How can I tell which denomination I'd feel comfortable with, let alone select a specific church to attend? Toss a coin? Throw a dart at the phone book? Throw a dart at the next Christian who starts a new church?

It's easy to be dazed and confused by all the options, but there is hope (and with this guide, you might cut five years off your search). While I can't tell you which specific congregation to attend, I can help you sort through the liturgy, the lingo, and the lunacy. In some churches, people stand up and wave their hands in the air whenever they want to, in others

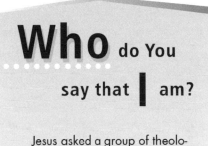

Who do You

say that **I** am?

Jesus asked a group of theologians who they believed him to be. They answered, "You are the eschatological manifestation of the ground of our being, the *kerygma* in which we find ultimate meaning, the leap into the impenetrable unknown."

And Jesus said, "Huh?"

that's a no-no and you're expected to stand, sit, and kneel as an synchronized unit. Some pastors wear hoods and flashy robes while others show up in jeans and T-shirts. You may have wondered what the Eucharist, Communion, and the Lord's Supper have in common, and which churches encourage you to join in the festivities and which don't. To help sort through the menagerie, you'll find some categories to understand what a church is all about.

What is a Heretic?

In some ways, you could say that church history is also a record of heresies, because many of the church's creeds, statements of faith and denominational splits were in response to real or imagined heresies. Technically, a heretic isn't someone who simply has a difference of opinion (although often people were persecuted solely on their beliefs). Nor is a heretic someone who is mistaken or confused (who isn't?). A heretic, in the true sense of the word, is someone who comes up with his or her own ideas that are in opposition to "orthodox" teaching, and then actively persuades others to alter their beliegs, thereby dividing the church.

Who is a teacher of the truth and who is a heretic can depend on one's perspective. One church's heretic may be another church's founder. Protestants were seen as heretics because they disagreed with Roman Catholicism, actively persuaded others to alter their beliefs, and, intentionally or unintentionally, split the church. On the other hand, Protestants accused Roman Catholics of being heretics by distorting the original truths of Scripture through tradition. And the Orthodox think we're all heretical. According to someone's standards, you're a heretic. And if you changed your beliefs, someone else would find your new views heretical. You can't please everyone.

More of a reference guide than a read-from-beginning-to-end kind of book, this book is designed to explain in normal English what various Christian churches are about. A number of denominations are reviewed so that you can get an idea of the big picture—such as why a particular denomination was set up in the first place, what do these people believe in now, or what to expect so you don't stick out like a sore thumb when you visit for the first time.

As much as I can, I will acknowledge my personal biases, which are many. I was raised in the Church of the Nazarene and have been shaped (and here and there misshapen) by that experience. I've also attended services in nearly every Christian group listed in this book at some point in my life. With this as a backdrop, I need to clarify the criteria I used to pick the churches included here.

First, I narrowed my focus to those I view as distinctly Christian. This is not to say that every individual who attends the churches listed here, or even all of the clergy, share my view of what it means to be a Christian. Nor am I saying you have to agree with me to be a follower of Christ. I do believe that Christianity is unique in asserting that God became one of us in the person of Jesus—that Jesus was both divine and human simultaneously. This claim is paradoxical, to be sure, but the heart of Christianity nevertheless. No other spiritual path makes such a claim. Jesus said, "I am the way, the truth and the life. No one comes to the Father except through me" (John 14:6).

Making such a statement in this age of pluralism can ruffle some feathers and smack of exclusionism. In a turbulent world where religious fanaticism can prove deadly, it may be tempting to smooth out any differences and focus solely on the common elements held among all world religions. However, respecting our differences is only possible when our differences are acknowledged. Anyone open to understanding and respecting the Christian tradition is challenged to take into account the significant and mind-boggling view of Christ as both God and human.

Consequently, I draw a somewhat arbitrary line in the denominational sand. I believe that any of the denominations described in this guide can support and strengthen your spiritual development as a sincere follower of Christ. But please don't assume the denominations left out can't simply because they're not listed. Including every Christian group is impossible due to space constraints (there are two hundred and fifty Lutheran denominations alone).

Which brings me to my second criterion—I focus on denominations that represent broad theological and historical movements. Even though all of these churches share a respect and reverence for Jesus, they differ widely in how they live out their view of Christ. The reason there are so many churches to choose from is that there is a great deal of disagreement among Christians about what to believe and how faith should be practiced. Let's face it, Jesus may have preached a gospel of love and forgiveness, but his followers have had a hard time getting along with each other (or anyone else who disagrees with us, for that matter). That's the bad news.

The good news is that now there are so many approaches to worship, you'll probably find one in which you can grow. Take time to find a good fit. There's no reason for you to invest in a congregation where the teaching constantly rubs you the wrong way, you're tempted to wear ear plugs during the music, it takes all your strength to stay awake during the homily, or you feel perpetually unfulfilled spiritually. Neither theology nor history lend themselves to neat and tidy categories, but I've done my best to capture the essentials of each denomination— poked a little fun at them all and hopefully been fair about what they have to offer.

Faith Survey

Let's start with focusing on where you are at this point in your spiritual journey. Being aware of what you believe will help you line up your convictions with those of a particular church. To that end, take the following short quiz. If appropriate, check more than one answer for each question, and fill in additional thoughts you may have. There's nothing scientific about this survey. It's simply intended as a springboard for you to ponder your own hot buttons, pockets of doubt, and personal preferences.

1. God:
   - ☐ is a Being who relates to me personally
   - ☐ is a Being who relates to humankind as a whole, but not to me personally
   - ☐ is the unifying energy of the universe
   - ☐ is a mystery no one can know
   - ☐ expects me to behave and, if I don't, will punish me
   - ☐ really loves me
   - ☐ is confusing to me and I'm not sure what I believe right now.
   - ☐ other:

   _____

   _____

2. Jesus Christ
   - ☐ is God in the flesh who was raised from the dead
   - ☐ is a special human being who was raised from the dead
   - ☐ is a special human being who taught important spiritual truths, but who was not raised from the dead
   - ☐ is significant, but I'm not sure how
   - ☐ is a transcendent concept found in most religions, not just Christianity
   - ☐ was a good teacher, on par with Buddha or Mohammed
   - ☐ other:

   _____

   _____

3. The Bible
- ☐ is the Word of God and should be interpreted literally
- ☐ is the Word of God and should be interpreted contextually
- ☐ is a collection of stories written by people who believed they encountered God
- ☐ is a collection of stories, myths, and fairy tales
- ☐ is an interesting read, but I'm not sure what I believe about it
- ☐ other:

_____

_____

4. To encounter God:
- ☐ one must have faith in Jesus alone
- ☐ one must have faith in Jesus and demonstrate faith through actions
- ☐ one must adhere to the teachings of the church
- ☐ one must participate in the sacraments
- ☐ one must do the best one can to live a moral life
- ☐ one must follow a spiritual path, but Christianity is not the only way to God
- ☐ I have no idea how to relate to God.
- ☐ other:

_____

_____

5. The Holy Spirit:
- ☐ is God's living Spirit on earth
- ☐ gives each believer at least one spiritual gift
- ☐ is revealed through signs such as healing, speaking in tongues, and being slain in the spirit
- ☐ is overemphasized in some churches
- ☐ empowers believers to live in faith
- ☐ seems a bit spooky to me
- ☐ other:

_____

_____

6. The sacraments:
- ☐ are central to experiencing my faith
- ☐ are symbolic and central to my faith
- ☐ aren't central to my faith
- ☐ What in the world are sacraments?
- ☐ other:

_____

_____

7. I want a church that:
- ☐ has clear guidelines for morality and takes a stand for what is right
- ☐ is flexible about morality issues and accepts a wide range of behaviors
- ☐ expects members to submit to the teachings and guidance of the pastor
- ☐ encourages members to question or disagree with the pastor and make their own personal decisions
- ☐ clearly states a political agenda (whether right, left, or whatever) and is active in the community to bring about social and legislative change
- ☐ refuses to align the church with a specific or partisan political agenda
- ☐ expects me to actively participate in church activities and community
- ☐ other:

_____

_____

8. I feel most comfortable in worship services:
- ☐ that are highly structured with inspiring liturgy and steeped in tradition
- ☐ that are filled with classical choral and organ music
- ☐ that utilize liturgical dance, drama, and other creative forms of worship
- ☐ with a wide variety of musical styles
- ☐ with a contemporary worship band, consisting of guitars, drums, and keyboard
- ☐ where we sing traditional hymns, like "Amazing Grace"

☐ that are loosely structured so the Holy Spirit guides
☐ where I'm left alone in my own thoughts
☐ where I can participate in group worship and prayer
☐ other:

_____

_____

9. When I pray,
☐ I envision talking to God the Father
☐ I envision talking to Jesus Christ
☐ I envision talking to the Holy Spirit
☐ I'm not sure who, if anyone, is listening
☐ other:

_____

_____

10. In figuring out what I believe:
☐ I rely solely on what the church teaches
☐ I place a great deal of importance on my personal experience
☐ the Bible is the one and only authority
☐ if it doesn't make sense to me, I don't buy it
☐ there's a great deal that confuses me and I simply take it on faith
☐ I check my beliefs against several check points including Scripture, personal experience, feedback from other believers, and tradition
☐ other:

_____

_____

Add anything else that comes to mind regarding your beliefs and how you want to express your faith.

Does **Size** matter?

There's no way of telling, by size alone, whether a congregation is spiritually healthy or the right place for you to worship. Small, medium, and large churches may teach the same truths and foster spiritual maturity, and churches of any size can be dysfunctional and dangerous. It's estimated that only 1 percent of churches today have more than 700 members. Over 50 percent have 100 or fewer regular attenders. Megachurches, those boasting of at least 2,000 members with some at 20,000 plus, are popping up all over the country. Each size of church has benefits and dangers.

Smaller Churches

Since smaller churches are the norm in America, you will find a wide variety to choose from. Also, a number of small-church movements are gaining popularity, offering worship in homes as "cells" of an institutional church or simply a small church like the one that meets down the street from where you live. These movements are promoting the benefits of small congregations, claiming to model themselves more closely to the early church than larger affiliations. For more information about their beliefs and how to locate a congregation in your area, contact House Church Central at www.hccentral.com, Network of Open Church Ministries at www.openchurch.com, or Cell Church International at www.cellchurchint.co.za/

The benefits of small churches are many. They can provide members with a strong sense of belonging and a place to serve. You'll probably have the opportunity to get to know most everyone in the congregation and may be able to develop deeper relationships than in a larger spiritual community. If you miss a service, you can be assured you'll be missed. Dangers of a small congregation include the possibly becoming an exclusive clique, having limited resources for services and programs, and having the leadership stuck in a rut.

Megachurches

On the other end of the continuum are megachurches where thousands worship weekly. Large churches tend to be seen as "user friendly," providing a variety of smaller subgroups such as young married couples, teenagers, people in recovery, adult singles, or senior adults. With more financial resources, these churches may provide a gymnasium, day-care centers, elementary and high schools, health services, recovery groups, seminars, concerts, and counseling centers—a one-stop spiritual center. There's something for everyone in the family, a place to serve and socialize. Dangers of a large church include getting lost in the crowd, mistaking glitz with genuine spiritual depth, and leadership that may judge success by the numbers instead of the genuine ministry taking place.

Two of the most well-known megachurches are Willow Creek Community Church in Illinois and Saddleback Church in Southern California. Willow Creek started out in the early 1970s with a handful of students, and today over 17,000 people attend weekend services. Under the leadership of Bill Hybels, the church is developing the Willow Creek Association that now has over 7,200 churches in affiliation. For more information, contact www.willowcreek.org.

Saddleback Church in Lake Forest, California, stresses a casual atmosphere, upbeat music, and practical messages to its 15,000 weekly attenders. Pastor and author Rick Warren promotes the concept of the purpose-driven church. Along with selling over a million copies of his book, *The Purpose-Driven Church*, Warren has facilitated the training of more than 175,000 church leaders in his principles. Saddleback Church can be contacted at www.saddleback.org.

Middle-Size Churches

Churches in the middle range can provide some of the programs available in megachurches but are still small enough to notice if you play hooky. Many offer programs for children, youth, adults, and seniors, but not quite as elaborate as those in megachurches. The dangers of middle-size churches are those besetting smaller and larger churches—developing meaningful relationships with other members, getting caught up in program rather than spiritual growth, and taking pride in numbers rather than quality of ministry.

Take a look at your personal needs and those of your family. As a good friend of mine, Lynnette Martindale, said, "If our church doesn't meet the needs of every member of my family, it won't work for any of us." Find a spiritual home that is big enough or small enough to nurture all involved.

Personal Needs Survey

In addition to the content of your theological beliefs, locating the right church for you is influenced by your personal needs. A congregation may teach all the right doctrine in your estimation but be wholly unsuitable for you due to age, marital status, or racial background.

Age

What we need from a church body differs depending on our age. We all need peers with whom we can share our lives, and at specific times in our lives we may need extra support. A lot has been written about the various generations—Baby Boomers, Gen Xers, Millennials, etc. I have found that the most helpful distinction involves whether you look at the world through a pre- or post-World War II lens. Those who were born before World War II had to grow up quickly and tend to have more respect for authority. If you're in this age group, you're probably an older adult who would benefit from a strong network of senior adults. Plus, you may be more comfortable in traditional style worship services.

Those born after World War II are often referred to as postmodern. If you're a Baby Boomer, you'll have to decide for yourself if you're modern or postmodern. Gen Xers are definitely postmodern and place a high value on relationships and equitable power sharing, and may view their pastor more as a coach than a spiritual authority. Most people in this category are drawn to either end of the worship continuum—toward liturgical or contemporary worship styles, usually avoidant of traditional services.

How many postmodernists does it take to change a lightbulb?

Each and every one of us.

If you're a parent, the ages of your children will also come into play. For many, a church is a family experience where both parents and children find safe, nurturing relationships. This may be especially important to parents of teenagers, a time when peer group influences are at their highest. Looking for a church with a strong children and youth program where kids receive moral teaching and core Christian doctrine may be a significant need for you and your family.

What to Do With These Women!

Why all the controversy over ordaining women? Scripture, being as it is, offers us enough ammunition to argue either side of the issue. Those who oppose women in church leadership cite passages such as 1 Timothy 2:12 in which the Apostle Paul wrote, "I do not permit a woman to teach or to have authority over a man, but to be in silence." Sounds pretty clear, doesn't it?

The problem is that in other letters, Paul seems to contradict himself when he writes that ". . . there is neither male nor female; for you are all one in Christ Jesus" (Gal. 3:28). In addition, there are several references of specific women who held positions of church leadership, such as Phoebe who was a deaconess (Rom. 16:1), and four sisters who spoke publicly about their faith in God (Acts 21:8–9). Perhaps the strongest case for equal treatment of women within the church can be made by Jesus' treatment of women—even though it was against the custom of the day, he had close friendships with women and first revealed himself to women after his resurrection.

Those who interpret Scripture more literally usually use one verse or passage to support a view. Those who see Scripture as presenting principles are more likely to base their beliefs on themes, rather than individual verses. You'll have to decide for yourself whether you can benefit from the spiritual wisdom and teaching of women.

Marital Status

Your marital status can be a significant factor in selecting the right church for you. Most churches easily accept married couples. You may run into some trouble if you're single, since many churches are oriented to mom, dad, and 2.5 kids.

Single adults may find a sense of family within the church. This is sometimes achieved through special programs designed specifically for single adults. Check to see if the church you're interested in has a singles group and/or a pastor who is assigned to minister to this population. You may not need or want to be a part of this kind of group, and that's fine too. Just be aware that if you join a small church of married couples, you may spend most of your weekends alone.

Some churches go out of their way to reach out to people who are divorced or widowed by offering programs such as grief recovery groups. Others frown on divorce to such a degree that only widowed or never-married adults feel welcome. If you're divorced, my advice is to avoid any church that has a judgmental attitude about your marital status and go where you can be loved and accepted.

Ethnicity

In the Jewish world in which Jesus lived, devout Jews went to extreme lengths to keep themselves "clean"—physically, spiritually, relationally, symbolically. It was considered unclean to associate with unclean people—those considered immoral (like prostitutes), those of other ethnicities (like Samaritans), or even those of a perceived lesser gender (like women). Jesus broke every taboo—such as the time he spoke to a Samaritan woman (of ill repute), in public no less.

Following Jesus' example of crossing social barriers, especially ethnic ones, the early church welcomed believers from any and all racial backgrounds. This ran against everything these early Christians had believed as devout Jews, but their openness to ethnic diversity played a major role in how the church grew in size and span. No church can follow Christ's example without crossing over racial lines and making room for everyone who desires to worship.

Ideally, any church you'd walk into would have a mixture of ethnicities that mirrors the community in which it resides. But for the most part, churches are comprised of one predominant ethnic or socio-economic group. Perhaps it is because we feel safer and more at home when we are with people like ourselves. Regardless of sociological influences, Christ set an example that turned social norms upside down, and churches today are challenged to do the same.

Nonnegotiables

We all have values that are nonnegotiable—that reach to our very core. I encourage you to take time to identify these for yourself. If you're clear on these, you'll be able to disqualify some denominations from the get-go. Here are four of mine:

1. I need to worship in a church that understands and promotes a personal relationship with God through Christ. Some people refer to this as being "born again" or "saved." Whatever the term, I can sense on a spiritual level if I'm with people who know God in the same way I do. I need that to feel at home spiritually.

2. I need peers with whom I can develop deep friendships. I am a single adult, but singles groups don't appeal to me. What's important to me is finding a subgroup in the church, usually formed around a ministry or program, that has married *and* single people. I'm a Baby Boomer, but have found I relate primarily to post-

modern folks and thoroughly enjoy the creativity, flexibility, and informality of contemporary worship.

Purity vs Unity

If you look at the people who set up new religious movements, you'll often see folks who adamantly assert that the church is about purity. It takes courage to stand up for truth, especially back in the days when it meant putting your life in jeopardy. Most church founders fought to recapture what they saw as the original or true essence of Christianity. I agree with these people—standing up for truth is important.

The downside of taking a stand is that a schism is usually the byproduct. Churches break off from other churches with both sides convinced they represent the truth. Sometimes, after a church has been around a while, the original fervor fades a bit. The congregants look around and ask, "Why are we so mad at those Christians who meet down the street?" Being embarrassed at the discord and the sheer number of different denominations, attention is given to building bridges. For churches engaged in merging with other denominations or involved with the ecumenical movement, unity is the focus. I agree with these people too—being unified in love is a significant witness for Christ and his message of forgiveness.

There is a tension between purity and unity that the church has struggled with from day one. I support both sides of the issue and find no easy answers. No church can balance these perfectly. Those churches that take clearly defined stands are often accused of being exclusive and divisive. On the other hand, those who focus on similarities and unity have been criticized for watering down truth and selling out. Take a look at this issue for yourself. You may feel differently about this at various times of your life. Sometime you may value unity over purity and other times purity over unity. You'll feel most comfortable in a church that parallels your concerns and convictions.

3. I was raised in the Church of the Nazarene which is, on many counts, a very conservative denomination. However, the Nazarenes ordained women from the church's inception back in the late 1800s, and I grew up believing that God loved me as much as any male-type person. Many women have felt oppressed and unable to express what they believe is their true calling from God. I've never struggled with that. I've always known that I could be all I am within the church. So, as I survey the possible congregations, I personally could not attend any congregation that formally limited the role of women (politics and latent sexism usually exist even in the most progressive of churches). You may agree with me, or maybe you feel the exact opposite. There are some who believe Scripture clearly states that women should not be in spiritual authority over men. Or, it may be no issue for you at all. Whatever you believe, I've included information about each church to let you know which ones ordain and do not ordain women into the clergy.

4. My political leanings have been shaped by my Christian experience, but I do not believe that it is more Christian to be Republican, Democrat, or Independent. Quite frankly, this world is so complicated, most of the time I don't know what I think our government should do. I look to church as a place to talk about issues, but not as an authority to tell me how to vote or which political views are "Christian" and which aren't. I think for myself and cringe when a church correlates biblical truth with a specific political agenda. However, you may feel that a local congregation or even an entire denomination should play a direct role in politics. If so, you'll want to look for a church that has combined its spiritual message closely with its political one. Joining some churches is tantamount to declaring your political party, so be sure you're in the right crowd.

What are your nonnegotiables? There are many issues that have divided the church over the years, and identifying which of these is important to you will help considerably in finding a congregation in which to worship God.

You now have a faith survey and a personal needs survey, which should give you a clearer sense about what you believe and need in a church community. In the next chapter, you'll gain some categories by which to further assess the churches you may want to visit.

Further Info

- Philip Yancey, *Church: Why Bother?* (Zondervan, 1998)

- Henri J. M. Nouwen, *Life of the Beloved: Spiritual Living in a Secular World* (Crossroad/Herner and Herder, 1992)

- C. S. Lewis, *Mere Christianity* (Harper San Francisco, 2001)

- Leonard Sweet, *Post-Modern Pilgrims* (Broadman and Holman, 2000)

- Richard Cimino and Don Latti, *Shopping for Faith* (Jossey-Bass, 1998)

two

Sorting through the **Liturgy, Lingo,** and **Lunacy**

According to my meticulous count, there are exactly 29816 gazillion denominations to choose from. As I've sorted through this mishmash, I've looked for common or contrasting characteristics, which is like trying to match up my socks on laundry day. The bad news about sock sorting is that there are always two or three left over without a partner, but the good news about socks is you generally have consistency of color. Denominations, on the other hand, are continually changing their colors. Where they started out is rarely where they are today, what was important to the founders may be a source of embarrassment now, and the groups so ferociously opposed in the last century may now be their new best friends.

Denominations are moving targets, nearly impossible to pin down and sort into tidy categories. Churches can be grouped in a myriad of ways—by doctrine, church structure, musical preferences, or if you can expect to be splashed, sprinkled, or plunged for baptism—or simply put in alphabetical order. The sorting possibilities are endless, and each one that I've tried always leaves me with one or two churches that don't fit the mold.

Having complained about that, I have come up with five categories by which to evaluate potential churches. These are:

- Kind of Church
- Church Structure
- Worship Style
- Trinity affinity
- Clout Continuum

In addition to the issues presented in this chapter, you may want to look at A Few Items to Help Make More Sense of It All in the third section of this book. I've put together some charts, lists, and a timeline of major dates. I hope these aids help to clarify rather than further confuse this church thing.

Kind of Church

The church was one big happy family for the first thousand years. That's an exaggeration. Okay, it's a downright lie. But believe it or not, all of the denominations included here are offshoots of same original church that began in Jerusalem. From the get-go, early Christians struggled over what was the true faith and what was heresy. For example, Christians argued about whether or not new converts had to become Jewish (meaning be circumcised and follow Jewish tradition). Peter said yes. Paul said no. The prospect of adult men having their private parts pruned diminished the new religion's attractiveness. This and a myriad of less personal and more theological reasons prompted the new movement to break with its Jewish heritage and spread throughout the world.

The early "church" evolved into five major Christian centers that worked cooperatively (at least some of the time), each with its own bishop. Three of these centers were more or less taken over by the Muslims in the seventh century, leaving Rome and Constantinople to argue over turf.

It's hard to say whether the schism between the Eastern (Greek-speaking) and Western (Latin-speaking) portions of the church was motivated by a desire to remain theologically pure as much as by cultural and language differences or political shenanigans. Regardless of the causes, in A.D. 1054 the Bishop of Rome (the West) and the Bishop of Constantinople (the East) got into a big theological battle, excommunicated each other, and severed organizational ties. Roman Catholicism expanded west into Europe and eventually the Americas. Eastern Orthodoxy spread into Eastern Europe, Russia, Turkey, and the Middle East, making a late but rapidly growing appearance in the United States.

About five hundred years after the Roman Catholic Church and the Orthodox Church parted ways, the Roman Catholic Church experienced another giant schism—the Reformation. Medieval culture proved to be no match for Renaissance thought, art, and science as it challenged and transformed all aspects of society. Humanism influenced religious as well as secular thinkers, challenging the authority of political powers and, specifically, the role of the Rome-based church. Those who valued the individual and innovation over a feudal caste system identified with the Renaissance movement; Christians who elevated a personal religious experience over a corporate hierarchy were known as Protestants.

Due to these three major schisms, Christian churches can be grouped into three broad categories:

- Orthodox
- Roman Catholic
- Protestant

Orthodox Church

The Orthodox Church claims to be **the** church (which I suppose may account for taking on the name "orthodox" as opposed to "heretical" church). It's clear from their letterhead that Christians in the East see themselves as remaining true to the original vision of Christianity, which they believe is more mystical and less cognitive than their Western counterparts.

Orthodox churches don't have a single hierarchy, but they are nevertheless one denomination. Most Orthodox churches are organized around nationalities, with congregations worshiping in their native language and continuing to be influenced by geographical culture and customs. Consequently, we have Greek Orthodox, Russian Orthodox, Ukrainian Orthodox, Romanian Orthodox, etc., that all embrace the same theology but express their faith with a distinctively ethnic flare.

Roman Catholic

The Roman Catholic Church also claims to be **the** church, tracing its authority back to Peter (a disciple of Jesus), who was killed in Rome by Nero for his faith. The name Peter means "rock," and the Roman

Catholics believe that Jesus personally told Peter that the church would be built "upon this rock," making Peter the first pope.

Roman Catholicism has made a valiant effort to make sense of the mystery of Jesus by developing elaborate theological constructs, some so complex that only the church's reps were trained and authorized to interpret them. Fortunately, in recent years, specifically since Vatican II (1962–1965) and recent challenges to clerical misconduct and authority, the church has translated ancient doctrine into everyday language. The church is slowly becoming more accessible to the average person. Most of the sacraments and rituals are intended to be rooted in the five senses as a way to bring together the spiritual and tangible realms. The primary spiritual duty of a "practicing" Catholic is to participate in these sacraments on a regular basis.

Protestants

If the Christian church you're sitting in isn't Orthodox or Roman Catholic, then you are in a Protestant church of one variety or another. The thing to remember about Protestants is that they protest. Martin Luther spearheaded the movement in the 1500s, but even now, some five hundred years later, the name is still used to describe this brand of Christian. Protestants react against whatever religious movement proceeds them, often splitting off into separate groups, creating one

Oops

You know you're a Protestant in a Catholic church when you're the only one saying "for Thine is the Kingdom and the power and the glory for ever. Amen" at the end of the Lord's Prayer. The Catholic version is the same as the Protestant version, only one phrase shorter.

church after another and then sometimes doubling back and merging with former foes. There are lots and lots and lots of Protestant churches.

Church Structure

Due to evangelistic fervor and religious persecution, the apostles left Jerusalem, spreading out to other parts of the world and organizing communities of believers as they went. These moving evangelists left others to administrate the many aspects of church life. By the second century it was standard practice for a bishop to oversee the local church, aided by priests and deacons.

Churches today may or may not use these terms for its leadership, but every church has a power structure for those who administrate and serve congregants. A church's identity is formed not only by what doctrines and practices are espoused but also by how these beliefs are determined and by whom. Who has the power and who doesn't is formally decided by the form of church government adopted, which can be divided into three categories: episcopal, congregational, and presbyterian.

Episcopal

The "episcopal" form of church government (not to be confused simply with the Episcopal Church) gives those at the top final say over what happens in the denomination and the local church. Those in leadership are called "bishops"—a word derived from the Greek word we translate as "episcopal." Some denominations enforce homogeneity, while others give the local church enormous latitude, but ultimately the final power rests in the hands of the central headquarters.

Usually there is more consistency of faith and practice in churches with centralized authority. Change rarely occurs rapidly, and decisions are made formally through prescribed hierarchical steps and procedures. If you want a church that is anchored in tradition and alters long-held beliefs at a snail's pace, then an episcopal church structure will best suit your spiritual needs. Churches in this category include Orthodox, Roman Catholic, Episcopal, and Lutheran.

Congregational

On the other end of the power spectrum are independent or "congregational" churches (not to be confused with churches formally named Congregational). These local congregations are independent of any other congregation, fully self-supporting, and answering to no one but their own members.

Some independent and nondenominational churches have banded together into loose associations on the basis of shared ministry or theological beliefs, like the Willow Creek Association or the Purpose-Driven Community spearheaded by Saddleback Church.

Churches bound together under the term "conventions" have a stronger link to one another in order to pool resources for missions, fellowship, doctrinal direction, and financial concerns such as pensions and insurance. The Southern Baptist Convention, the Northern Baptist Convention, and the American Baptist Convention fall into this grouping.

Technically, none of these groups are denominations. This may seem like a matter of semantics, but it's an important distinction to those who view themselves outside denominational boundaries. Many Christians believe that there is no church other than the local church, and denominations are in variance to Scripture. Churches who belong to associations or conventions are independently governed and beholding to no outside entity. Most nondenominational churches fall into this category.

Presbyterian

In between congregational and episcopal forms of government stands the "presbyterian" structure (again, not to be confused with Presbyterian denominations). Presbyterian church government gives quite a bit of autonomy at the local church level but with an overarching center of administrative and theological power. As a result, these churches often have oodles of committees comprised of laity and clergy who participate in lots of discussions and tedious agendas, but with wide representation.

Take notice of the degree of autonomy afforded the local congregation. If you prefer some flexibility on the local level but look for a uni-

Sacraments vs. Ordinances

Sacraments are Christian rituals that are believed to be outward signs of inner spiritual realities. The more liturgical the church, the more significance is placed on the transforming nature of sacraments. For example, liturgical churches assert that Christ is actually present in the elements of Holy Communion. They may differ in how they envision that happening, but basically the act of sharing communion is being spiritually nurtured by Christ. While Episcopal and Lutheran churches tend to view the Eucharist as making Christ "really present," most other Protestant churches view the sacraments as ordinances—as symbolic expressions of a spiritual truth. In this view, a believer participates in communion to remember and acknowledge Christ's sacrifice on the cross.

fied theology and vision, the presbyterian approach may be for you. Churches included in this category are the Church of the Nazarene and Presbyterian churches of all varieties.

Worship Style

Worshiping God with other believers is, for many Christians, the most significant reason to participate in church. Worship is expressing one's devotion and esteem for God through actions that could include prayer, Scripture reading, singing, telling others about your spiritual experiences—not necessarily limited to the confines of corporate gatherings. However, in general, Christians refer to "worship" as an activity occurring in a group of believers who participate together in rituals and spontaneous activities aimed at giving glory to God.

Before the early Christians broke with Judaism, believers met in local Jewish temples for worship. But around A.D. 75 they moved to private homes, which became the norm for the first 300 years or so. From the New Testament and writings of early Christians, we know that these early worship services included reading Scripture, prayer, preaching, singing, baptism, and sharing the Lord's Supper. As time went on, additional activities were added to worship, often reflecting the culture of the believers. Worship became more structured and ritualized, which brings us to four types of the worship style: Liturgical, Traditional, Contemporary, and Free-Form.

Liturgical

Liturgy is simply a prescribed order or structure of worship. In a way, you can say that any worship gathering that has been planned ahead of time is "liturgical." But liturgical worship is generally considered those services that are highly structured, often including an ear-splitting pipe organ (don't sit in the balcony with the pipes), where the clergy are more prone to wear special robes and headgear. The congregation moves in unison—whether sitting, standing, or kneeling—leading up to the main event: the celebration of the Eucharist (also called the Lord's Supper or Communion). The Roman Catholic, Eastern Orthodox, Episcopal, and Lutheran churches are usually considered liturgical.

Historically, liturgical churches practice the following order of activities:

- Confession of Sins
- Pronouncement of Absolution
- Acknowledgment of God's Authority
- Reading of God's Word
- Hymn of Praise
- Sermon
- Taking the Offering

Icons

Icons are used in personal and corporate worship in the Orthodox Church. An icon, or picture, is "meant to be a window into the spiritual world, used to help us contemplate spiritual matters or to put us into a prayerful frame of mind, as a reminder of events in the Bible, the life of Christ and the Saints. Icons were never meant to be worshiped or venerated as something holy in themselves. The reverence shown to an icon must be done with the understanding that it is not the icon or artwork itself we are respecting, but rather the person or event it portrays."

- Prayers of the Church
- Lord's Supper (Communion, Eucharist)

Orthodox churches focus on experiencing a mystical union with God through a variety of highly symbolic spiritual practices. Every item used, every movement made, and every word spoken has meaning. Incense is burned in Orthodox services to signify prayers rising to God (creating great ambience but murder for us allergy sufferers), along with the use of icons and other cool religious aids.

The Roman Catholic Mass, available everyday and several times a day, is a structured service with a prescribed order and written liturgy leading up to the sharing of the Eucharist, which is based on Jesus' last supper with his disciples. The cultural climate of the church influences the style in which this service is executed—some long-standing congregations are more traditional, using long-cherished music and time-efficient homilies; contemporary and youth-oriented parishes may use guitars to create a more casual atmosphere; an African-American Mass may last for a couple of hours, incorporating a number of choirs, lots of swaying, and hand clapping and "amens" from the congregants. Each congregation has flexibility in how to interpret the Mass, but the basic service is the same across the world.

Along with the Orthodox and Roman Catholics, Episcopal and Lutheran services are considered liturgical. While the Protestants did away with their affiliation with Rome, they kept many of the same rituals of their Catholic ancestors. All elements of a liturgical service lead up to the sharing of the Lord's Supper, which is viewed, in one way or another, as an encounter with Jesus.

Traditional

Traditional worship is primarily a Protestant invention comprised of what I call "three songs and a sermon." The congregation sings hymns (mostly written by Protestants) from a hymnal, with a choir and an electric church organ and/or piano as accompaniment. Whereas the elements of liturgical worship lead up to the Eucharist, traditional services often focus on a sermon that is usually evangelistic or instructional in nature. Traditional sermons may last from twenty to forty-five minutes and usually contain at least one good joke and three theological points. Churches with traditional services include Methodists, Presbyterian, Reformed, and Nazarene. Communion is shared on a regular, although rarely weekly, basis.

The Lord's Supper

Sharing the Lord's Supper is standard fare for most churches, but the concept was mind-boggling to people of the first century. Everyone was divided into distinct social groups, from the Emperor on down. Class distinction wasn't reserved for the Romans. Ancient Jews were extremely conscious of of social standing. The more religiously upright a person was, the more aloof he or she would be from anyone who was "unclean" or beneath their station. And here were these Christians breaking bread with anyone who confessed a belief in Christ. Slaves and their masters, men and women, educated and illiterate, rich and poor gathered on equal ground and shared the Lord's Supper. We all come to God on even ground when we participate in the Lord's Supper—no matter who we are, what we've done, or what we own. Jesus invites all who believe to share in the meal.

Contemporary

Contemporary worship is informal, with musical accompaniment as simple as a couple of folks on acoustical guitars or a full-fledged band with electric guitars, electric keyboard, and drums. While occasionally drawing from standard hymns (but sung with a folk, R&B, or rock beat), most songs or choruses have been written in the last fifty years. The words are often displayed on the wall via overhead projector for the congregation. The musical portion of worship takes high priority and may share equal time with the sermon. Pastors in contemporary services rarely wear suits and ties, most often donning casual wear and comfortable shoes. Communion may be included on special occasions.

Some contemporary services are very loose—following a basic plan of singing, preaching, group prayer, and more singing—although no one seems overly concerned with structure. As long as no bodily harm is inflicted on fellow worshipers, you can do pretty much what you want—while standing, sitting, kneeling, listening, or speaking up as the Spirit moves.

Charismatic and Pentecostal services tend to be contemporary. In addition, a number of liturgical and traditional churches have incorporated contemporary worship into their services or offer a separate contemporary service in addition to the regular Sunday morning gathering.

Free-Form

I came up with this category to encompass any service style that doesn't fit into the previous three. Some churches include sermons and some don't; some sing a cappella and some chant; some wave their hands and shout "hallelujah" while others sit quietly and meditate together; some include sacraments and some have done away with the sacraments altogether.

Trinity Affinity

In the Old Testament God's identity was clear—there was one and only one God—the God of Abraham, Isaac, and Jacob. With the appear-

Nicene Creed

Figuring out who Jesus is has divided and united the church over the years. It's a balancing act of faith to accept Jesus as the most amazing expression of God's love in the history of the planet. It's easy to fall off one side and say that Jesus was just a human, a good teacher, or at best God spoke through him. Or you could fall off the other side and believe that Jesus was divine and his human nature was absent or irrelevant. How far a doctrine tips to one side or the other I believe determines how true or heretical a particular teaching may be.

To sort this and other issues out, a number of creeds were written, the most universally accepted being the Nicene Creed. Two versions of the Nicene Creed—the first drafted in 325 and the second modified in 381— are used by most churches today. The Roman Catholic and most Protestant denominations use the second version, while the Orthodox Church uses the first. The disagreement centers on three words, "and the Son" (called the filioque clause), which were added to the second version. Even though the Orthodox Church believes in the Trinity, this little phrase served as one of the reasons the East and West divided in 1054. With these exceptions in mind, here is a summation of what most Christian denominations affirm:

ance of Jesus, and later the Holy Spirit, the Christian concept of God got a little more complicated. Christians retained the "one God" idea from Judaism, but now had three variations of God to deal with. I don't believe that any mortal really understands the mystery of divinity in general, let alone fully grasps a three-in-one God. (When Jesus prayed to the Father was he talking to himself?) Yet this unfathomable God is at the heart of Christianity—an unsolvable mystery who asks for our devotion. Every church in this book formally affirms the doctrine of Trinity—that God is one, comprised of three persons: the Father, Son, and Holy Spirit.

We believe in one God, the Father, the Almighty, maker of heaven and earth, of all that is, seen and unseen.

We believe in one Lord, Jesus Christ, the only Son of God, eternally begotten of the Father, God from God, Light from Light, true God from true God, begotten, not made, of one Being with the Father; through him all things were made. For us and for our salvation he came down from heaven, was incarnate of the Holy Spirit and the Virgin Mary and became truly human. For our sake he was crucified under Pontius Pilate; he suffered death and was buried. On the third day he rose again in accordance with the Scriptures; he ascended into heaven and is seated at the right hand of the Father. He will come again in glory to judge the living and the dead, and his kingdom will have no end.

We believe in the Holy Spirit, the Lord, the giver of life, who proceeds from the Father and the Son,* who with the Father and the Son is worshiped and glorified, who has spoken through the prophets.

We believe in one holy catholic and apostolic Church. We acknowledge one baptism for the forgiveness of sins. We look for the resurrection of the dead, and the life of the world to come. Amen.

* "and the Son" is the filioque clause

We humans have a hard time holding irreconcilable concepts in perfect balance. Consequently, we tend to identify a bit more with one aspect of the Trinity than the other two. For example, I address my prayers to God the Father. But I know some Christians who pray to Jesus and others who pray to the Holy Spirit. It's just human nature to have a favorite. Like the people who make up the church, various denominations tend to emphasize one aspect of God over the others. One way to sort out which church best suits you is to see if their Trinity affinity matches yours.

God the Father

The churches that have an affinity with God the Father use the word "God" more than "Jesus" or "Holy Spirit" in sermons and writings. Not only is Jesus not the center of attention, the term "Jesus" may be used less frequently and the term "Christ" used more often. Listen to the sermons and prayers to pick up on this. While there are certainly exceptions to this rule, I put denominations such as Methodists and Episcopalians in this category. I also think Reformed churches could be included here because of their emphasis on the sovereignty of God, but I'm not sure they'd agree with me—I suspect they perceive themselves as Christ-centered, which brings us to the next person of the Trinity.

God the Son

A number of denominations are "Christ-centered," with prayers addressed directly to Jesus or, at the very least, offered "in the name of Jesus." I suspect the air of exclusivity floating around many of these churches is an unintended consequence of being convinced that "Jesus is the answer." People of all kinds, sizes, and ethnicities may be welcome, but all belief systems are not.

A number of evangelical and conservative denominations would fall into this category, such as Congregational, Nazarene, and Baptist.

God the Holy Spirit

The Holy Spirit takes center stage in some denominations—especially Pentecostal or Charismatic churches. While God the Father and Jesus

Mary, Mother of God

The Roman Catholic Church and the Orthodox Church have brought another dimension to the discussion of the Trinity—Jesus' mom, Mary. How can a human being give birth to God? If you're the mother of God, does that change your humanity in any way? The answers to these and other questions has helped Mary rise to a status of honor unparalleled in other parts of Christendom.

It's important to note that Mary is not worshiped in the same way as the Trinity. She is honored and revered not because she is divine but because she willingly gave birth to divinity. Mary played a necessary role in our salvation. She stayed with Jesus to witness his death and his resurrection, actively sharing in his sacrifice and triumph. Catholics and Orthodox Christians believe that Mary didn't die a normal physical death, like other human beings, but was taken, body and soul, directly to heaven, known as the Assumption.

If you've wondered why Catholics and Orthodox Christians pray to saints, and specifically to Mary, it's because they believe that the "communion of saints" refers to both the living and the dead. Asking Mary (or another saint) to pray for you is no different than asking a friend to pray for you. If you want to get Jesus to do something for you, wouldn't getting his mother on your side help your cause? Mary is definitely a significant player, and, perhaps most importantly, a feminine player in a faith that is otherwise dominated by male images.

are central to worship in these groups, the Holy Spirit holds the most sway for those who believe that what was true for the early church (as described in the Book of Acts) is good enough for the church of today. I consider Assemblies of God, VineyardUSA, and most Pentecostal churches to be included in this category.

Clout Continuum

Churches make some amazing claims—all claim to have important spiritual knowledge, some claim to speak directly for God, others even claim to be Christ on earth. On what basis can these churches claim spiritual authority? Generally, churches point to three sources to support their beliefs and actions: Scripture, their particular traditions, and the personal experience of the believer. But these three forms of clout are not valued equally. Some stress Scripture over tradition with personal experience coming in third. Some change the order and claim that a personal experience with God takes first place, with Scripture and tradition bringing up the rear. Tradition takes the lead in several denominations, with Scripture and personal experience in second and third place. In each church description I've listed the order in which these three forms of Christian clout are valued.

Scripture

In the year 393, the Synod (or council) of Hippo (the town not the animal) agreed on the sixty-six books of the Old and New Testaments we now refer to as the Bible. All the denominations I'm reviewing accept this listing or basic "canon" of the Bible. The Eastern Orthodox, Roman Catholic, and Episcopal churches also include additional books called the Apocrypha.

Scripture holds a place of authority in all Christian denominations, but what kind authority varies greatly. The Roman Catholic and Orthodox Churches both revere Scripture but also value tradition and declarations of the church. Martin Luther broke with this

How the Bible
Came to be

Those who saw and spoke with Jesus after his resurrection became known as apostles—including but not limited to the twelve disciples. These folks were seen as having substantial if not full authority in representing Jesus and his message. At first, oral tradition seemed adequate. Why read a story when you can talk directly to someone who talked to Jesus? But as the apostles were martyred or died of old age, people realized that they needed to get some of this down on paper.

The four Gospels were written describing Jesus' ministry, death, and resurrection—two ascribed to apostles (Matthew and John) and two to close associates of the apostles (Mark and Luke). In addition to writing one of the Gospels, Luke wrote a fascinating record of the successes and mistakes of early believers in what is called The Acts of the Apostles. These pioneer Christians enthusiastically laid the framework for the church we have today.

The remainder of the books in the New Testament were originally letters and writings shared among the newly formed churches, written by apostles or their representatives (the authors of a few books are still matters of debate). It is widely believed that all of the documents we now have in our New Testament were authored between 50 and 100 A.D.

The church in the first two or three centuries debated which of the apostolic writings were authoritative. This distinction became especially important when Roman Emperor Diocletian issued a series of edicts from 302–304 to "to tear

view by declaring "Sola Gratia, Sola Fide, Sola Scriptura." If you're not up on your Latin, it means we are saved by grace alone, through faith alone, based on Scripture alone.

Protestants emerged by challenging not only the authority of the Catholic Church but also by redefining authority altogether. Without pointing to the sole authority of Scripture, Protestant churches don't have a theological leg to stand on. If Protestants gave up this tenet,

down the churches to the foundations and to destroy the Sacred Scriptures by fire; and commanding also that those who were in honourable stations should be degraded if they persevered in their adherence to Christianity." A number of Christian writings were in circulation at the time, some believed and some not. In the face of torture and death, you'd probably want to be certain that the documents you had in hand were worth dying for.

Twenty books—the four Gospels, Acts, the letters attributed to Paul (excluding Hebrews), the first letter of John, and the first letter of Peter—were readily acknowledged and accepted as Scripture, now referred to as the *"homologoumena,"* or acknowledged books. Seven additional books, now called *"antilegomena,"* or disputed books, required more discussion. These books are Hebrews, the second and third letters of John, the second letter of Peter, Jude, James, and Revelation. The matter wasn't resolved until quite a few years after the Diocletian persecution had ended. After much scrutiny and a number of councils, the twenty-seven books we know today as the New Testament books were accepted as Scripture. Most churches point to the Council of Hippo held in 393 in North Africa or to the Council of Carthage held four years later in 397 as authoritative councils. Both councils were in agreement.

The New Testament was then added to the Jewish Scriptures, what Christians call the Old Testament. Evidence points to around 400 B.C. as the period in which various Jewish writings, dating as far back as 1400 B.C., were gathered and agreed upon as making up the Old Testament.

they would have no viable recourse but to rejoin the Roman Catholic Church (or the Orthodox, depending on which one they saw as the real original church). You can see that biblical authority is no minor issue for Protestants, so it comes as no surprise to find that Protestants have created many terms with which to dissect, discuss, and debate the nuances of scriptural authority and interpretation.

Protestants argue about Scripture amongst themselves, often between conservative and liberal perspectives. Stated loosely, the more conservative a Protestant denomination, the more literally the Bible is interpreted; the more liberal the denomination, the more leeway is given in biblical interpretation.

Fundamentalist churches take a "plain sense" approach, asserting that the Holy Spirit essentially dictated the Bible to the human authors. Every detail in Scripture, including historical events, time frames, and issues of nature and science, is literally and factually accurate. Churches on the conservative end are more likely to use terms such as "inerrant" and "verbally inspired" to describe the Bible.

A softening of this view asserts that Scripture is comprised of both human and divine elements and contains "all truth necessary to faith and Christian living." This view rejects the idea that the Bible states factual information the way we might state baseball scores or the highs and lows of today's weather. While insisting that the Bible is reliable in areas of God's intention—specifically to communicate to us about our spiritual condition—Scripture is to be studied and interpreted from a historical context, taking into consideration the personality and culture of the authors. Nazarene pastor Dennis Bratcher writes, "The significance of the Bible is not what it tells us about history, science, or the future, but rather what it communicates about God and how human beings should respond to Him."

The further you travel from inerrancy, the more flexibility you have in interpreting and applying Scripture. In addition to relying on the actual words on the page, it is believed that the Holy Spirit assists people to make Christian truth applicable to today's society. Scripture is seen not only as God's Word but also as literature and historical narrative. The focus shifts from citing specific verses or passages to identifying scriptural principles. In the extreme, liberal churches can interpret themselves clear out of Christianity (as I define it) if they're not careful. I personally draw the line when theologians tinker with the divinity of Christ.

That's Only My Opinion

As all these denominations squabble over doctrine and practice, remember that the Bible is a complicated compilation of books, letters, poetry, and stories written by many different authors of varying cultural backgrounds over hundreds of years. A number of paradoxes are presented within its pages, such as God is sovereign and yet human beings have free will, Jesus is fully God and yet fully human, or God is just and yet ordered the massacre of entire races of people—enough paradoxes to keep any thoughtful person up at night.

Sometimes theologians try to tidy up this very messy spirituality by making up systems to explain it all. No matter how complicated or jargon-laden, every theological system has a few significant biblical concepts left over (God is a tad too big to get our heads around . . .).

As a result, the next generation of theologians grab hold of the leftovers and create new doctrinal statements. While the newer approach may solve the previous problems, new loose ends are left. And so the doctrinal dance continues.

I believe that "systematic theology" may be an oxymoron, and that tolerating unresolved tensions inherent in the Christian faith is part of our mysterious journey of learning about a Being beyond our wildest imagination. But that's only my opinion.

Tradition

No matter what a denomination overtly states, it's my observation that the longer a denomination has been in existence, the bigger role tradition plays in their beliefs and practices. I guess that's because they've had time to develop some traditions. The Orthodox and Roman Catholic churches are tied for first in this category, the epitome of ". . . because that's the way we've always done it. . . ." Both believe that God is alive and well inside the church organization itself. They're big on councils, diets (formal gatherings, not the fat-burning kind), and synods that create creeds, dogmas, and elaborate declarations of faith.

It wasn't until the early 600s that Pope Gregory I first declared himself and subsequent popes to be infallible in regards to matters of Roman Church doctrine. This authority was qualified somewhat at Vatican II by requiring a pope to gain approval of a council of bishops before any new doctrinal declarations are made. While specific practices, such as mandatory celibacy of the priesthood or methods of birth control, are arenas for intense debate and disagreement, doctrinal stands are nonnegotiable until, if ever, modified by the pope.

Protestant denominations threw out the pope but not all of them tossed out tradition. Embracing a bit of pomp and circumstance are the Lutherans and Episcopalians. Martin Luther asserted that if Scripture didn't speak about or against an issue, then it was permissible to include in church tradition. Many of the terms and rituals used in these denominations are borrowed directly from the Catholics.

In contrast are those who believe that if it isn't in the Bible, then it shouldn't be in the church. While these congregations may hold to their own recently developed traditions, they try to eliminate anything that isn't "scriptural." In the extreme are those Christians who are suspicious, if not downright hostile, to any tradition or practice created by previous generations. A tension exists between those who grow spiritually by participating in long-held spiritual practices and traditions and those who want to reframe the faith in such a way as to be relevant to today's worshiper.

Experience

Spiritual experience is defined differently by various denominations. The Orthodox refer to a believer experiencing the sacramental mysteries. The Orthodox and the Roman Catholics believe that congregants are spiritually fed through the Eucharist, and also endorse a long line of saints and mystics who had personal encounters with God. Both of these denominations emphasize personal experience within the context of church life, as do the Lutherans and Episcopalians.

Most Protestants promote a more strictly personal experience of faith that may or may not take place within the context of community. Luther talks about the moment in which he felt "reborn altogether and had entered Paradise," which was not, by the way, while participating in the sacraments of the Roman Catholic Church. John Wesley points to an evening while worshiping with a group of believers called Moravians when his heart was strangely warmed. No one knows the exact nature of John Calvin's "sudden conversion," or whether he was participating in corporate worship, with a small group, a friend, or by himself, but for Calvin, his conversion was convincing and life-changing. The term "born again" is often used by those who have had an experience resulting in a personal relationship with Jesus.

Churches from the Holiness and Pentecostal movements take this a step further by emphasizing an additional spiritual experience for the already converted. A second blessing, attributed to the Holy Spirit, is promoted as sanctification by holiness groups and is evidenced by speaking in tongues and other gifts in Pentecostal churches.

You now have your faith survey, your personal needs survey, and some ways to evaluate the churches you're planning to visit. In the next chapter we're going to discuss what to look for when you're actually sitting in the pew (or standing, if you're visiting a Russian Orthodox Church).

Further Info

- James F. White, *A Brief History of Christian Worship* (Abingdon Press, 1993)

- Paul R. Spickard and Kevin M. Cragg, *A Global History of Christianity: How Everyday Believers Experienced Their World* (Baker, 1994)

- Ian Bradley, ed., *The Book of Hymns* (Testament Books, 2000)

- Frank S. Mead, Samuel S. Hill, and Craig D. Atwood, *Handbook of Denominations in the United States*, 11th edition (Abingdon Press, 2001)

- Arthur J. Magida and Stuart M. Matlins, *How to Be a Perfect Stranger: A Guide to Etiquette in Other People's Religious Ceremonies* (Skylight Paths Publishing, 1999)

- John McManner, *The Oxford Illustrated History of Christianity* (Oxford, 2001)

three

Checking Out a Church

After you've narrowed your search to denominations you think may be a good match, here are suggested steps to follow in checking out specific churches:

Check out the denominational web site

Most denominations are into the Internet and have web sites. A lot can be learned about a denomination from the web site. Most have sections that describe their history, their current beliefs, ministries they offer, and other interesting info. Also, most have links to their network of congregations, and this can be an easy way to find a church near you.

Visit the worship service at least three times before making a decision

Just like people have "off days," churches may not best represent themselves on any given Sunday. Perhaps you are visiting on a special day set aside for raising funds for the new sanctuary (and you feel pressured to give money), or when one of the founding members is being honored (and you feel like an outsider), or on bring your pet to be blessed day (and you're allergic to cats). A guest speaker may be on the docket who in no way reflects the tone of a typical service, or the pastor may simply be having a bad day. Since you are not (yet) a part of the group, there may be in-jokes that make no sense to you or may even seem offensive from your point of view.

Give yourself a chance to get to know what the church is really like. Assume good faith. If you walk in and no one greets you, don't assume you're not welcome. People in that church may not want to seem intrusive, or maybe the welcome team was around the corner and didn't see you. Be as open minded about the church as you want them to be about you.

Review printed materials

I've never visited a church that didn't have plenty of printed material to hand out—worship bulletins, service guides, denominational magazines, missions updates, weekly activity notices, even personal ads and service listings. Check them all out. If you want a church that is open to a variety of perspectives, look for discussion groups led by people who are outside the denomination, or even outside Christendom. On the other hand, if you want a traditional, more conservative congregation, a class on the similarities between Buddha and Christ may not be your cup of tea.

You'll discover quite a bit from these small publications—what is of concern on a denominational level, how this particular congregation falls into line or differs from the larger organization, groups to which you or other family members could belong.

Don't only read what these publications say; also read between the lines. What aren't they including? Is a big election coming up, yet

What the Building Says about a Church

For the first three hundred years, buildings weren't intentionally built to function as places of Christian worship—believers gathered in private homes. A residence might be renovated into a place of worship by tearing down an interior wall or two and making space for believers to meet, but it wasn't until the 300s that buildings were built specifically to function as a "church."

After legalizing Christianity, Roman Emperor Constantine got into the church building business big time. Churches sprang up all over the known world, designed primarily after pagan and civil architecture. As a result, Christians began gathering together in large numbers rather than in smaller home-based groups. Huge meeting places were constructed sans seats, giving the Eastern and Western portions of Christianity something else to argue over—whether or not seats should be allowed inside the church. The West brought in benches (the precursor for the pew), but the East insisted on standing for the entire service. Today many Orthodox churches have succumbed to the need for seating, but many Russian Orthodox churches are still holding onto a standing-only policy for worshipers.

You can tell a lot about a church just by checking out the building, since the way a church is constructed usually reflects the theology and spiritual practices of the congregation.

Craig McNair Wilson, an author and friend of mine, observed that a church's mission and the structure of the sanctuary may seem to contradict each other—congregations that worship in tall church buildings are often focused on reaching out to the community and maybe a bit less concerned with personally relating to God; flat or rambling churches often house congregants who are more likely to focus on relating to God and less likely to be involved in their communities. Go figure.

Liturgical Worship

Liturgical churches demonstrate the importance they place on the role of clergy in worship by providing separate places for the laity (sitting in the pews) and those in charge (up front on stage). Since sharing the Eucharist is the climax of most liturgical services, their churches have an altar, front and center, with a rail at which congregants can kneel to receive the elements. In addition, there is an area for a formal choir, but not necessarily facing the congregation, and most likely an organ. Off to the side you'll see a raised podium or pulpit for the priest to deliver the homily. The ceiling may be vaulted, encouraging the eye to go upward. Around the sanctuary you may find a variety of symbols—stained glass windows, statues, paintings, and additional altars. When you walk into one of these churches it's easy to feel transported to a different time and place.

Traditional Worship

Since the sermon is more highly revered in churches with traditional worship services, the pulpit is usually the main focus of attention, raised so everyone can see. Behind the pulpit you'll often find seating for the choir, which faces the congregation. On one side of the platform, you'll probably find an organ and on the other side a piano. As is true for liturgical churches, pews are the preferred seating, bolted to the ground and facing forward. The words and music for congregational singing are usually in a hymnal provided in a shelf on the back of each pew. If the church has stained glass windows, they are rarely as elaborate as those in liturgical churches. You may find some symbols around the church, such as banners or paintings or crosses, but traditional churches are usually more simply adorned than liturgical churches. The Lord's Supper is not a weekly occurrence, so you'll rarely, if ever, find a permanent altar at the front of the church. Most will have an altar rail, which may be used as a place to serve communion or for prayer.

Contemporary Worship

It's hard to generalize about churches that provide contemporary worship services—their surroundings will reflect the values of that particular congrega-

there's not one word about promoting a particular candidate? This is probably a church that encourages each member to make political decisions for themselves. On the other hand, if you're handed voter guides with instructions not only about how to vote but also for whom you should vote, you've walked into a group that feels strongly about the issues, and you might be uncomfortable if you differ in political leanings.

Check out the quality of the paper. Sounds odd, but this will also help you gather important information. Are the materials on good quality paper, perhaps in color? Photocopied onto inexpensive color stock? These observances may indicate that the congregation has substantial funds and is concerned with presenting a more polished image,

tion. For example, contemporary services may be held in a rented high school auditorium, a large room with chairs set up in the round, or huge church structures designed to seat thousands. Generally speaking, however, buildings used for contemporary worship provide space for a worship band, a stationary or moveable podium for the pastor (although many walk around while they preach), and an overhead projection screen for the words of the worship songs. Rarely, if ever, will contemporary services use a hymnal.

Free-Form Worship

There is no way to make generalizations about free-form worship other than to say that whatever they believe will be reflected in their surroundings. Some meet in church buildings, some in rented halls, others in homes to illustrate their belief in low overhead and intimate, less formal services. Chairs in a circle usually mean less centralized authority and more lay participation; rows of seats facing forward may indicate less interaction among members and more clerical authority; no seats at all is, in my estimation, a bad sign and a bit too austere for me, but maybe you like standing for long periods of time. Just keep your eyes open and you can learn a lot about what a church believes.

that this is a wealthy congregation that doesn't want to appear slick, or that it is simply a congregation with limited funds trying to get the word out the best they can. In which of these groups would you feel most comfortable? Remember, none of the ten commandments mention publishing standards, so there's no right or wrong on this—just what suits your style.

Visit a Sunday school class or small group

It's hard to really get to know people in a church by visiting a few times, especially for larger churches of four hundred members or more. Most churches have Sunday school classes before or after the primary worship service or small group meetings during the week. These may be organized around age, marital status, common interests, or areas of service. Take time to check these groups out. Wonderful friendships have developed through small groups in church settings. It's a great place to find out more about the informal nature of the congregation.

And don't send your kids off to Sunday school without checking out the curriculum and the teachers. Go with them to their Sunday school classes and see how well they are received into the group. Listen to what your children will be taught and make sure you agree with the perspective. Get to know your child's teachers. Before you entrust your child's spiritual development to strangers, check them out thoroughly.

Talk to the pastor(s)

Regardless of what perspective is promoted by the headquarters of a denomination, each congregation has its own personality that is shaped in large part by the personalities of the senior pastor and pastoral staff. Ultimately, the senior pastor controls the shots, so if you don't like his or her style, this probably won't be the church for you.

Even if you don't want to call a lot of attention to yourself in the long run, I recommend shaking hands with the senior pastor each Sunday you visit simply for the information you'll gather. Do you feel comfortable in each other's presence? Is there good eye contact? Are you remembered the second time you meet? Is this someone you want to influence, even shape, your spiritual experience?

If you're visiting a large church with an extensive pastoral staff, I'd also recommend you introduce yourself to the pastor who oversees your small group or area of interest. If you're single, speak to the singles' pastor. If you have children, talk with the children's pastor or director of Christian education. If you're a senior adult, talk to the person pastoring people in your peer group. See if you are comfortable with this style of leadership.

Once you're seriously considering regular attendance, the next step is to determine what kind of relationship you can expect from your pastor(s), which often depends on the size of the church. In some extremely large churches the senior pastor is not available to meet with individual members simply because its impossible for one person to minister to hundreds, if not thousands, of people. In these churches, additional pastors serve on staff to minister directly to congregants.

Say What?

The first time I visited a local church, the people were so friendly. After the service a sweet woman came to me and asked if she could "pray over" me. I'd never heard that phrase before and heard it as "prey over" me! I had visions of satanic altars and it scared me so much I rudely excused myself and ran from the church. Once I calmed down I realized what she had actually meant, and then had a good laugh at myself.

—Carol

Pastor availability is also influenced by the pastor's personality. Some pastors prefer to see their role as preacher/teacher or administrator and develop personal relationships with a restricted number of people. On the other extreme are those who are available to everyone at all hours, night and day. To find out where your prospective senior pastor falls on the continuum, call the church office during the week and set up a short appointment—fifteen minutes or so. If the pastor is not available for individual meetings, you'll know not to expect a visit at the hospital if you are ill . . . at least not by the senior pastor. However, I recommend that you then make an appointment with the pastor in your ministry area and develop a relationship with him or her. If you want to be in a church where the senior pastor knows you by name and will be there for you in times of crisis, you may want to select a smaller congregations. If you're happy with relating to someone else on the pastoral team, then a larger church may be the place for you.

And Now a Word on Spiritual Abuse

Not only is it wise for you to be clear about what you are looking for in a church, I strongly encourage you to be clear about what you don't want. Nearly everyone I know has had some kind of negative experience with a church group or pastor or member—some minor run-ins and some major abuse resulting in serious spiritual or emotional damage. Some people are spiritually abusive and don't know it—they think they're doing or teaching the right thing. Others have a good idea that what they're up to isn't good. It matters not what the perpetrator intends, if the outcome spiritually damages someone else's relationship with God then it's abuse. In cases where people physically assault or sexually molest others, it's important to get the police involved. But it doesn't have to be that overt to be hurtful. I think the most destructive kind of spiritual abuse is perpetrated by those in leadership—whether they be ordained or lay leaders—and can be subtle manipulation, intimidation, or teaching distortions of the truth.

The church has demonstrated time and again that it can be a powerfully destructive force. Shall I name a few? Well, there were the Crusades where thousands of Orthodox Christians were killed when Western Christian Crusaders invaded their cities and raided their churches; the iconoclastic persecutions where thousands of Christians who used icons in their worship were killed by Christians who didn't; the rise of Protestantism when Christians on all theological sides warred against each other and beheaded, stabbed, and burned each other at the stake. And this is just how Christians have treated other Christians. The church hasn't been any kinder to those outside the church.

Granted, it is rather unlikely that, should you have a falling out with a particular denomination at this point in history, in America, you'll find your life in danger. But remember—just because people claim to be Christians doesn't make them moral, kind, or wise; just because a building has a cross on it doesn't make the people who worship there safe and trustworthy. It's foolhardy to let your guard down just because you're hanging out with Christians. I've listed five characteristics of congregations to avoid. You know you're in a spiritually dangerous church if:

The pastor is a control freak

The person in charge may have the best intentions, but any group led by someone who wants to control what everyone thinks and does is dangerous for you and your loved ones. How to detect a control freak masquerading as a benevolent pastor?

Listen between the lines. There is a difference between providing guidance and spiritual instruction and attempting to control the thoughts and choices of the congregation. A pastor may feel very strongly about his or her convictions—that does not make someone dangerous in and of itself. In fact, a pastor who is clear, honest, and direct lets you know just where they stand on the issues—even if that includes not taking a stand on every issue.

Take a look around. Do you observe other congregants engaged in open discussion about Scripture, church policy, or ministry methods? Or is it assumed that everyone will agree and simply follow the leader? If there is pressure for you to conform your beliefs and actions simply because you're "supposed" to submit to the leadership, my recommendation is to walk out and don't come back.

Watch how decisions are made. Is there discussion and healthy debate? Or are important decisions made behind closed doors? Does the pastor resent working with a governing board? Can other pastors on staff share differing opinions without reprisal? Is telling the truth discouraged? Are open dialog and conflict resolution common occurrences?

Check our how the pastor relates to the congregation. Do you see the pastor everywhere? A pastor who has to go to every activity, coordinate every ministry, and be the center of the church's attention is excessively controlling. Even in a small congregation, an emotionally healthy pastor will delegate responsibilities to staff and church members and create a sense of shared ministry. If your pastor tries to be all things to all people, burnout is sure to follow, and everyone gets hurt when a pastor crashes.

Do you see the pastor nowhere? Do you only catch glimpses of your pastor on Sundays as he or she scurries from the sanctuary to locked offices? Is getting past the church secretary to set up a personal appointment comparable to gaining admittance to the Oval Office? Do you get the feeling that the pastor is preoccupied or downright uninterested in what you have to say when you do speak face to face? Either the pastor is such an introvert that a career change is in order or your spiritual leader is in the last stages of burnout. Self-isolation on the part of a pastor is a warning sign—especially when you recall that one of the tasks of church leadership is to facilitate community. A spiritually healthy pastor is an emotionally healthy pastor—you can't have one without the other.

The congregation is mean and nasty

Church members can talk all they want about God's love, but if they don't live daily in an atmosphere of forgiveness and reconciliation, churches can become critical, self-righteous, and contentious. Snoop around and find out how long the current pastor has served this con-

Top 10 Signs You Are
in the Wrong Church

10. The church bus has gun racks.
 9. The church staff consists of senior pastor, associate pastor, and sociopastor.
 8. The Bible they use is the Dr. Seuss version.
 7. There is an ATM in the lobby.
 6. The choir wears leather robes.
 5. The worship services are B.Y.O.S. (bring your own snake).
 4. There's no cover charge, but communion is a two-drink minimum.
 3. The pastor regularly attends meetings in Las Vegas and Atlantic City.
 2. The ushers ask, "Smoking or nonsmoking?"
 1. The women's quartet are all married to the pastor.

gregation. Under what conditions did the last pastor leave—retirement, mutual agreement, a tar and feathering? Listen to what people say behind the pastor's back (and behind each others'). Are they kind, understanding, and forgiving? Or are they rude, two-faced, and arrogant? Do they violate each others' privacy by passing on negative information disguised as a prayer request?

Another great tip-off to a critical spirit is when someone says, "Well, bless her heart." Listen closely and you'll probably hear something negative about the person who needs his or her heart blessed. I don't understand how this works exactly, but it's somehow okay to gossip as long as somewhere along the way you say, "Well, bless his heart." Even

Spiritual abuse

Spiritual abuse is any behavior on the part of a Christian or a church that damages your relationship with God. This can occur in many ways—a particular pastor or leader can misuse spiritual authority within the context of your personal relationship, a group of church members can become toxic, you can be taught to believe false things about yourself or God . . . the list is long.

If you suspect you've suffered from spiritual abuse, I recommend logging on to Jeff VanVonderen's web site at www.spiritualabuse.com. He's the guru on recovering from and avoiding spiritual abuse. His web site can get you in touch with resources. Another good place to look is on www. christianrecovery.com, the web site for the National Association for Christian Recovery. Their materials are solid (I wrote some of them myself, so I'm biased), and their network can get you in touch with groups and therapeutic support.

What to Do If Your Church Splits

As history demonstrates in spades, churches are known to split over just about anything. To our shame, Christians have had a hard time discussing and resolving our differences within the context of community. All too often we get mad at each other, break into factions, and split into pieces. Usually one group gets to keep the building while the other(s) start their own thing or join another existing congregation. I'm sad to say that it happens all the time.

I don't know how one can go through a church split and not be wounded in some way—by losing respect for a leader, hearing (and maybe spreading) malicious gossip, having people say untrue or cruel things about you behind your back, losing important relationships, and even questioning how God could let this happen. If you've been caught up in a church split, here are a few pointers that a friend of mine, Rev. Mike Platter, gave me in a recent conversations. They may help you heal and figure out what to do next:

1) Somehow stay in Christian community.

Even though you've been wounded within and by a congregation of Christians, you'll only compound the damage you've suffered if you withdraw from the church entirely. I'm not saying you need to continue attending *that* particular church. In fact, distancing yourself from toxic Christians is a wise thing to do. You may want to attend "Bedside Baptist" and find your church on TV (just avoid weird televangelists who ask for money). Whatever it takes, find some kind of Christian community in which you can heal.

2) Let the church you pick be a "transitional" community.

We need different things at different times in our lives. When we're in good shape, most of us need a place to serve and share out spiritual giftedness. But if you've just been beaten to a pulp, jumping into the middle

meanness can sound spiritual if it's said with a smile and the right religious jargon.

of activity in another congregation may not be good for a while. Give yourself permission to attend a church that will love you without expecting much back, knowing that you're in transition. Eventually, you'll be back to your old self, but hopefully wiser and more forgiving, and you can return to nurturing others. You may end up staying at this new church or moving on. Either way, right now it's your turn and it's not the time to make long-term commitments.

3) Pick a church that tells the story of God and how you fit into that story.

Perhaps a more liturgical church may be a good place to heal, or a megachurch with contemporary music that really speaks to you, or even a small traditional church where they sing all of your favorites—any congregation that understands the transforming power of Christ. Pick one where you can have God's story told to you over and over again, where you're invited to God's table to be fed and fed and fed until you are full. There is spiritual healing in the middle of the ritual and tradition and singing and praying. God truly is present within the worship of believers. Just be there and let God heal your hurts. Before long, you'll find yourself in much better shape.

4) Live in your faith and visit your doubts.

I suspect that you'll never get all of your questions answered or feel totally vindicated or satisfied with your "old" church, but you'll most likely gain enough insight and transformation to continue in your faith. Eventually it will be time to get up, dust yourself off, and get back into the game. When you're ready, look around and I'm sure you'll notice other people who are hurting as badly as you once were who could use your support, prayer, and counsel.

No group is perfect because no human being is perfect—health is a matter of degree. Each congregation will have its own personality, idiosyncrasies, and flaws. You need to use wisdom in discerning whether or not a particular group is "normally" dysfunctional and able to nurture your spiritual walk or has crossed over the line and is a genuine spiritual danger. A church that doesn't understand honest communi-

"Where Should I Go?"

How baffling you are, oh Church,
and yet how I love you!
How you have made me suffer,
and yet how much I owe you!
I should like to see you destroyed,
and yet I need your presence.
You have given me so much scandal
and yet you have made me understand sanctity.

I have seen nothing in the world
more devoted to obscurity, more compromised, more false,
and I have touched nothing
more pure, more generous, more beautiful.

How often I have wanted to shut the doors of my soul in your face,
and how often I have prayed to die in the safety of your arms.

No, I cannot free myself from you, because I am you,
although not completely.

And where should I go?

cation, taking responsibility for wrongs committed and making amends, and facilitating forgiveness and reconciliation is a church that doesn't understand the most basic principles of Christianity. Your best move is to a spiritual community that does.

Guilt is used as a spiritual motivator

God created guilt to let us know when we've failed to act in loving ways. In response, we're expected to take responsibility for our actions, ask for the forgiveness of anyone we've harmed, and make some form of restitution. Guilt is not to be used as a way to get you to give more money, serve on another committee, come forward in a public meeting to "get saved," or any other human intention.

Beware of this aspect of spiritual abuse—for your own protection and certainly for your children. Jesus said that his yoke was easy and his burden light (Matthew 11:30). Those struggling under the load of obligation know little about God's love and too much about the manipulative misuse of guilt on the part of the church.

The church is a financial mess

How financial decisions are made is another significant indicator of the spiritual life of a church. Like people, church organizations can live beyond their means. However, if you go into debt, you're the only one who will suffer the consequences. But when a church accumulates debt, its members are saddled with an unreasonable financial burden. If you become involved in a spiritual community, that means you will become partially responsible for the debt, whether or not you had any input into financial decisions.

Back-breaking debt often results when those in leadership, which includes lay leadership as well as clergy, get their egos overly involved in the church. Often believing that "bigger is better," emphasis is placed on building larger facilities or trying to meet every need in the surrounding community. A spiritually healthy congregation is a realistic one, one with goals that facilitate the spiritual growth of its members rather than submerge them in debt.

Ask a pastor or call the church office and see how easy it is to get copies of financial reports. Find out if there is open disclosure regarding budget expenditures and proof that funds raised for a specific purpose actually go to that purpose. Are financial decisions made behind closed doors and hidden under the mislabel of "confidentiality"? Remember, if there is nothing to hide, nothing will be hidden. You will have found a healthy church where the ministry goals liberate, not obligate, its congregants.

The church teaches a distorted view of God

Identifying abusive Christian teaching isn't as simple as checking everything the pastor says against the Nicene Creed. A church may have its theological ducks in a row and still be a spiritually dangerous place. As Dale Ryan, the executive director of Christian Recovery International, writes, "Our theological convictions may be thoroughly orthodox, but we may actually serve a god who is quick to anger and slow to forgive. Or a god who shames his followers. Or a god who is punitive and rejecting."

Being on solid spiritual ground is more than giving an intellectual nod to the right creeds; it's about participating in a healthy relationship with God. If we misunderstand who God is, our relationship suffers. Spiritually abusive teaching promotes, either overtly or covertly, God as being punitive, vindictive, inattentive, impotent, and shaming. There are more distortions of course, but you get the idea.

If a church doesn't help you fall in love with God, then it's not a church that knows God. No matter what they've got on paper, it's not in their hearts. Such a church can only undermine your spiritual growth, so check that congregation off your list. Ask God to lead you to believers who have encountered the most loving Being in the universe.

Further Info

- Gene Edwards, *Crucified by Christians* (The Seed Sowers, 1995)

- Donald E. Sloat, *The Dangers of Growing Up in a Christian Home* (Nelson, 1986)

- Stephen Arterburn and Jack Felton, *More Jesus, Less Religion: Moving from Rules to Relationship* (Waterbrook Press, 2000)

- David Johnson and Jeff VanVonderen, *The Subtle Power of Spiritual Abuse* (Bethany House, 1991)

- Mary Alice Chrnalogar, *Twisted Scriptures* (Zondervan, 2000)

- Juanita and Dale Ryan, *Life Recovery Guides* (InterVarsity Press, 1992)

Part 2

Denominational
Groupings

A number of denominations are described in this section to let you know what they believe, how they practice their beliefs, and what they might expect from you if you join.

Finding a way to list churches that didn't make things more confusing was a challenge. I decided to group them according to worship styles and then roughly (and I do mean roughly) by historical sequence.

In case your mind doesn't work that way, here's an alphabetical listing of all the churches mentioned. Also, in Part Three churches are grouped in a variety of ways to help you compare one with another. The index gives you every reference to particular churches or religious movements—so that may help you as well.

Churches described in this book listed in alphabetical order:
African Methodist Episcopal Zion Church
African Methodist Episcopal Church
American Baptist Churches in the U.S.A.
Assemblies of God
Christian Church (Disciples of Christ)
Christian Methodist Episcopal Church
Christian Reformed Church in North America

Church of the Nazarene
Churches of Christ
Conservative Congregational Christian Conference
Cumberland Presbyterian Church in America
Episcopal Church
Evangelical Lutheran Church in America
Greek Orthodox Archdiocese of North America
International Church of the Foursquare Gospel
Lutheran Church-Missouri Synod
Mennonite Church USA
Moravian Church in America
National Association of Congregational Christians Churches
National Association of Free Will Baptists
National Baptist Convention of America, Inc.
National Baptist Convention, USA, Inc.
Old Catholics
Orthodox Church in America (Russian Orthodox)
Presbyterian Church in America
Presbyterian Church USA
Progressive National Baptist Convention
Protestant Reformed Churches in America
Reformed Church in America
Roman Catholic Church
Salvation Army
Southern Baptist Convention
United Church of Christ
United Methodist Church
VineyardUSA
Wesleyan Church

Selecting a spiritual community is one of the most significant deci-sions you can make in life. Those who travel alongside you will undoubtedly influence and enhance (or possibly undermine and sour) your spiritual experiences. The better informed you are about the Christian faith, as well as specific denominations—their history, views, and practices—the more wisely the choice can be made.

four

Orthodox
Churches

For the most part, American concern with historical Christianity has focused on the Roman Catholic Church and its Protestant offshoots—a bias that is illustrated by this book. The majority of my overview (I'll be honest . . . every section except this one) describes denominations that developed in the West. I feel it's important to acknowledge that one section cannot adequately represent the Eastern portion of Christendom, which makes up the second largest organized body of Christians in the world, but I hope this overview gives you a place to start should you want to explore more fully the various expressions of the Orthodox Church.

A Brief History of the Orthodox Church

How did this approach to Christianity develop? Why is it similar to yet different from those denominations from the West? To get a glimpse of the Orthodox Church's unique perspective on doctrine and worship, it's important to see how the church and the history of the Byzantine Empire are intertwined.

From Byzantium to Constantinople

The heart of the Orthodox Church beats in the city of ancient Byzantium (renamed Constantinople in 330 and Istanbul in 1930). In 667

Constantine's
Unusual Conversion

According to the account Constantine told Eusebius, a historian who chronicled the story, Constantine's conversion occurred immediately before the battle of Milvian Bridge. Factions within the Roman Empire were struggling for power and Constantine decided he could use all the help he could get. So, in the middle of the day, he prayed for assistance. He and his army saw a vision in the sky of a cross and the words, "in this sign you'll be victorious" (in Latin). That night he had a dream that confirmed his daylight vision. The next day he instructed artisans to construct the sign that was the intersection of the Greek letters chi and rho in gold and stones. The image was carried into battle and Constantinople won a decisive victory. Once in power, Constantine put an end to the persecution of the church, elevated it, and participated in establishing doctrinal orthodoxy.

B.C., Byzantium was founded at the entrance of the Black Sea by Byzas as a colony of Greek city-states. Alexander the Great (356–323 B.C.) conquered Byzantium as his empire expanded into India. Alexander's empire was divided up after his death and then reconquered by the Romans.

From the obscure Roman-occupied city of Jerusalem, a new religion rapidly spread throughout the Empire. Roman Emperors intermittently persecuted the church until Constantine came to power. Emperor Constantine did (at least) three things that significantly affected the church: he legitimized Christianity, called the first ecumenical council, and moved the seat of the empire from Rome to Byzantium, renamed Constantinople.

Within this new political center, the East and West met and intermingled. The elite of Constantinople spoke Latin while the general population conversed in Greek. The church from the West provided religious and cultural teaching, yet also supported the study of ancient Greek classics, including literature, medicine, art, and science. Constantine imported the finest Greek and Roman art from all areas of his empire, which included Europe to the West and to the East—southwestern Asia, northeastern Africa, today's Balkan Peninsula, Syria, Jordan, Israel, Lebanon, Cypress, Egypt, and part of Libya. The best of both worlds were combined in Constantinople.

Constantine died in 337, with Thedodosius taking the throne. Under Theodosius's rule two important church meetings took place. The Second Ecumenical Council was held in Constantinople in 381 with the patriarch of Constantinople, St. Gregory of Nazianzus, presiding. This council denounced the Macedonius movement, which promoted the idea that God is two persons—Father and Son—while the Holy Spirit is simply a power of God. To combat this notion, the filioque clause, "and the Son," was added to the Nicene Creed. In 393, the Synod of

Hippo agreed upon a list of inspired writings now referred to as the New Testament.

The Roman Empire Breaks in Half

When asked the question, "When did the Roman Empire fall?" it would be quite appropriate to answer with a question of your own, "Which one?" We in the West usually refer to the fall of Rome itself as the mark of the end of the Roman Empire. However, the Empire had already been divided when the German tribes conquered Rome. The Eastern portion, now called the Byzantine Empire, continued until captured by the Ottoman Turks over a thousand years later. There's a bit of a controversy about who deserves the name of the Roman Empire since both saw themselves as a continuation of the same kingdom. For the sake of clarity I'll refer to the Western portion as the Roman Empire and the Eastern portion as the Byzantine Empire.

Ecumenical Councils

Councils are assemblies of clergy and theological bigwigs that gather to discuss and establish church doctrine and discipline. An ecumenical council is made up of representatives from the worldwide church—not one, two, or even three denominations—but from the entire church. For the first several hundred years the church was united enough to hold true ecumenical councils. But as the splintering of the church increased, more and more parts of Christendom were excluded or refused to attend the gatherings. Today, many denominations are trying to establish relationships with other branches of Christianity with a goal of, someday, holding true ecumenical councils once again.

The division of the Roman Empire wasn't caused by outside influences, but by the empire itself. After Theodosuis died in 395, this massive Roman Empire was ruled by his two sons, Arcadius, who was seventeen, and Honorius, who was ten. The Western portion didn't last long. Just fifteen years later, Rome was invaded and pillaged by the Visigoths. Internal rebellions further weakened Rome, and by 476, the

'Tis the Day of
Resurrection

St. John of Damascus, considered by some the last of the Greek church fathers, is credited with writing the first ode in the Golden Canon for Easter Day. He lived part of his life as a Christian representative in the court of Damascus and later in the remote monastery of St. Sabas in between the Dead Sea and Jerusalem. Not only did he defend the use of icons in the church, he wrote the book, *The Fount of Wisdom,* that proved to be foundational in Orthodox doctrine. At midnight on Easter eve, Greek Orthodox all over the world sing St. John's words as candles are lighted throughout the gathering.

1
'Tis the day of Resurrection,
    Earth, tell it out abroad!
The Passover of gladness,
    The Passover of God!
From death to life eternal,
    From earth unto the sky,
Our Christ hath brought us over
    With hymns of victory.

2
Our hearts be pure from evil,
    That we may see aright
The Lord in rays eternal
    Of Resurrection-light;

And, listening to his accents,
    May hear, so calm and plain,
His own 'All hail,' and, hearing,
    May raise the victor strain.

3
Now let the heav'ns be joyful,
    Let earth her song begin,
The round world keep high triumph,
    And all this is therein;
Invisible and visible,
    Their notes let all things blend,
For Christ the Lord is risen,
    Our joy that hath no end.

last Roman emperor, Agustulus Romulus, was overthrown by German invaders.

While the political system in the West was coming undone, the Eastern portion survived. When Emperor Arcadius died in 408, his son, Theodosius II, was crowned Emperor in Constantinople. Attila the Hun invaded a few times in the early 400s, but the Byzantines either fought him back or paid him off. Theodosius II died in 450 and Byzantine Emperor Marcian stepped into power.

As the Empire was splitting in two, the church tried to hold itself together. In 451, the Fourth Ecumenical Council was called in Chalcedon in response to a schism in the church between the Orthodox and Monophysite factions. The Monophysites believed that Jesus' humanity was dissolved into God's divinity, making him solely divine. The Council reiterated that Jesus was wholly God and wholly man simultaneously. In addition, five official Christian centers were recognized, each with its own patriarch: Rome, Constantinople, Alexandria, Antioch, and Jerusalem. These centers were referred to as patriarchates. Rome was considered the first among equals, but essentially the structure was democratic. As you might guess, cooperation didn't last long.

A few emperors came and went, some murdered to make room for their successors. The next major player was Emperor Justinian (483–565), who recaptured Western territory that had been lost to invaders—Italy, Sicily, Sardinia, parts of Spain, and northern Africa. Contributing to Constantinople's grandeur, Justinian built a number of amazing buildings, including the domed church of Hagia Sophia (Holy Wisdom), completed in 537, and a monastery on Mount Sinai, completed in 565. Under his rule, the Fifth Ecumenical Council met in Constantinople confirming (once again) that Jesus has two natures, divine and human. But the Orthodox Christians were not able to get the upper hand until the Monothelites were banned in the Sixth Ecumenical Council of 680.

The early 600s were hard on the Eastern empire. In 614 the Persians captured Jerusalem and carried off what was believed at the time to be the cross on which Jesus was crucified. The Persians then attacked Constantinople, but the city valiantly fought back. After ten years of war, the Byzantines finally won in 627. Twelve years after that victory, the Empire experienced defeat when Syria, the Holy Land, Egypt, and Jordan were taken over by Islamic armies in 639. Three of the five Christian centers were significantly stifled by the Muslims, leaving Rome to oversee in the West, and Constantinople the primary church in the East. The Muslims declared jihad or holy war on Constantinople in 670 and again in 717, but both times the city successfully defended itself.

The next major threat to the church came not from invading armies but from within the empire. In 726, Byzantine Emperor Leo III launched a violent religious oppression called the Iconoclastic Controversy (which might better be labeled the Icon Massacre, if you ask

Jihad

Jihad is a term few of us knew prior to September 11, 2001. Today, Americans connect the term with terrorism; Christians in Constantinople would probably agree with our association with the term. Technically "jihad" is Arabic for "struggle" and can refer to one's own struggle with his or her own sin. To some extremist Muslims, this struggle should be carried out against others, even through violence. Though the Koran condemns acts of warfare, after Mohammed's death his followers came up with the concept of jihad to justify their military exploits. Their goal has been to "conquer the rest of the non-Muslim world 'so that the world could reflect the divine unity [of God]'"

me). The Byzantine church used icons, or sacred images, in worship. Some of the Orthodox leadership tried to convince Emperor Leo III that honoring icons was idol worship and in direct violation of the Old Testament commandments. He was unconvinced until an underwater volcano erupted in the Aegean Sea, dark volcanic ash spewed into the sky, and huge tidal waves swept over coastal areas. The emperor took this as a sign that God was miffed and he sided with the "iconoclasts." Leo III launched his attack on icons and a vast number of religious works of art, and those who defended them were obliterated.

Leo's son, Constantine IV, continued his father's campaign. In 754 he gathered 338 hand-picked bishops for the Council of Hieria. The council dubbed itself the Seventh Ecumenical Council and rejected the use of icons in worship. During the "decade of blood" from 762 to 775, thousands of people who tried to protect icons were exiled, publicly humiliated, tortured, or killed.

Constantine IV died in 775, succeeded by his son, Leo IV, who, fortunately, was not as aggressively anti-icon. Leo IV died after ruling five years, and his wife, Irene, ruled as regent for their son. Irene had secretly been pro-icon and, once in power, reversed direction. In 787 Irene called together a council that is now considered the authentic Seventh Ecumenical Council. The Council stated, "We declare that one may render to icons the veneration of honor (*proskunesis*), not true worship (*latreia*) of our faith, which is due only to the divine nature." The Seventh Ecumenical Council marked the last time such a meeting was honored by the Orthodox portion of the church.

In 790, Constantine V got tired of Irene running the show. He took his rightful claim to the throne and removed his mother from power. He unwisely trusted her and decided not to have her imprisoned. After seven years of conspiring behind her son's back, Irene had her son seized, his eyes gouged out, and then imprisoned him in a monastery. For the first time, a woman claimed the throne on her own behalf.

The Church Breaks in Half

While all this intrigue was occurring in the East, huge news was about to pop in the West. Charlemagne, King of the Franks, wanted what the Byzantine Empire had—a vast kingdom that was seen as the continuation of the Roman Empire. In 800, he got the patriarch in Rome, Pope Leo III, to crown him "Emperor of the West." To further drive his point home, Charlemagne called his kingdom the "Holy Roman Empire." Not only did he take the title Roman Empire, he made it holy on top of that. Since the Byzantine Empire thought of itself as the Roman Empire, this proclamation didn't make Empress Irene happy. Furthermore, the church in Constantinople was very upset about the role the church in Rome was playing in this drama.

Before Empress Irene could do much about it, in 802 she was seized in the night, taken to a convent, and forced to take the vows of a nun. She was replaced by Nicerphorus, who died in 811. His son-in-law, Michael Phangable, was in power for one year, just long enough to recognize Charlemagne as the Emperor of the West. Charlemagne had what he wanted.

Emperor Phangable was tossed out by one of his soldiers, Leo V. In 815, Emperor Leo V once again abolished icons, a decision that was overturned by Empress Theodora in 843. Theodora's final and lasting decision put an end to the iconoclastic persecutions.

The Past and the Future

The true orthodox way of thought has always been historical, has always included the past, but has never been enslaved by it . . . [for] the strength of the Church is not in the past, present, or future, but in Christ.

Fr. Alexander Schmemann

But as the conflict over icons was cooling off, the clash between Orthodoxy and Roman Christianity was heating up. Empress Theodora's son, Michael III, replaced the ruling Orthodox patriarch Ignatius with Photius in 867. Photius squared off with the patriarch in Rome by challenging clerical celibacy, rejecting the filioque clause that was added to the Nicene Creed, and denouncing the crowning of Charlemagne as the Emperor of the Holy Roman Empire. The patriarch in Rome denounced him right back.

While the church was squabbling, Michael III developed a drinking problem (earning the nickname Michael the Drunkard). He also had a problem with picking his friends. In 867, his drinking buddy, Basil of Macedonia, had him murdered and then took over as emperor. Basil was the first of the Macedonian dynasty that ruled Constantinople for nearly two centuries. Under his leadership, the Eighth Ecumenical Council met from 869 to 887 in Constantinople, wherein Photius was condemned for his stand against the West. The Orthodox Church did not (and still doesn't) recognize the legitimacy of this council.

For the next 167 years the tension between the two factions of the church intensified until 1054 when the Pope of Rome and the Patriarch of Constantinople excommunicated each other. This date is called the Great Schism, marking the break between the Eastern and Western portions of the church. But it seems to me that the final break between the two came a little over a hundred years later during the Fourth Crusade.

Crusaders to the Rescue . . . Sort Of

Muslim Turks declared jihad on Constantinople and it soon became clear that the Empire needed help fighting back. Byzantine Emperor Alexius I asked Pope Urban II of Rome to send soldiers to help in the battle. Even though Muslims hadn't invaded Europe, European Christians viewed Muslims as the aggressors as they conquered territory previously "Christianized." This sentiment was especially true when Muslims took control of the Holy Lands. In addition, Western Christians feared that the Muslims would not stop until they had conquered Europe as well.

Pope Urban II not only agreed to help Constantinople, he expanded the vision to include liberating Jerusalem from "the unbelievers." The pope called the Council of Clermont in 1095 and declared that anyone who would fight in the Crusade against the Muslims in occupied Jerusalem would receive full pardons of their sins and any criminal offenses they may have committed. Approximately sixty thousand men and women volunteered. For the next three years the Crusaders pillaged across Europe, losing two-thirds in battle. Reinforcements were sent and Jerusalem was finally captured, launching the Latin kingdom of Jerusalem.

Some fifty years later the descendents of these Crusaders sent word to the West that they were starving to death within the city walls. The Muslims controlled the area around Jerusalem and kept food from getting through. The Second Crusade (1145–1149), led by Louis VII of France, tried to come to their aid. Most of the Crusaders died in route and the rest were killed in battle. In 1187, the Muslims recaptured Jerusalem. Not known for their ability to lose well, Western Europeans planned their next attack.

From 1187 to 1192 Richard I (the Lionhearted) led a combined effort of German, French, and English Crusaders to restore Jerusalem to Christian control. The Third Crusaders were not up to the task and the Muslims retained control. Six years later, the Fourth Crusade was launched with the purpose of trying once again to invade Jerusalem. Unfortunately for the Byzantines, and for Christendom in general, these Crusaders got sidetracked by greed and an intense desire to win at least one battle. They attacked their unsuspecting allies in Constantinople instead of the powerful Muslim army in Jerusalem.

Even though Constantinople was a "Christian" city and had originally asked for military support, the Roman Catholic Crusaders ripped the city apart. Orthodox churches were plundered, with an enormous amount of religious art stolen and taken to the West. Libraries that included irreplaceable sacred documents were destroyed. The devastation of the most cherished aspects of the Orthodox Church at the hands of Roman Catholic Christians was the last straw. The break between the two churches was complete and lasting.

Protestantism and
Orthodoxy

Luther and the Orthodox Church had several things in common—all related to the Roman Catholic Church. Both rejected papal supremacy, celibacy for the clergy, indulgences, and Communion by bread alone. In fact, Luther was known to point to the existence of the Orthodox Church as evidence of how far Roman Catholicism had strayed from original Christian ideas.

I guess Luther had his hands full renovating Europe, as he never made any effort to connect with the Orthodox Church. But his colleagues did. The Lutherans saw linking up with the Orthodox against Roman Catholicism a victory. The Lutherans and Orthodox engaged in an open six-year dialogue starting in 1575, resulting in over four hundred pages of correspondence. But by the time they sorted out various doctrines and worship practices, the Orthodox found they had much more in common with the Catholics than the Protestants. Certainly the Protestant propensity to break away and form new denominations was utterly unacceptable to the East.

The last four Crusades—the Fifth (1217–1221), the Sixth (1228–1229), the Seventh (1248–1254), and the Eighth (1270–1272)—were fought against the Muslims, leaving untold desolation in their wakes. It's hard to justify such horror as a Christian endeavor, although there are some who try. Ultimately, the Crusades sowed seeds of hatred in the hearts of the Muslims who saw the Crusaders as thieves trying to take the lands they believed were rightfully theirs. Perhaps the deepest wound inflicted by the Crusades was on the church itself, which resulted in a vast chasm of animosity between Christians in the East and West that is still reaping a sorrowful harvest today.

The Turks Triumph

After keeping the Muslims at bay for a great many years, Constantinople finally fell captive to the Ottoman Turks in 1453. The Orthodox Church found itself surrounded by an Islamic sea of hostility. The Orthodox community in the Balkans and the Near East was largely cut off from the rest of Christendom for the next four hundred years.

Hagia Sophia and the Parthenon were turned into mosques. Many smaller churches, however, were left untouched, and Christianity was tolerated to the extent that Jesus was recognized as a prophet by the Muslims. But the church was not allowed to share Christian teaching with Muslims. While it was legal to convert to Islam, converting to Christianity meant automatic execution. No new churches were built, no church bells rang, and many Orthodox believers found converting to Islam preferable to living marginal or short lives as Christians.

In addition, corruption was rampant in the Orthodox Church under Ottoman rule. Few Patriarchs died natural deaths—most succumbed to one kind of assassination or another at the hands of so-called church leaders. Power, rather than any spiritual calling, brought leadership into the church.

But Wait, It Gets Worse

The Russian Revolution of 1917 and the expansion of the Soviet Union brought an even graver threat to Orthodoxy. Communism wasn't just another oppressive government, it was an overtly *anti-Christian* regime. Plus, the Russian Orthodox Church in particular was associated with the czars. While Christians had been persecuted over the years because they wouldn't worship the Emperor or Allah or whomever, it wasn't until the communists took over that Christianity was directly targeted for annihilation. Thousands of Christians, clergy and lay people, were systematically hunted down and killed within the confines of the Soviet Union. The exact numbers are not known, but may exceed those who died at the hands of the Roman Empire.

While systematic persecution of Christians occurred in the background, the Soviets forced remaining clergy to support the communist regime and set up a bogus church structure called the Renovated, or Living, Church. The government reached around the world with this power and was able to seize church property in the United States using this ruse. Orthodox Christians who did not support the Living Church were harassed, tortured, and executed by the Soviet government. The stripping and demolishing of churches continued so that by World War II, the Orthodox Church, especially the Russian Orthodox Church, was all but destroyed. Most clergy loyal to Orthodoxy had been imprisoned in concentration camps or were in hiding.

The Second World War brought about an odd, tenuous alliance between the Soviets and the church. Seeing the church as a source of moral support during a time of invasion, in 1927 Stalin enlisted the aid of all resources in the war, including the Orthodox Church. The Living Church was disbanded and suddenly, traditional Orthodox churches were open for services and clergy were released from the camps. The church gave assistance freely. Stalin actually met with church leaders in 1943. However, under Khrushchev, thousands of Orthodox Churches were closed again "for ideological reasons."

The dismantling of the Soviet Union put an end to an era of tyranny for Orthodox Christians within its borders. Now under the rule of smaller governments, some branches of the Orthodox Church are experiencing more freedom and safety while others continue under oppressive regimes. With internal corruption and external oppression, it is a miracle that the Orthodox Church survived in any form, let alone with its traditions and beliefs intact.

What Makes a Church Orthodox?

The Orthodox Church goes by a wide variety of names, which can be quite confusing. It is sometimes called Eastern Orthodox, Oriental Orthodox, or, to really complicate things, the Orthodox Catholic Church. All of these names are interchangeable and refer to the Orthodox Church in general.

The Orthodox Church is similar to the Roman Catholic Church in that it has managed to retain doctrinal unity while allowing for unique cultural expressions of faith. For example, Catholics in Ireland differ in culture from Catholics in Spain or in Africa, but they are Catholics all the same. As Orthodox missionaries spread throughout Eastern Europe, Russia, Turkey, and the Middle East, the liturgy was translated into the language of the people, and each nationality developed its own variation on the theme.

Unlike Roman Catholicism, however, Orthodoxy does not have one overarching governing body. Even though all Orthodox churches recognize the spiritual preeminence of the ecumenical patriarch of Constantinople, each major Orthodox center has its own bishop who is independent of any other bishop. Consequently, along with cultural differences among Greek Orthodox, Russian Orthodox, Ukrainian Orthodox, and Romanian Orthodox, you'll also find different organizational hierarchies.

If you visit an Orthodox Church without understanding the symbolism and meaning of the worship and surroundings, you may find the experience romantically mystical, or simply like watching a bunch

Orthodox **Saints**

The Orthodox Church reveres saints who are seen as people who have shared in the holiness of God. They have several classifications of saints, such as the holy fathers, apostles, specific monks and nuns, and righteous lay people. They even have a special category called "fools for Christ's sake," those who abandoned normal necessities to witness for Christ.

Studying and revering the writings and lives of the saints is believed to contribute to one's spiritual growth. Their writings are not seen as infallible, but they can be helpful when interpreted in light of the tradition of the church. To genuinely gain from this endeavor, one needs some wisdom and the ability to discern the difference between fanciful tales and authentic experience. It is asserted that "a careful reading of the lives of the saints will almost always reveal what is authentic and true in the realm of the miraculous. Also, the point has been rightly made that men can learn almost as much about the real meaning of Christianity from the legends of the saints produced within the tradition of the Church as from the authentic lives themselves."

The Orthodox are big on church fathers (the church mothers are mostly neglected) including Saints Basil the Great, John Chrysostom, Gregory of Nazianzus, Cyril of Jerusalem, Gregory of Nyssa, Ignatius of Antioch, Irenaeus of Lyons, Athanasius of Alexandria, Maximus the Confessor, John of Damascus, Photius of Constantinople, Gregory Palamas, Anthony of Egypt, Macarius of Egypt, John of the Ladder, Isaac of Syria, Ephraim of Syria, and Simeon the New Theologian, to name a few.

men in strange outfits conducting unintelligible rituals. Behind the many faces of Orthodoxy stands a common theological, sacramental, liturgical, and spiritual identity.

One and Only One Church

The Orthodox Church considers itself to be the one and only true church. While the Orthodox Church has its "human" organizational elements, it is fundamentally a divine mystery, alive and dynamic. It is also the only Christian body that has kept its teaching free of heresy, retaining "its absolute integrity in the face of the changes and innovations that have occurred within Christianity." Furthermore, it claims to be the kingdom of God on earth glorifying God "with the right worship," the living embodiment of the undivided church.

Protecting the purity of truth has been possible, in part, to the "Greekness" of Orthodox tradition. Some (especially Protestants) argue that translating Hebrew thought-forms and language into the Greek translations of the New Testament has altered and somewhat corrupted the original message. But, along with Father Georges Florovsky, the Orthodox believe that "Hellenism is not simply a phrase in the history of Christianity but a cornerstone in its life." From their perspective, three major cultures came together to create the truth of Christianity. The original Judeo-Christian message was transmitted through the Jews, in the Hebrew language. The Roman Empire provided a unified political world in which to spread this message. But Greek, not Latin, was the language of the people. They point to the fact that Paul, an apostle and author of several books in the New Testament, wrote his letters in Greek, not Hebrew or Latin. Even the liturgy in the church in Rome was Greek until the third century. The Orthodox Church holds onto its Greek heritage as inherently engrained in true Christian teaching.

This is not to say that you have to be Orthodox in order to be a Christian, or that everyone who is a member of the Orthodox Church is thereby a Christian. The state of a person's soul is ultimately judged by God. But according to Orthodoxy, if you worship with other believers on a Sunday morning and it doesn't say "Orthodox" out front, you're not *really* or fully in church.

The claim of exclusivity can be a bit off-putting in our culture of "whatever works for you is fine." And, not being Orthodox myself, it's a little hard to swallow that I'm not a part of the real church, not even a marginally enlightened part. But researching this denomination has given me a lot to think about, and I hope you will give the Orthodox a chance, even if they may sound amazingly arrogant to some ears. In some respects this denomination isn't any different than all the others who believe they have a corner on truth. And who knows? Maybe they're right . . .

Theosis

The concept of theosis, deification, or "becoming God" is at the

Major Orthodox Feast Days

Exaltation of the Holy Cross:
September 14

Presentation of the Theotokos in the Temple:
November 21

Christmas (Nativity of Jesus Christ):
December 25

Epiphany (Baptism of Christ):
January 6

Presentation of Christ in the Temple:
February 2

Annunciation (Evangelismos):
March 25

Easter (Pascha):
(Varies from year to year)

Ascension:
40 Days after Easter

Pentecost:
50 Days after Easter

Transfiguration of Christ:
August 6

Dormition (death) of the Theotokos (also called *Kimissis*):
August 15

heart of Orthodoxy. They believe that "God became man so that man might become God." When I first read this and similar statements, I thought they were promoting the idea of our becoming absorbed into God (similar to Hinduism) or becoming little gods (similar to Mormonism or some New Age ideas). Both of these concepts are outside Christianity as I understand it. I mused, "These Orthodox folks aren't as orthodox as I thought."

But on closer look, I discovered that the doctrine of theosis is unique, but very Christian. First, there is a difference between how Orthodoxy and churches in the West view the current state of humanity. Orthodoxy believes that humanity was created in both the image and likeness of God. The fall of humanity resulted in the loss of our likeness to God, but not our image. In marked contrast, most Western denominations claim that the fall of humanity had a more debilitating impact on us. The most extreme in this category is the Calvinist who believes that fallen humanity is totally depraved. The Orthodox believe that God's image remains intact and effective in humanity, and our Christian journey is the process of "restoration of the lost likeness to those who have been redeemed in Christ."

The Orthodox believes that "the energies of God" radiate from God's essence. The Holy Spirit communicates God's energies to us so that we personally partake in the divine nature. Although we will never be fully divine or lose our personal identities, by following the teachings of the Orthodox Church we can come as close as possible to being God-like.

The Mystery of Orthodox Worship

The Orthodox Church exists for the purpose of revealing the Christian mystery through the divine liturgy. Within the Orthodox worship experience, Christians communicate with God, learn more about God, and become more like God. Eventually the kingdom of God, which is life in and with God, will "come with observation, with power and glory, when Christ will be revealed and God will be 'all in all.'" But for now the kingdom of God is here in the form of the Orthodox Church through "symbol and sacrament."

Since humanity is believed to retain God's image, the Orthodox Church celebrates creativity and beauty in a way that is distinct from the West. Symbols and sacraments have provided a variety of artistic expressions through architecture, music, sculpture, needle-work, poetry, icons, and vestments, and are seen less as teaching tools or depictions than as avenues through which one can experience God.

The architecture of the church is designed to help believers to experience the kingdom of God on earth. Orthodox churches are some of the most magnificent in the world. The layout of the buildings with their domed ceilings and the use of icons and other artistic expressions draw worshipers out of everyday life and into a world of spiritual mystery.

The icon has been called Orthodoxy's highest artistic achievement. In itself, an icon is a beautiful piece of art. But spiritually, the icon is the combination of divinity and humanity, the spirit and material worlds. Depictions of Christ, Mary, the apostles, saints, and sacred events bring believers into the experience of the mystery of Christianity. Not merely a reproduction of a person or an occurence, icons are "an inexhaustible source of revelation of the Orthodox doctrine and faith."

The divine liturgy guides Orthodox worship, utilizing these various creative forms, leading to the apex of worship: Holy Communion—a true act of communing with the Trinity.

Orthodox Sacraments

Like the Roman Catholic Church, the Orthodox Church holds to seven sacraments, although they stress that a life filled with the Spirit of God is itself a sacrament.

- Baptism: The Orthodox baptize infants and adults as an individual's personal Easter—a celebration of participating in Christ's death and resurrection.

- Chrismation: Through chrismation, or confirmation, a person receives the "seal of the gift of the Holy Spirit." One is able to live a life of love and participate in theosis by the power of the Spirit of God. This can be viewed as an individual's personal Pentecost.

- Holy Communion: Considered the "sacrament of sacraments," Holy Communion is the fulfillment of every other sacrament in which believers share the banquet of the kingdom of God, the body and blood of Christ. When bread and wine are consecrated by the Holy Spirit through the bishop or priest, the elements are mystically changed into the body and blood of Christ.

- Marriage: In Orthodox marriages, Christ transforms human love into divine and unending love.

- Anointing of the Sick: Human suffering is consecrated with the suffering of Christ, thereby transforming our wounds as the way to eternal life instead of death.

- Confession: Through the sacrament of repentance, believers receive Christ's forgiveness.

- Holy Orders: A sacrament for the clergy, holy orders maintain the continuity of the church from the first church in Jerusalem to the many congregations throughout the world today. Clergy are comprised of three orders: deacon, presbyter, and bishop. A priest can be married if he was married before he entered the priesthood. The position of bishop is reserved for monastic clergy who have taken the vow of celibacy.

Orthodox Church in America (formerly Russian Orthodox)

Approximately five million Americans have found a spiritual home in Orthodox churches. While one church structure developed in many of the countries evangelized by the Orthodox, this model was not replicated in the United States due, in part, to the fact that the Orthodox Church was cut off from the West when America was being established. You can find a variety of Orthodox churches to choose from. Only recently has the Russian Orthodox Church taken the lead by changing its name to the Orthodox Church in America.

The Russian Orthodox Church traces its roots to 954 when Princess Olga of Kiev was baptized as a Christian. The Christianization of the Russian people is marked by Prince Vladimir's baptism in 988. Some of the most breathtaking Orthodox churches were built in Russia beginning in the tenth century. Monasteries in the eleventh century served as religious and educational centers for the Russian people. Historical records, art, and literature were gathered, developed, and protected by the monasteries. In addition, iconography and other art forms flourished. Over the centuries, as Russia was invaded by outsiders, these libraries and art collections served as reference points for retaining the Russian culture.

In Russia today the church is experiencing a renewal under the leadership of his holiness Patriarch Alexy II of Moscow and All Russia. The Russian Orthodox Church has 128 dioceses compared to 67 diocese in 1989; 19,000 parishes compared to 6,893 in 1988; and nearly 480 monasteries compared to 18 in 1980.

Just the FACTS

Orthodox Church in America

Kind of Church:	Orthodox/Russian
Worship Style:	Liturgical
Church Structure:	Hierarchical
Trinity Affinity:	Father
Clout Continuum:	1st place: Orthodox tradition
	2nd place: Personal experience through sacraments
	3rd place: Scripture
Founded in USA:	1794/1970
Members In USA:	1,000,000
Churches in USA:	710
Headquarters:	P.O. Box 675, Sysosset NY 11791–0675
Phone:	516-922-0550
Web site:	www.oca.org

The first Russian Orthodox missionaries arrived in Alaska, then a part of Russia, in 1794. By 1840 a bishop was assigned to the area. With further expansion, the seat of authority was moved from Alaska to San Francisco in 1872. By 1905 the administrative headquarters were relocated once again, this time to New York City.

The church was formally known as the Russian Orthodox Greek Catholic Church of America. After the patriarche of Moscow granted the church the right to govern itself as an independent, indigenous body in 1970, the name was changed to the Orthodox Church in America. Today the Orthodox Church in America maintains filial ties with the Holy Patriarchate of Moscow and All Russia and is in communion with other autocephalous churches and patriarichates of the Orthodox Church around the world.

According to their web site, "The Mission of the Orthodox Church in America, the local autocephalous Orthodox Church, is to be faithful in fulfilling the commandment of Christ to 'Go into all the world and make disciples of all Nations, baptizing them in the name of the Father, and of the Son and of the Holy Spirit, teaching them to observe all [things that He has] commanded' so that all people may be saved and come to the knowledge of the truth:

> To preach, in accordance with God's will, the fullness of the gospel of the Kingdom to the peoples of North America and to invite them to become members of the Orthodox Church

> To utilize for her mission the various languages of the peoples of this continent

> To be the body of Christ in North America and to be faithful to the tradition of the Holy Orthodox Church

> To witness to the truth, and by God's grace and in the power of the Holy Spirit, to reveal Christ's way of sanctification and eternal salvation to all."

(Adopted in 1990
by the Holy Synod of Bishops
of the Orthodox Church in America)

How to Speak
Orthodox-ese

Autocephalous: Orthodox churches that operate independently of the patriarchates churches.

Patriarchates: Church centers that are recognized by and work in association with the Orthodox Church in Constantinople.

Greek Orthodox Archdiocese of North America

The first Greek Orthodox Church in America was founded in 1864 in New Orleans, Louisiana. Soon after, a large number of Greek immigrants came to the U.S. between 1890 and 1929, making Greek Orthodoxy the largest Orthodox body in America. Getting established and including new members has been a challenge for cultural and language reasons. (Except for a few seminary students and Greek immigrants, who knows Greek?) In addition, church organization has been a source of confusion.

The problem began in 1453 when the Ottoman Turks captured Constantinople. The Muslims subjugated all Orthodox Churches within the empire to the ecumenical patriarchate of Constantinople, disrupting the structure of the Greek Orthodox Church. In the 1800s an independent but cooperative Holy Synod was set up in Greece. Both bodies sent priests to serve in Greek Orthodox Churches in the United States. The situation was further complicated between 1908 and 1922 when the jurisdiction of U.S. churches moved from Constantinople to Greece and back again. The issue was resolved in 1922 with the establishment of the Greek Orthodox Archdiocese of North and South America.

Today, the Greek Orthodox Archiocese in America has been led by His Eminence Archbishop Demetrios since 1999, the sixth archbishop since the church was established in 1922. One of his predecessors, His Eminence Archbishop Iakovos, negotiated a new charter with the ecumenical patriarchate in 1978. As a result, New York was established as the center of an archdiocesan district with ten dioceses: New Jersey, Chicago, Atlanta, Detroit, Toronto, San Francisco, Pittsburgh, Buenos Aires, Boston, and Denver. The Archdiocese is governed by the archbishop and the Synod of Bishops comprised of the ten bishops presiding over the dioceses. A Clergy-Laity Congress, comprised of delegates selected by parishes, submits decisions for approval and ratification to the ecumenical patriarchate. Local parishes are governed by their priest and a parish council. Ultimately the parish priest is responsible to the bishop.

Just the **FACTS**

Greek Orthodox Archdiocese of North America

Kind of Church: Orthodox/Greek

Worship Style: Liturgical

Trinity Affinity: Father

Christian Clout: 1st place: Tradition

2nd place: Personal experience through sacraments

3rd place: Scripture

Founded in USA: 1864/1922

Members in USA: 1,000,000

Churches in USA: 540

Headquarters: 8–10 East 79th St., New York NY 10021

Phone: 212-570-3500

Web site: www.goarch.org

What to Expect When You Visit

Visiting an Orthodox Church can be a challenge on two counts—first, you may be unacquainted with the church traditions and, second, each church will have an additional cultural overlay with which you may or may not be familiar. You'll encounter different expressions and symbols of the same faith depending on whether the church has been shaped by Greek, Russian, Ukrainian, Romanian, or other nationalities. Understanding the theology as well as the culture can present some obstacles to Americans who are new to Orthodoxy. Here are some pointers that may help the first time you visit.

Orthodox Churches are about as "high" church as you can get—formal liturgy that is rooted in tradition and steeped in symbolism. To fit in, I'd recommend that your dress be on the formal side. I'm not insinuating you don your tux or tiara, but women should avoid pantsuits in favor of dresses or skirts, and a suit and tie would be best for men. On special occasions, or if it is especially hot, some congregations may allow more casual attire, but jeans, t-shirts, and flip-flops are definitely out.

Try to be early or on time. Once the service starts, it will be hard to slip in unnoticed. If you do come late, ask an usher to show where to sit or stand and when to enter. If you cannot stand for an extended time, let the usher know so seating can be made available to you.

Since Orthodox Churches are liturgical, improvisation is frowned upon. Unless participation somehow violates your religious beliefs, follow the crowd in kneeling, reading, standing, sitting, singing, etc. Do not participate in the Holy Communion, which is restricted to members. When the priest invites congregants to come forward to the altar and receive communion, stay in your seat and admire the architecture. Most, but not all, Orthodox services are conducted in English with the native language sprinkled in here and there. You may want to call ahead to make sure you'll be able to understand a majority of the service or ask an usher for a translation of the service.

A special note to allergy sufferers—incense is used extensively in Orthodox services. Smoke from the incense represents prayers rising to heaven, adding a sensual element to worship. Take your antihistamine ahead of time so you can thoroughly enjoy (rather than sneeze through) the service.

The Orthodox Church is enjoying a wave of popularity today in the U.S., in spite of the cultural and language obstacles. I urge you to let the mystery draw you in rather than turn you off. It may take a bit more time to understand the complexities of the faith than it would some other denominations, but I suspect your efforts will be well rewarded.

More Orthodox Churches

Albanian Orthodox Archdiocese in America
www.oca.org/oca/al

American Carpatho-Russian Orthodox Greek Catholic Church
www.goarch.org

Antiochian Orthodox Christian Archdiocese of North America
www.antiochian.org

Holy Eastern Orthodox and Apostolic Church in North America, Inc.
www.theocacna.org

Malankara Orthodox Syrian Church
www.malankara.org/American.html

Mar Thoma Orthodox Syrian Church
www.marthomachurch.org

Romanian Orthodox Episcopate of America
www.roeg.org

Serbian Eastern Orthodox Church
http://oea.servian-church.net

Syrian Orthodox Church of Antioch
www.syrianorthodoxchurch.org

Ukrainian Orthodox Church of the U.S.A.
www.uocofusa.org

Further Info

• Charles Bell, *Discovering the Rich Heritage of Orthodoxy: As Discovered by One Who Came to Orthodoxy from the Evangelical and Charismatic Traditions* (Light and Life, 2001)

- Kallistos Ware, *The Orthodox Way* (St. Vladimirs Seminary Press, 1995)

- James H. Forest, *Praying with Icons* (Orbis Books, 1997)

- Demetrios J. Constantelos, *Understanding the Greek Orthodox Church: Its Faith, History and Life* (Hellenic College Press, 2001)

five

Catholic
Churches

The growth and survival of the early church, especially the church in Rome, cannot be separated from the politics of the Roman Empire. The first goal for early Christians was to avoid being fed to the lions. While some historians assert that persecution was much less severe than popularly believed, Christians were at the mercy of the emperor's whims and decrees. It was not the best of times.

Physical persecution may have posed a threat to individual Christians, but a greater challenge to the survival of Christianity as a whole came in times of relative peace. The separation of religion and state was an unthinkable concept. Consequently, to live within the Roman Empire—to engage in business, attend a school, learn a trade, or participate in most aspects of public and private life—

required taking part in rites and festivals honoring Roman deities. Clothing of the day often sported symbols honoring Roman gods, presenting Christians with the dilemma of blending in but dishonoring their faith or dressing differently and drawing unwanted attention to themselves. Christians struggled being true to their faith within a polytheistic (thereby idolatrous) society.

No Longer Center Stage

Having persevered in a hostile culture for over three hundred years, I imagine that Christians throughout the Roman Empire breathed a sigh of relief when, in the early 300s, Emperor Constantine identified himself as a Christian and legitimized the faith. Christians found themselves in the position to influence culture rather than simply survive it.

But before anyone in Rome could get too comfortable, Emperor Constantine uprooted the center of his empire and moved to Byzantium (renamed Constantinople). The church in Rome found itself no longer in the center of political activity. Instead, Constantinople was where the action was taking place. Constantinople grew in grandeur and influence as Emperor Constantine and subsequent emperors built monuments and churches to attest to their prowess.

Emperor Constantine wanted the church as a whole to stop squabbling, so he convened the first ecumenical council, which was comprised of three hundred and eighteen bishops, in 325. The controversy centered around Arianism, which rejected the Triune God. The result was the first version of the Nicene Creed.

But writing up the creed didn't stop Arian Christianity from spreading. A Visigoth named Ulfilas came to Constantinople and converted to Christianity—Arian style. He became a bishop in 341 and returned to the Visigoths as a missionary. He translated the Bible into Goth, the first Germanic language to be put into print, and the Visigoths converted to Arianism.

A few years later the Huns were out and about causing trouble, and around two hundred thousand Visigoths asked Emperor Valens to give them safe haven within the Roman Empire. He did, but didn't treat them well once inside. After a couple of years, in 378, the Visigoths got fed up with the abuse, revolted, and killed Emperor Valens. Theodosius I became the next emperor.

Theodosius, hoping to avoid his predecessor's fate, made peace with the Visigoths. Furthermore he tried to get the Visigoth Christians (who didn't believe in the Trinity) and the majority of the church (who did) to iron out their differences. No such luck. The church wasn't interested in including "outsiders" and was busy defending itself from another heresy started by Macedonius, who asserted that the Holy Spirit was not divine. A second ecumenical council was called in 381, this time meeting in Constantinople. As a result, the clause referring to the Holy Ghost and the remainder of the Nicene Creed was added.

The next big jolt to the church came in 395 when Emperor Theodosius died, leaving his two sons, Arcadius, age seventeen, and Honorius, age ten, to run the Roman Empire. The older boy, Arcadius, already lived in Constantinople, having been installed as Augustus in 383. When their father died, ten-year-old Honorius became responsible for the western portion of the empire while his brother ruled in the east.

Too young to lead with wisdom or genuine authority, the boys were easily manipulated by their advisers. Rufinus (in the east) and Stilicho (in the west) hated each other, ambitiously competing for power. Weakened internally, the Empire was unable to effectively protect itself from outside invasions. The east and west began looking after themselves as separate territories rather than one unified empire. While the empire was disintegrating, the Visigoths elected Alaris as their king. Not a shy, retiring type, Alaris set his sights on Rome. The eastern part of the empire was able to deflect invasions and survive for a few more centuries, but Rome's days were numbered.

The Goths Are Coming! The Goths Are Coming!

Imagine you're a Roman soldier on watch at an outpost far from Rome. Life's not too bad, really. Sure, you're stuck out here at the edge of nowhere, but you still feel very much a part of the orderly Roman world back home. You've been trained in the art of combat within a highly structured military and have successfully shown your courage in several battles. Your rank and duties are clear, and you fear, if not respect, your commanding officer. Plus you get to wear armor, carry a shield, and use a sword (always a hit with the ladies). You're feeling pretty cool. After all, your empire (thanks to you and your comrades) rules most of the world.

From over the horizon, like a swarm of locust, hundreds, maybe thousands, of half-naked, screaming men flood in your direction. Wow, they're tall! You sound the alarm as you watch the unruly mass approach, flailing homemade weapons. From your perch you can see that women and children are right behind their fighting men, contributing to the clamor—a shrieking reminder that, if the battle is lost, their families will become spoils of war. What are these people doing? Put on some armor (or at least some shorts) for Pete's sake! Get a decent sword . . . and leave the wife and kids at home! Don't these people understand the right way to fight a war?

The fierce Germanic tribes that pestered the parameters of the Roman Empire were anything but uniformly organized. They can be traced back to northern Germany, southern Sweden, Denmark, and the coast of the Baltic Sea. As they migrated in warlike waves across Europe, separate tribes formed including the Angles, the Alemanni, the Saxons, the Lombards, the Vandals, and the Goths. The Vandals (from which we have the word "vandalism") and the Goths (who split into the Visigoths and the Ostrogoths) were the first to terrorize Rome.

Did **Ancient Goths** Wear Black **Eye Shadow?**

The definition of "Goth" has changed over the years being applied to Germanic tribes that invaded Rome, a type of architecture that developed during the European Renaissance, and the Gothic Romance genre full of horror, mystery, and romance. Gothic Romance novels are often set within an eerie medieval, Edwardian, or Victorian backdrop, focusing on the dark, untamed, morose, and mysterious.

The most recent usage of "Goth" was coined by Anthony H. Wilson, manager of a punk band called Joy Division, on a British Broadcasting Corporation television program aired in the early 1980s. He referred to the band's music as "gothic" rather than pop mainstream or traditional punk. First established at a nightclub in London called the Batcave, the Goth subculture split off from the punk movement and has survived.

Today's Goth subculture contains many variations on the original theme, so it's hard to accurately define. But, of course, I'm going to try anyway. As a generalization, Goths tend to wear black clothing of various styles, whiten their faces and use contrasting black eye makeup, have various parts of their bodies pierced, and create elaborate and unusual hairstyles. Goths have been blamed for acts of violence, but most Goths are nonviolent. If you're interested in getting a taste of today's Goth, check out *The Crow* horror movies or pick up a CD by the Bauhaus, the Sisters of Mercy, or Dead Can Dance.

They were pretty scary people to the Romans, who never quite understood what made these ferocious warriors tick. The Germans were generally taller and physically stronger than their southern Roman counterparts. Bravery in battle was highly valued and cowardice was unforgivable, since they relied more on brute strength than weaponry or military strategy.

If the deciding factor was military sophistication, there would have been no contest between the highly disciplined Roman army and the unruly Germanic invaders—hands down, the Romans should have won. Had the Roman Empire remained united and wisely ruled, its skilled armies could have continued to effectively defend against the tribes. But by the early 400s, the empire had conquered too much territory to adequately protect every mile of border. And outside invaders weren't the only enemies to fight—Roman soldiers warred amongst themselves in support of their favorite emperial candidate. Civil rebellions were common, further depleting soldier-power and finances. There just weren't enough loyal soldiers to cover all fronts of conflict. If only those Germanic tribes had given up, but they never did. Slowly encroaching further and further into the Empire, by 410 the Visigoths, under the leadership of King Alaric, made it to Rome itself. The once proud bastion of military prowess was plundered, broken in spirit and authority.

The Romans made a futile effort to keep an emperor in place after King Alaric plundered the city, but Rome never recovered. It took some sixty more years for the western empire to officially "fall," when the Goth General Odacer overthrew the last Roman Emperor, Augustulus Romulus in 476. Byzantine armies played tug of war with the Goths until 552 when the Goths' power was destroyed, but no one seemed to hold onto Rome for long. Rome was invaded repeatedly, first by the Visigoths, then the Vandals, with the Franks not far behind. One Germanic tribe after another blustered through the region—the Saxons,

Danes, Alemanni, Lombards, and Burgundians. Every so often another Byzantine emperor would storm into town recapturing the territory once again. Everyone wanted a piece of Rome—but the unifying power of the city and the empire it represented was shattered. Europe broke into a myriad of small regions controlled by whoever had the most tenacious army. By the time the invaders were through dismantling Roman culture, the medieval era was in full swing.

One thin thread wove through this chaos—Roman Catholicism. Former Roman citizens were well versed in the faith, with local churches still operating throughout the former empire. A lot of criticism has been aimed at the hierarchical, if not controlling, personality of the Roman Catholic Church. But I don't think their penchant for centralizing power came about simply because some guys wanted power (although this propensity has contributed greatly to their stance over the years). It's human nature to grab for control in the middle of a crisis, and it must have seemed like the whole world was falling apart in a swirl of competing cultures, divergent languages, and a succession of invading tribes. The church in Rome saw itself as a point of reference in a savage world.

A Quick Trip through the Middle Ages

The Roman Catholic Church provided a sense of stability and gave people in Europe a way to make sense out of the craziness. God was in heaven, the Earth was the center of the universe, and the church mediated between the earthly and spiritual realms. Throughout the ensuing medieval centuries (from approximately 476 with the fall of Rome to 1350ish with the start of the Renaissance), the church played a major role in shaping feudalism with its hierarchical loyalty to authority. We might look on the Middle Ages with a bit of disdain from our democratic vantage point, but the rigidity of medieval society was, in part, a reaction against the turbulent fall of the Roman Empire.

In addition, the church preserved classical literature and education through monasteries, convents, and universities. The arts and architecture were supported and advanced through the creation of churches, the duplication of valued manuscripts, and the commission and promotion of religious paintings and sculpture. Much of what remains from our Greek and Roman heritage is due to the value the church placed on art and the written word. The Germans were illiterate and placed no value on written documents of any kind. If it had been up to the tribes, books and other papers would have been used for kindling.

On the downside, the Roman Catholic Church amassed more and more power, wealth, and status so that it became nearly impossible to differentiate the church from any other political power. Through a series of legitimate ecumenical councils and backroom political maneuverings, the church in Rome bolstered its power and position. Many have believed that the more power you have the better off you'll be, but this seldom proves true. Paradox-

What's that Monophonic Sound in the Air?

Along with expanding the political muscle of the Roman Catholic Church, Pope Gregory I is credited with compiling plainsong liturgies during his rule. There's some doubt about his role, but the unharmonized chant became a mainstay in medieval worship throughout the church. Plainsongs date back to the early church, and may have originated in Jewish synagogues and Greek musical practice. From 1889 onward, Gregorian chants became the official music of the Roman Catholic Church thanks to the effort of the Benedictine monks of Solesmes.

ically, the stronger the church became in the temporal realm, the more vulnerable it became to internal corruption and spiritual bankruptcy. Once the Catholics placed institutional loyalty over spiritual clarity, it was only a matter of time before the spaghetti hit the fan.

A major turning point occurred under the rule of Pope Gregory I (590–604). At that point, Rome was under the Byzantine control, but the city was left essentially leaderless. When the Lombards attacked in 592, the Byzantines did nothing to help. Pope Gregory I reasoned that it was the church's mission to protect anyone being mistreated, and he set out to negotiate directly with the Lombards. The Byzantines didn't back him up, so the Lombards resumed their attacks. But that didn't stop Pope Gregory I. He expanded the role of the Roman Church from mediating spiritual affairs to include military and civil power. This precedent set the stage for an increasing political presence of the church throughout the Middle Ages.

In 740 the concept of a papal state was introduced, giving the church "permission" to rule territories independently of any other governmental control. By the time this practice was modified in 1859 the church had amassed about 16,000 square miles of territory—reaching across the Italian peninsula from the Adriatic Sea to the Tyrrhenian Sea. This was a bit more than owning a corner lot for a neighborhood church.

In addition to expanding its real estate, the Roman Catholic Church shaped the political landscape far beyond it's own domain. For example, Pope Leo III (795–816) played a major role in legitimizing the Franks' claim to the West, much to the dismay of the Byzantines and the church in Constantinople. A few years after Leo III was elected pope, some of his enemies in the church attacked him, trying to maim and disfigure his face and eyes. They hoped that he would be unable to perform his duties if he were unpresentable. He fled to Charlemagne's protection. They struck a deal. Charlemagne used his military might to reinstate

Leo III as pope and, in return, the pope crowned Charlemagne the emperor of the Holy Roman Empire. The Byzantines' hopes of recapturing the West essentially ended on Christmas day, 800.

In the years that immediately followed, the Orthodox patriarchs and the popes jockeyed for control. The struggle increased in 869 when the

Gothic Cathedrals

In Renaissance Europe, anything or anyone referred to as Goth-like was being likened to the invading Germanic tribes that plunged the Roman Empire into the Dark Ages. It wasn't a compliment. Some folks valued only Greek and Roman architecture, much of which the Goths destroyed. So when a new form of architecture emerged from the Normans and Franks, there was no more contemptuous term to be given than "Gothic." In actuality, the architecture has little to do with the Gothic peoples, since they had been assimilated or expunged long before the first Gothic structure, the Abbey of Saint-Denis, appeared in France around 1140. But the term was still in use, even though the tribes were long gone, as a reference to all things barbaric, uncultured, and disgusting.

Today Gothic architecture is revered as one of the most beautiful in the world. Rather than depend on massive walls for stability, Gothic structures rely on the balance of opposing forces through the use of buttresses and arches. As a result, walls weren't needed as supports and became prime spots for the display of elaborately beautiful stained glass windows and other displays of art. Walking into a Gothic cathedral, one feels transported upward into the light—a symbolic experience of interacting with the divine.

Those churches with Gothic architecture tend to be more liturgical in worship style, more rooted in tradition and history than newer styles. This isn't a hard and fast rule, but if you're looking for "high" church, look for the tallest spire in town.

Eighth Ecumenical Council was held in Constantinople under Byzantine Emperor Basil with Pope Hadrian II presiding. The council condemned Photius, the Patriarch of Constantinople, for challenging clerical celibacy, the addition of the filioque clause to the Nicene Creed, and the crowning of Charlemagne as the emperor of the Holy Roman Empire. The Orthodox Church washed its hands of this and any future ecumenical councils.

It took a couple hundred more years, but the church formally split in half in 1054. Depending on if you listen to the Orthodox or the Roman Catholics, the fault rests with the other side. From the Catholic's viewpoint, Michael Cærularius, patriarch of Constantinople, was ambitious and unwilling to submit to any authority but his own. (Is that the pot calling the kettle black?) The pope and Patriarch excommunicated each other and went their separate ways—a split often referred to as the Eastern Schism.

About fifty years later the Roman Catholic Church launched the first of eight Crusades against the Muslims who had captured Jerusalem—not one of the Roman Catholic Church's more stellar ideas. Over the next five hundred years, Crusade after Crusade was waged with no one really coming out the winner, although a great deal of wealth ended up in Catholic hands.

In 1512 the Eighteenth Ecumenical Council met in Rome under Roman Catholic Popes Julius II and Leo X. One of their agenda items was to gain support for a ninth Crusade. No one was interested. The church hadn't counted on one small thing getting in the way of their plan—the Protestant Reformation.

Those Pesky Protestants

Since the remainder of this book consists solely of Protestant denominations and associations, there's no need to go into the Reformation from a Protestant perspective here. From the Roman Catholic vantage point it's safe to say they were not happy with Martin Luther or his fellow reformers. The Reformation utterly disrupted business as usual for the Roman Catholic Church, and few Catholics today believe that the Protestants should have left the church (which, of course, is why they're still Catholics . . .). But the Catholic Church was never the same after being forced to address its own corruption and clearly articulate its beliefs.

In 1521 three Christians forces collided in the city of Worms. Martin Luther represented the Protestant perspective by promoting a theological reformation. Charles V from Spain advocated for a revival within the church, keeping the power of the pope and tradition unchanged, working cooperatively with secular authorities to purge and persecute anyone who deviated. Finally, there was Girolamo Aleander who represented the pope. Aleander stubbornly resisted any kind of reform at all. No formal changes were made for the next twenty-five years or so until the Nineteenth Ecumenical Council was called.

From 1545 to 1563 the Nineteenth Ecumenical Council was held in Trent to address the abuses of the church that had been so embarrassingly pointed out by Luther and other reformers. It lasted so long that five popes came and went—Paul III, Julius III, Marcellus II, Paul IV, and Pius IV. Included were five cardinal legates of the Holy See, three patriarchs, thirty-three archbishops, two hundred and thirty-five bishops, seven abbots, one hundred and sixty doctors of divinity, and seven representatives from monastic orders. In its first phase, Protestants were invited to participate. But as hostility grew between the groups, the council took on a "counter-reformation" air, with the council digging in its heels and enshrining certain Catholic doctrines. For eighteen years this impressive crowd worked to reform the church from the inside, with some important changes in moral discipline and the formalization of theological perspectives. The Society of Jesus was a shaping force in internal reform.

The council articulated its theological defense, which was intertwined with the church's hierarchy and papal authority. A process of eliminating the immoral and corrupt behaviors on the part of clergy was initiated. The Mass was revised, firmly delineating the doctrines of transubstantiation and eucharistic sacrifice. This Mass was used exclusively for four hundred years—from 1570 until 1970. Through the turbulence of the Reformation and then the Enlightenment, the Catholic church relied more and more on the pope to be the protector of doctrinal purity and institutional longevity.

Raising the Stakes—Vatican I

Even though the first Vatican Council was held some three hundred years after the Council of Trent, they are viewed as being linked in purpose and perspective. The authority of the pope was incrementally increased in nearly all of the ecumenical councils, but it wasn't until the first Vatican Council, held from 1869 to 1870, that the pope was declared to be infallible in matters of faith, practice, and morals.

For many Roman Catholics, Vatican I simply put into words what had been believed for some time. Some Catholics, however, were strongly opposed to the idea of papal infallibility. A group of Dutch Catholics had been at odds with the papacy in the 1700s over doctrines of determinism and grace, but when the pope was declared infallible by Vatican I, a large number of Swiss, German, and Austrian priests joined the Dutch in opposition to the ruling. These priests were excommunicated in 1871, resulting in a group called the Old Catholics.

A More User-Friendly Roman Catholicism— Vatican II

Big changes occurred between 1962 and 1965 with the decisions of the second Vatican Council (the Twenty-first Ecumenical Council). The council was first called by Pope John XXIII and reconvened after his death under the leadership of Pope Paul VI. In some ways the Roman Catholic Church integrated some Protestant ideas without abandoning their uniquely Catholic roots. Laity were encouraged to participate in parish ministry and worship in ways they hadn't been able to before. The Mass was translated into the language of the people, so your average Catholic (who probably wasn't a Latin scholar) had an idea what was going on in the service. Focus was placed on group and personal Bible study, giving Catholics the opportunity to become more informed in their faith.

Perhaps the biggest change was becoming a part of ecumenical dialogue. Prior to Vatican II it was forbidden for Catholics to participate in any meeting or activity sponsored by the World Council of Churches. Even though the Roman Catholic Church isn't a formal member of WCC, Catholics participate in an observer status and are engaged in dialogue in a variety of interfaith venues.

The Pope is the Man

The authority of the church is traced back to Jesus' commissioning Peter as the first pope. Not only is the pope the man, he has to *be* a man, since only men are allowed in the priesthood.

What Makes a Church Catholic?

From the outside looking in, Catholicism can appear rather

superstitious. Skeptically viewing Catholicism from the outside, however, is quite different from practicing this faith from the inside. An outsider may see a statue; a Catholic sees the face of Christ. What may look like a string of beads to an observer is a spiritual discipline with transforming power to a praying Catholic. What may seem like gadgets and jingles to a nonparticipant are catalysts for spiritual transformation and psalms of praise to devoted converts. We can all see the stuff (and compared to many other churches, Catholics do have a lot of stuff) from holy water to holy cards, but it takes the eyes of faith to see these items as points of contact between matter and spirit. Matter is easy to see; I can see the candles, the oil, the bread, and the wine, and so can you. But recognizing how these items combine matter and spirit requires a different kind of eyes and a heart that can contain mystery.

It is tempting to eliminate the mystery of Christ through linear and so-called logical thought processes. We prefer Jesus to be either divine or human, but not both simultaneously. It's bothersome to try to live with such contradiction, and it's easier to say that bread is just bread and wine is just wine than to consider the possibility that the presence of Christ could actually inhabit or transform these commonplace items.

In spite of theological challenges and political factions, Catholics relentlessly hold to a sensual approach to spirituality—one that includes the body as well as the spirit of the participant. For example, there's nothing magical about genuflecting, but in the act of kneeling one has the opportunity to be a respectful worshiper. By making the sign of the cross, you move your body in harmony with your faith—spirit and matter are unified. It's one thing to think about your failings in the privacy of your own mind, but quite another to take responsibility for your misconduct by telling someone who wants to help you reconcile with God. These spiritual activities have been trivialized in the media, and granted, they can be practiced without personal change

The Society of Jesus

A wayward cannon ball can be credited for turning a soldier into a saint in 1521. Ignatius Loyola, at the age of thirty, urged his Spanish comrades to fight against all odds in their battle with the French. His speech was cut short when a cannon ball smacked him in the leg and the white flag was waved.

His recuperation was lengthy because his broken leg didn't heal well and had to be rebroken and reset (ugh). While reading *The Life of Christ,* written by a Carthusian monk, he was spiritually transformed. Even though he now walked with a limp, he went on a pilgrimage where he hung his sword over the altar in a church in Montserrat. He then lived in a cave as a hermit to study *The Imitation of Christ* by Thomas á Kempis (this was the book that led to the conversion of John Newton, the author of "Amazing Grace"). It's believed that he wrote his *Spiritual Exercises* while a hermit, a book of prayer and meditation that Catholics and Protestants alike continue to enjoy to this day.

His views were rooted in devotion to Christ rather than institutional correctness, so once Loyola left the cave, he got into trouble with the Catholic Church. He was imprisoned twice during the Spanish Inquisition for preaching as a layman. He was instructed to keep silent about his beliefs for three years.

In 1534, he and six friends formed a group with the goal of traveling to Jerusalem to preach the gospel to the Muslims. A war in Palestine disrupted their travels, so the group offered its services to Pope Paul III. They called themselves the Society of Jesus, but were nicknamed Jesuits. They were ordained to the priesthood and focused on the reforming of the Catholic Church from the inside, promoting missionary efforts to non-Christian areas and developing a cogent response to the Reformation.

The Jesuits hit a tough patch in 1773 when Pope Clement XIV authorized a papal decree to suppress the order. Property was taken and schools were shut down. Some Jesuits were imprisoned and held in miserable conditions. Fortunately, in 1814, Pope Pius VII rescinded the order, restoring the Jesuits worldwide.

By the time Loyola died in 1556, about a thousand priests had joined the order. Through missions, educational efforts, and parishes, the Jesuits have nearly twenty-five thousand members and are respected for their scholarship and missionary vision.

or authenticity, but sincere participation in traditions that blend physicality with spirituality can, without a doubt, change your life.

Whereas a Protestant may view faith as a personal, even private, relationship with God and view church attendance as optional, the Catholic faith emphasizes participation in the spiritual community to experience God's grace. Catholics of all varieties see their church as Christ-on-earth. It follows, then, that in order to be in relationship with Christ,

Connie's Story

"When people talked about experiencing the Eucharist not as a symbolic ritual but a transforming encounter with Christ, something started yanking on me. I became more and more dissatisfied with seeing communion as merely a symbol. When Catholics go up to receive either the body or the blood, they are taking into themselves Christ's essence.

"I now believe that the very presence of Christ is present in the bread and wine, once it is blessed by the priests. It looks like bread. It tastes like bread, but it is Christ's body. He is present. I've always sensed something amazing, or holy, when I walked into a Catholic church, and I've always enjoyed the beauty of the liturgy. The holiness I feel is Christ's presence in the bread and wine that's kept at the front of the church. In fact, I don't feel comfortable taking communion anymore in a Protestant church. It feels like a mere shadow of the reality. I don't want to be mean or critical about other churches. I just don't see why I'd want a symbol when I can have the real thing.

"Without a doubt, the Eucharist is the catalyst that pulled me into the Catholic Church. Some of the high churches, such as Episcopal or Lutheran believe that Christ's essence is present in the host, but only when the congregation is there to partake. In the Catholic church, the host is present constantly. Once the elements have been blessed and the Holy Spirit has per-

one would be in relationship with the Catholic Church. Catholic churches honor seven rituals, called sacraments, all of which are administered by the members of the priesthood.

Baptism

The journey of faith is launched through baptism, a declaration of unity with Christ and the church. Parents raising their children in the

formed the mystery of turning it into the essence of the body and blood of Christ, they keep it up in the front, in the tabernacle. He's always there.

"The point of no return came last year, on Good Friday. I decided to go to the afternoon mass. One thing I like about the Catholic church is how they decorate the sanctuary with colors associated with the time of the year. The color for lent is violet, and the last time I'd attended, I enjoyed the rich decorations. They had two huge purple banners, from ceiling to floor, and a big banner in the back with a picture of a heart that said, 'Lord, change our hearts.' In front of the altar stood an arrangement of greenery and flowers, so full of color. That's what I expected to see when I walked into the church on Good Friday. Instead, I entered a sanctuary that was totally barren. All the candles were gone, the banners were gone, not a hint of color anywhere. Most startling was that the door of the tabernacle where the host is kept was open and the host was gone.

"My first thought when I walked through that door was, 'Where did they take Him?' Not 'Where did they take it?' Not 'Where did they take the host?' but Him. 'Where did they take Him?' I realized I was no longer searching for what I believed, I already believed it. I knew in the core of my being that the presence of God, of Christ, is in that host.

I'm now in classes preparing for my confirmation. I'll take my first Communion at Easter this year. I'm certain that this is where I belong. I've found my spiritual community."

faith have their infants baptized, while adult converts are required to receive instruction prior to baptism. Some Catholic churches recognize the validity of baptism conducted in other denominations and fellowships.

Confirmation

Confirmation, which occurs when a bishop lays hands on you, marks the fuller presence of the Holy Spirit in your life. Most of the time con-

Old Catholics

Old Catholics isn't a name for the senior citizens in the local diocese—it's a term referring to a group that broke away from the Roman Catholic Church in order to restore the church to the "old" ways. The Old Catholic Church movement began in Holland in the 1700s when the See in Utrecht wrangled with the pope over doctrinal issues of grace. When the Roman Catholic Church declared papal infallibility in 1870, the movement gathered more Catholics, including priests from Switzerland, Germany, and Austria. They were promptly excommunicated, so the bishops in Utrecht led the way and ordained other clergy for service.

In 1889 the Old Catholics completed the Declaration of Utrecht, which outlined their basic beliefs that centered on the Catholic tradition until the Great Schism in 1054. In particular, Old Catholics reject papal infallibility, the immaculate conception of Mary, and compulsory celibacy for clergy.

Old Catholics came to America in the late 1800s, setting up their episcopacy in 1914. Things went well until 1958, when their leader, Father Carmel Henry Carfora, died. In similar fashion to the Protestants, the Old North American Old Catholics splintered into a dozen or more groups, some that are recognized by the Old Catholics in Europe and some that are not.

firmation occurs some time after baptism, although adult converts may be baptized and confirmed in one event.

Eucharist

In each Mass, Christ is spiritually present as an ongoing sacrifice and physically present in the bread and wine. Catholics believe that, once consecrated, the bread becomes Jesus' actual body, and the wine becomes his blood. This may sound a bit creepy—who wants to really eat human flesh or really drink someone's blood? But remember, the central focus of Catholicism is sensual spirituality. Spirit and matter are united. So eating the bread or drinking the wine is taking Christ literally into your body and spirit. No mere symbolism here. You actually encounter Christ and are changed by this encounter—you receive atonement for sins and are spiritually nourished.

> **The Roman Catholic Church is coming out with a new low-fat Communion wafer called, "I Can't Believe It's Not Jesus!"**

Confession

In addition to regularly attending Mass, Catholics are expected to participate in confession. Confession in the Roman Catholic Church gives a three-step process of reconciliation with God: (1) a sense of sorrow over sin, (2) verbal confession to a priest, and (3) absolution of your sins by the priest. In the past, Roman Catholic priests would require some kind of penance be performed, such as praying specific prayers or other activities that weren't especially pleasant. Today's Roman Catholic priests tend to tie penance more directly to the problem area, such as having someone make amends for harm they might have caused or spending time in silent self-reflection to review their behavior. Since Vatican II, more importance is placed on a person's spiritual growth than being punished.

Old Catholic Churches tend to use the term "reconciliation" rather than "confession" for this sacrament. Confession can be expressed in two ways—by an individual who confesses personal sins to a priest or by a group of people who corporately acknowledge personal sin and receive general absolution from the priest.

Anointing

What has commonly been referred to as the last rites has been refocused as the anointing of the sick, sacrament of the sick, or unction, with an emphasis of healing rather than saying goodbye. I've often thought how upsetting it must be to someone who is sick to see the priest coming with his vial of oil. Clearly it would be a signal that everyone's

Wardrobe Changes

What's the difference between a Roman Catholic priest, monsignor, and bishop? No, this isn't a set up for a joke. All of the men in leadership are, first and foremost, priests. As they climb the church ladder, they change titles and color-coordinated outfits. The priests who serve in a local congregation wear black with white Roman collars. If your priest has purple piping on his collar and robe, you know he's a monsignor, an honorific title. The next step up from a priest is bishop, and he gets to wear a pointy hat and purple skull cap during Mass and oversees a parish (a local area) or diocese (a group of parishes). The more authority you have, the more elaborate your ensemble.

Just the FACTS

Roman Catholic Church

Kind of Church: Catholic/Roman
Worship Style: Liturgical
Church Structure: Hierarchical
Trinity Affinity: Son
Clout Continuum: 1st place: The pope and Catholic tradition
2nd place: Personal experience through sacraments
3rd place: Scripture
Founded in USA: 1565
Members in USA: 61,200,000
Churches in the USA: 22,728
Headquarters: National Conference of Catholic Bishops, 3211 Fourth St., Washington DC 20017
Phone: 202-541-3000
Web site: www.uscccb.org

given up hope and you're about to die. The church approaches this sacrament more positively, offering hope of healing rather than signaling the end. And should a person pass on to eternity, he or she will be ready.

Marriage

We commonly think of marriage as an agreement between two people, but in the Catholic church you're never alone. When you marry there's three of you involved—you, your soon-to-be spouse, and Jesus. The covenant between you and your partner is supposed to be as unbreakable as God's love for the church. Old Catholic Churches view marriage as a sacrament, but will allow remarriage to occur in the church and will not refuse you communion if divorced. This is not the case with Roman Catholics. If you marry in the Roman Catholic Church, proceed very cautiously. Except for special cases, you're expected to stay married until death parts you, and being allowed to continue participating in the church after a divorce is much more difficult than in most other denominations.

Holy Orders

Finally we have the sacrament of holy orders, by which a person is ordained to the priesthood. A priest mediates between you and God, quite a powerful and significant position. Only a priest can offer you the bread (and sometimes wine) at the Eucharist or can forgive your sins during confession, and he must be present at your wedding or you're not married in the eyes of God. Catholics, in general, treat their clergy with a great deal more respect and deference than do their Protestant counterparts. Only men can be ordained as priests in the Roman Catholic Church. In some Old Catholic Church groups women can be ordained, as can gay and lesbian individuals.

Roman Catholic Church

What do the late Mother Teresa and Madonna have in common? Musical talent? I doubt it. They both won the Nobel Peace Prize for helping the dying in Calcutta? Uh, don't think so. They both accessorized with crucifixes? Perhaps. But the main similarity between them is that they have identified themselves with Roman Catholicism.

One of the better aspects of the Roman Catholic Church, at least at this point in history, is its ability to create an umbrella that encompasses people as diverse in self-expression as Madonna and the late Mother Teresa, as opposed to each other as Ted Kennedy and Pat

Buchanan, or as culturally divergent as attendees at a rowdy Irish wake and nuns in a cloistered convent. Catholicism has taken on the color and culture of its converts, incorporating portions of European, Native Indian, Celtic, Latin, African, and other indigenous belief systems while maintaining a distinctive Roman Catholic flavor.

Roman Catholicism in America

The Roman Catholic Church is the single largest church in the United States and has been operating longer than any other on American soil. Catholics can make claim to being one of the first arrivals via Christopher Columbus in 1492. Missionaries arrived on the ships of other Spanish explorers, and by 1565 they had set up the first Roman Catholic parish in St. Augustine, Florida.

About a hundred years later, in 1634, Maryland was founded by Roman Catholics escaping the persecution of the English Civil War and the Protestant/Puritan heavy-handed role in government. Life was better in America, but not stress-free. Since the colonies were dominated by Protestants, Catholics weren't treated equally until after the American Revolution. In spite of the prejudices against Catholicism, Roman Catholics gained prominence and stature for freedom's cause. Three Catholics, Thomas Fitzsimmons, Charles Carroll, and Daniel Carroll, have their signatures on the Articles of Confederation, the Declaration of Independence, and the U.S. Constitution aiding in the elimination of religious discrimination.

Institutionally, the Roman Catholic Church stands in variance with the American

How many Catholic nuns does it take to change a lightbulb?

The entire convent. The Reverend Mother to compose a homily for the occasion of the lightbulb changing while the rest of the nuns raffle off the old one.

ideals of individualism and self-governance. While your typical American chaffs under authoritarian constraints, Roman Catholics in America have one guy in charge—and he doesn't even live in the States. Catholic Bishops in America have had a tough time balancing these two belief systems, as has become evident in the controversy over the sexual abuse of children by Catholic priests. The bishops in America took the lead to propose changes that had not been forthcoming from the Vatican. Having continuity and centralized authority can be comforting at times, but also problematic when swift action is needed.

Presently there are eleven cardinals, forty-five archbishops, three hundred and thirty-six bishops, and over forty-six thousand priests in America. In addition, the church includes deacons who are most often married men who support themselves outside the church. Deacons are allowed to preach, baptize, assist with Holy Communion, and conduct weddings.

In America today, nearly every ethnic group imaginable is represented among the church's members, such as Italians, Spanish, Irish, Latin Americans, Hungarians, Germans, Filipinos, Portuguese, French, Poles, Austrians, and Belgians. In the U.S. you can find services in English as well as languages from all over the world.

If you express your faith most authentically within a liturgical setting, the Roman Catholic Church may be a good fit for you. The institution is not without its flaws, but this is true for every church organization in the world. If you're looking for perfection, no church will meet your needs, but Catholicism may be your church if you want to be rooted in the past. Within this structure people of all ages and races have found unique ways of expressing the Catholic faith—and there may be a place just made for you.

What to Expect When You Visit

Roman Catholic Churches are liturgical and tend to be on the formal side. The exception to this rule would be if a particular congregation has developed an individual style of dress due to locale, ethnic influences, or fashion. To be on the safe side and to show respect, it's a good idea for men to show up for their first visit in a jacket and tie. Women will be appropriate in a dress, skirt, or nice pantsuit. Head covering is no longer required.

As you visit Roman Catholic churches, feel free to participate in every part of the service except the Eucharist. It's important to remember that unless you have formally joined the Roman Catholic Church, you are not invited to share communion. This is not to say that

Celibacy and the Priesthood

Originally, priests were not required to live a celibate lifestyle. It took about a thousand years for the Roman Catholic Church to set this in stone. Perhaps partly because deciding between a career in the church and never having sex again is a rather difficult choice, the popularity of becoming a priest, especially in the United States, has dropped significantly. The scandal of child abuse on the part of clergy is forcing the celibacy issue to be reexamined. In some cases it's actually possible for a priest to be married. However, don't start eyeing your local priest hoping for a date. The only way to be a married priest is if a man was already ordained in another denomination *and* already married when he joined the Catholic priesthood.

Catholics aren't friendly. They are, and they welcome visitors. But the theology is church-oriented, and if you're not a full-fledged member please honor their beliefs by sitting quietly during the Eucharist.

More Catholic Churches

Old Catholic Church
   www.members.tripod.com
Old Catholic Church of America
   www.oldcatholic.org
Old Catholic Church of the United States
   www.angelfire.com
Old Roman Catholic Church in North America
   www.orccna.org

Further Info

- Bob O'Gorman and Mary Faulkner, *The Complete Idiot's Guide to Understanding Catholicism* (Alpha Books, 2000)

- Thomas Howard, *On Being Catholic* (Ignatius, 1997)

- Al Kresta, *Why Do Catholics Genuflect? And Answers to Other Puzzling Questions About the Catholic Church* (Servant Publications, 2001)

six

Lutheran
Churches

The granddaddy of all things Protestant is Martin Luther. Passionate, prolific, and sometimes profane, Luther was quite a character. He wasn't the first to call for reform within the Roman Catholic Church, but he was undoubtedly the most influential. Luther fiercely defended whatever he believed at the moment, even if that meant he doubled back, apologized for, and argued against his previous opinions. At various points in his life Luther was exiled, had a price put on his head, and was excommunicated, but Luther gave as good as he got. You were either with him or confronted by him. By the time Luther died of heart failure at the age of sixty-two in 1546 the entire course of European culture had been altered. I can't help but like the guy.

A Mighty Fortress Is Our God

I was surprised to learn that not only did Martin Luther write a total of thirty-seven hymns, he also participated in the very creation of the congregational hymn itself. Appalled at the way the Roman Catholic Church failed to engage congregants in worship, Luther made sure his songs were in the language of the people. Both the lyrics and the tune of "Ein' Feste Burg *(A Mighty Fortress Is Our God)*" were written by Luther and first published in 1529 and translated by Frederick H. Hedge in 1852. This is one of my favorite hymns. Luther captures the passion and danger of the war between good and evil, and I like it that good wins in the end.

1.
A mighty fortress is our God,
a bulwark never failing;
our helper he amid the flood
of mortal ills prevailing.
For still our ancient foe
doth seek to work us woe;
his craft and power are great,
and armed with cruel hate,
on earth is not his equal.

2.
Did we in our own strength confide,
our striving would be losing,
were not the right man on our side,
the man of God's own choosing.
Dost ask who that may be?
Christ Jesus, it is he;
Lord Sabbaoth, his name,
from age to age the same,
and he must win the battle.

3.
And though this world, with devils filled,
should threaten to undo us,
we will not fear, for God hath willed
his truth to triumph through us.
The Prince of Darkness grim,
we tremble not for him;
his rage we can endure,
for lo, his doom is sure;
one little word shall fell him.

4.
That word above all earthly powers,
no thanks to them, abideth;
the Spirit and the gifts are ours,
thru him who with us sideth.
Let goods and kindred go,
this mortal life also;
the body they may kill;
God's truth abideth still;
his kingdom is forever.

A Brief History of Lutheranism

As a twenty-one year-old law student, Luther was dashing across an open field, being pummeled by an unexpected thunderstorm, when a bolt of lightening struck so close to him that he was thrown to the ground. Terrified, he cried, "Help me, St. Anna, and I will become a monk!" True to his word, fifteen days later he entered a monastery, joining the Augustinian hermits. Martin Luther was officially on his way to becoming a monk.

There was something unique about this monk. Luther never did anything halfway. Just ask Johannes Staupitz, the priest who had the dubious honor of being Luther's confessor. Convinced of his personal wickedness, Luther agonized over minute details of his failings, sometimes for six hours at a time. Hoping to get Martin to focus on something other than his own wickedness (and perhaps to get a little more time for himself), Johannes urged Luther to advance in his education. And advance he did.

Luther had already earned a bachelor's and master's degree when he entered the monastery. He threw himself into theological studies and was ordained by the age of twenty-three, then completed a doctorate in theology at twenty-eight. That same year he began teaching at the University of Wittenburg. At thirty, his duties were expanded when he became priest for Wittenburg's city church, and two years later he was appointed the vicar for eleven monasteries. He was one busy, over-achieving guy.

Perhaps he would have turned out to be just another obscure, burned-out priest had he not gotten worked up over the fact that a noticeable number of his parishioners were no longer coming to confession. And why should they bother with confession when it was easier to buy letters of indulgence that covered all the sins they'd commit in this life, as well as the sins of their parents and grandparents who might still be stuck in purgatory? Such a deal!

In protest, Luther penned his Ninety-five Theses and posted them on the door of Wittenburg Castle Church (which served as the university web site of the day). It's safe to assume that Luther wasn't expecting to turn Europe upside down with this document, but it generated so much controversy that he was singled out by the pope.

Squaring Off with the Big Guy

Luther was repeatedly called on the carpet by the pope and his representatives. Pressured time and again to recant, Luther gave up no territory. If anything, he advanced in his divergence from Roman Catholicism.

Luther may have made his original mark by denouncing indulgences in defense of the sacrament of confession, but eventually he negated confession altogether. He believed we are saved by faith in Christ alone. Christians no longer needed to confess to priests for the forgiveness of sin. In fact, being in relationship with the Roman Catholic Church was no longer a requirement for salvation.

This was not good news for the pope or the Roman Catholic Church, which is inherently sacramental and expects full participation in the life of the church. Luther shifted the focus off of having a relationship with God's representatives to focusing on one's own conscience and having a personal relationship directly with God. Even though Luther still believed that the Communion bread and wine were the actual body and blood of Christ, Luther launched a line of reasoning that others followed logically, resulting in the eventual divorce of spirituality from a tangible experience of the divine. This may seem like a small deal to us at this point in history, but it had a revolutionary impact on the Western world in the 1500s. The Reformation had begun.

Setting a New Course

When Luther became a priest in his twenties, he took a vow of celibacy. By the age of forty-one, Luther had changed his mind and married a former nun with whom he sired five children. He broke the power of the clerical elite by translating the Bible from Latin into everyday German, and he challenged existing political systems, dislodged alliances, and disrupted business as usual. But when common folks applied Luther's teachings to their political situation and revolted, he penned *Against the Murderous and Thieving Hordes of Peasants.*

When Luther wasn't busy attacking nearly every social institution of his day, he focused on creating a new one of his own—a church restored to what Luther believed was the original message of the gospel. He wrote catechisms, articles, treatises, and confessions not only for his educated peers but also with children and the common adult in mind. The world in which Luther was born was reshaped and refocused by the time this reformer was laid to rest in 1546.

Lutherans in America

On Christmas of 1619, the first Lutheran service was held on

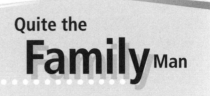

Quite the Family Man

Martin Luther may have been able to stand up to any man, including the pope, but, wise as he was, he deferred to his wife, Katherine von Bora, regarding matters of the heart and home. They met when Luther agreed to find husbands for nine nuns who had fled their convent. After eight of the nine were married, Luther and Katie decided to go for it, becoming engaged in front of friends on June 13, 1525. They married that same night in a private ceremony, launching a long and happy marriage. Luther said, "In domestic affairs I defer to Katie. Otherwise I am led by the Holy Ghost."

American soil. Immigrating primarily from German and Sweden, Lutherans poured into the colonies, mostly settling in the Pennsylvania area. Henry Melchior Muhlenber organized the first Lutheran synod in 1748, called the Ministerium of Pennsylvania. New York followed in 1786, North Carolina organized in 1803, Maryland in 1820, and Ohio in 1836.

Over one million German immigrants flooded into the States between 1850 and 1860. Local churches experienced huge growth in attendance, yet had to cope with conflict inherent in Americanized Lutherans and German-speaking Lutherans trying to share worship. At the same time, the country was divided by the impending Civil War. The combination of political animosity and cultural and languages clashes among Lutherans resulted in a fragmenting of the church. By the time the dust settled, as many as one hundred and fifty Lutheran associations existed in the U.S. Today, most of these groups have reunited and reorganized into a dozen or so. The two largest are the Lutheran Church–Missouri Synod and the Evangelical Lutheran Church in America (ELCA).

What Makes a Church Lutheran?

Enemies of the Reformation sneeringly called Luther's followers "Lutherans." Perhaps not the most creative slur, it seemed as good a name as any, and before long those who agreed with Luther's perspective adopted the term as their own. Today, Lutherans weigh in as the third largest group of Christians in the world, comprised of two hundred and fifty different autonomous varieties. Currently, twenty-one of these Lutheran groupings are in North America and hold the following tenets in common:

The Righteous Shall Live by Faith

Luther's genius was to boil down fifteen hundred years of Christian doctrine and practice into one simple truth: Anyone could be saved by grace through faith in Jesus Christ, alone. Period.

Luther wrote: "As a monk I had led an irreproachable life. Nevertheless I felt that I was a sinner before God. My conscience was restless, and I could not depend on God being propitiated by my satisfactions. Not only did I not love, but I actually hated the righteous God who punishes sinners. . . .

"Day and night I tried to meditate upon the significance of these words: 'The righteousness of God is revealed in that, as it is written: The righteous shall live by faith.' Then finally God had mercy on me, and I began to understand that the righteousness of God is that gift of God by which a righteous man lives, namely, faith, and that this sentence—The righteousness of God is revealed in the Gospel—is passive, indicating that the merciful God justifies us by faith, as it is written: 'The righteous shall live by faith.' Now I felt as though I had been reborn altogether and had entered Paradise."

This personal spiritual experience changed not only his life but prevailing culture as well. Building on this core tenet, Luther revised religious doctrine and practice.

Sacramental Changes

Of the seven Roman Catholic sacraments, only two are mentioned in Scripture: the Lord's Supper and baptism. Since Scripture, not church tradition, was his standard, Luther demoted the other five.

The Book of Concord

After Luther died, his followers argued amongst themselves (what a surprise). In less than forty years, Lutheran orthodoxy was declared through the Book of Concord (as in "harmony").

The Book of Concord is comprised of many separate documents, including:

- Apostles' Creed
- Nicene Creed
- Athanasian Creeds
- Augsburg Confession and Defense of the Augsburg Confession
- Small and Large Catechism
- Smalcald Articles

That's Only My Opinion

I see a tension between stating that Scripture is one's sole authority and then extending that "sole" authority to additional documents. Luther himself embodied this paradox. Even though Luther based his views on Scripture alone, he wrote voluminously in explanation of his interpretation of Scripture. Elaborate creeds, codes, and catechisms were developed to protect the purity and simplicity of the gospel. Ironic, don't you think? I don't see any way around it, however, since it's in our nature to split hairs and make things as complicated as possible. (And after all, life itself is pretty complicated.) Having acknowledged the impossibility of the task, I deeply respect the desire to hold true to Luther's original teachings. It is a worthy, if not altogether attainable, goal. But then, that's only my opinion.

- Treatise of the Power and Primacy of the Pope
- Epitome of the Formula of Concord
- Solid Declaration of the Formula of Concord

If you want to explore specific areas of faith in more depth, the Book of Concord can be downloaded or purchased in book form through most Lutheran web sites.

Lutheran Church–Missouri Synod

In spite of having the term "Missouri" in it's name, the LCMS extends far beyond one state in the union. Organized in 1846–47 as "The German Evangelical Lutheran Synod of Missouri, Ohio, and Other States," the LCMS has changed its name but not its beliefs or organizational structure.

Two terms that I believe capture the distinctiveness of LCMS Lutherans are "inerrancy" and "confessional." Scripture is seen as the sole authority of doctrine, being God's inerrant and infallible Word. A confessional Lutheran is one who embraces the Lutheran Confessions as "clearly, accurately and comfortingly" revealing God's Word and plan for salvation. In fact, the Lutheran Confessions are seen "as a true and unadulterated statement and exposition of the Word of God . . . because they are drawn from the Word of God and on that account regard their doctrinal content as a true and binding exposition of Holy Scripture. . . ."

Another distinction is the view LCMS holds on Communion. Luther believed that "the bread and the wine in the Supper are the true body and blood of Christ," but not quite in the same way the Catholics viewed it. This perspective is rather unique for Protestants in general, who tend to view communion as symbolic.

Just the FACTS

Lutheran Church—Missouri Synod

Kind of Church: Protestant/Lutheran/Conservative
Service Style: Liturgical
Trinity Affinity: Son
Clout Continuum: 1st Place: Scripture
2nd Place: Lutheran tradition
3rd Place: Personal experience through sacraments
Founded in USA: 1847
Members in USA: 2,582,440
Churches in USA: 6,220
Headquarters: 1333 S. Kirkwood Rd., St. Louis MO 63122
Phone: 314-965-9917
Web site: www.lcms.org

The conservative bent the LCMS has towards Scripture and adherence to Luther's teaching comes into play in regards to women's roles in ministry. Nearly half of the LCMS's full-time professional church workers are women. However, the LCMS does not ordain women as pastors. "The LCMS believes that those Scripture passages which say that women should not 'teach' and 'have authority' in the church (see, for example, 1 Cor. 11 and 14; 1 Timothy 2) mean that women ought not hold the authoritative teaching office in the church—this is, the office of pastor. Women are allowed to hold other offices in the church, as long as these offices do not involve the one holding them in carrying out the distinctive functions of the pastoral office (historically in the Synod this has included the offices of elder, chairman, and vice-chairman of the congregation)."

If you're looking for a church that has stayed true to Luther's original beliefs, then the Lutheran Church–Missouri Synod may be for you. Liturgical in worship and conservative in lifestyle, LCMS churches will provide you with a tradition that is over five hundred years old.

Evangelical Lutheran Church in America

Giving people the opportunity to worship and learn about God's Word in their native language was one of Luther's great gifts. In keeping with this value, Luther's writings were translated into a myriad of languages as Lutheranism spread throughout Europe. Ethnic and language groups developed their own approach to the Lutheran faith, and immigrants brought these practices with them to North America. A Lutheran wasn't simply a Lutheran, but a Scandinavian Lutheran, a Dutch Lutheran, a German Lutheran, a Danish Lutheran, and so on, many of whom worshiped in their native tongues.

In time, most Lutheran groups assimilated into mainstream American culture and adopted English as their primary language. This shift

Not His Finest Moments

In his late thirties, Luther authored *Jesus Was Born a Jew*, defending those of Jewish descent. But when the Jews did not accept his teachings, he turned on them in *Of the Jews and Their Lies*, written when he was fifty-nine. Luther's anti-Semitic rantings are inexcusable, and neither the LCMS or the ELCA now tries to excuse them. In 1983, however, the LCMS adopted a resolution denouncing Luther's racial views while maintaining support for Luther's theological position. For a copy of this resolution, go to www.lcms.org and check out FAQS–Luther's Anti-Semitic Remarks.

Just the **FACTS**

Evangelical Lutheran Church in America

Kind of Church: Protestant/Lutheran/Moderate
Worship Style: Liturgical
Trinity Affinity: Son
Clout Continuum: 1st Place: Scripture
2nd Place: Lutheran tradition
3rd Place: Personal experience through sacraments
Founded in USA: 1988
Members in USA: 5,125,919 (figure includes Caribbean)
Churches in USA: 10,816 (figure includes Caribbean)
Headquarters: 8765 W. Higgins Rd.
Chicago IL 60631
Phone: 773-380-2700
Web site: www.elca.org

laid the groundwork for merging distinct Lutheran groups. The Lutheran Church in America (LCA) was born in 1962 with the merger of German, Slovak, Icelandic, Swedish, and Danish congregations. By 1963, churches of German, Danish, and Norwegian backgrounds merged to form the American Lutheran Church (ALC). In 1976, a schism over biblical inerrancy occurred, with the Lutheran Church–Missouri Synod going in one direction and moderates in another, resulting in the formation of the Association of Evangelical Lutheran Church (AELC). Confused yet?

Allow me to skip the political intrigue and cut to the chase. These three groups: ALC, LCA, and AELC eventually merged in 1988 to form the ELCA, now referred to as the Evangelical Lutheran Church in America. The moderate arm of American Lutheranism was born.

Today the ELCA is the largest Lutheran denomination and accepts documents in the Book of Concord as "valid interpretations of the faith of the Church." Their confession of faith declares the "canonical Scriptures of the Old and New Testaments as the inspired Word of God and the authoritative source and norm of its proclamation, faith and life."

The ELCA has given the green light to ordaining women to the position of pastor. As of December 2001, roughly 14 percent of the 17,651 ELCA-ordained clergy were women.

Furthermore, the ELCA is trying to establish some kind of relationship with the Roman Catholic Church and other Protestant/Reformed churches, both of which Luther strongly opposed. Bridging difference in theology and practice requires loosening some of Luther's views, which may seem like a good thing to you, or maybe not.

What to Expect When You Visit

Lutheran worship services are liturgical, but may not be as formal as other liturgical churches. Like most Protestant churches, Lutherans place more importance on preaching, so more time may be given to the sermon portion of the service. As with other liturgical churches, it's best to stand, sit, or kneel along with everyone else.

As for nonmembers participating in communion, that practice varies depending on the congregation. Take a look in the bulletin to see if guidelines are printed. You could also ask an usher or someone who regularly attends. In the case that no instructions are given, I'd recommend not participating just in case it would be seen as offensive.

What is seen as acceptable attire also depends on the particular congregation. In general, a jacket and tie is the best bet for men if you're visiting a Sunday morning service. Women will be safe in a dress or skirt. In some areas, a pantsuit for women is quite suitable for worship. Steer clear of shorts, jeans, and low-cut tops.

More Lutheran Churches

Apostolic Lutheran Church of America
  www.apostolic-lutheran.org

Association of Free Lutheran Congregations
    www.aflc.org

Church of Lutheran Brethren of America
    www.clba.org

Church of the Lutheran Confession
    www.clclutheran.org

Evangelical Lutheran Synod
    www.evluthsyn.org

Wisconsin Evangelical Lutheran Synod
    www.wells.net

Further Info

- Robert Kolb and Timothy J. Wengert, eds., *The Book of Concord: The Confessions of the Evangelical Lutheran Church*, translated by James Schaffer (Fortress, 2000)

- Eric W. Gritsch, *Fortress Introduction to Lutheranism* (Fortress, 1994)

- Patti T. Arthur, *Stand Up, Sit Down, Sing, Pray: Why We Do What We Do in Lutheran Worship* (CSS Publishing, 1999)

seven

Episcopal Churches

Most church founders have been colorful, passionate people, and Henry VIII is no exception. Handsome, charming, quite the dancer, and adored by the English public, Henry VIII took the throne in 1509 at the age of eighteen. While other Protestant movements, by and large, arose from a passion for God and genuine spiritual conviction, Henry had one overriding obsession—to sire a male heir. He squared off with the pope, argued with Martin Luther, married six times, arranged a few executions, and set up a new state church with himself as the head during this endeavor. He was the kind of guy who did whatever it took to achieve his goal. You were either with him or you were headless.

A Brief History of the Episcopal Church

When Arthur, Henry's older brother, died in 1502, he unintentionally did Henry two favors—he made Henry VIII the heir to the throne and left a young widow who would, in Henry's estimation, make the perfect queen. As soon as his father, Henry VII, passed away, Henry VIII stepped into power and married Katherine of Aragon, daughter of King Ferdinand and Queen Isabella of Spain.

Katherine did her best to produce a male heir for Henry, but childbearing at that point in history was extremely dangerous to both mother and child. After numerous miscarriages and babies who died shortly after birth, Katherine gave her husband a daughter named Mary—not at all what Henry wanted.

Convinced that Katherine had failed him and would never produce a male heir, Henry's attention was caught by a flirtatious young woman with raven black hair. While other women of the court succumbed to his charms (Henry had many mistresses), Anne Boleyn refused Henry's advances. High spirited, intelligent, and strong-willed, Anne insisted on no hanky panky without a wedding, and Henry became a man obsessed. He pressured Thomas Wolsey, the Archbishop of York, to get the pope to grant Henry and Katherine a divorce. When Wolsey failed, Henry was outraged. He would have had Wolsey executed, except that he died of heart failure and saved Henry the trouble.

While Henry was lamenting his marital problems, Martin Luther was launching the Reformation on the continent. Realizing that he could grant himself a divorce if he were the head of the church, Henry turned to another Catholic priest, Thomas Cranmer, for help. Together they orchestrated a break with the Roman Catholic Church, and Henry became the self-declared supreme head of the Church of England. Cranmer annulled the marriage between Henry and Katherine, and Henry took Anne as his wife in 1533.

Anne soon gave birth to a girl named Elizabeth, and Henry's obsession turned to rage. He was going to have a son, or everyone else would die trying. Anne was convicted of incest and treason, trumped up to give Henry an excuse to have her executed. She was beheaded when Elizabeth was only two.

Almost immediately, Henry married the blonde and demure Jane Seymour, one of Anne's ladies-in-waiting. Jane gave birth to the son Henry been waiting for. His union with Jane promised to be a long and affectionate one, except that Jane never recovered from giving birth. She died less than two weeks later. Henry must have truly loved her, for he mourned her death for three years. She is the only one of his wives buried with him.

Henry's next marriage, in 1540 to Anne of Cleves, was purely a political affair, arranged by Thomas Cromwell to strengthen ties among Protestants. The fly in the ointment was that neither the bride nor the groom could stand each other. Henry had put on a few pounds over the years and, upon meeting, Anne made it quite clear that Henry repulsed her. He found her equally unattractive and refused to consummate the marriage. As much as he detested Anne, it was politically unwise to behead her, so Henry divorced her. Cromwell didn't fare as well. Blamed for the fiasco, he soon found his head on the executioner's block.

Henry was up in years when he took his next bride, the young, effervescent cousin of Anne Boleyn. Catherine Howard brought Henry back to life. He dieted, exercised, and reveled in his new-found virility. But, alas, Catherine was a girl who just wanted to have fun. After she was caught in an affair, she too was executed.

His sixth and final wife nursed him through the end of his life. Katharine Parr was a good egg and proved to be a stabilizing force for his three children. In his last days, Henry suffered from gout and arthritis, and Katharine was a great comfort to him. He died in 1547 having married six times, producing a total of three "legitimate" children—Mary, Elizabeth, and Edward.

A Bumpy Anglican Ride

When Edward was crowned King of England, he was only nine years old. Frail but good hearted, Edward VI was easy prey for his advisers. Henry VIII had tried to protect his son from exploitation by decreeing that a council would rule until Edward came of age, but his uncle, Edward Seymour, manipulated the Council of Regency to give him the titles of Lord Protectorship and Duke of Somerset.

Somerset isolated the young king while taking England in a decidedly Protestant direction. In 1549, Somerset instituted Archbishop Thomas Cranmer's Book of Common Prayer, making it mandatory in all churches in England. This act angered Catholics and Protestants alike. The Catholics were upset because their Latin Mass was abolished and the more conservative Protestants felt that the Book of Common Prayer sidestepped many controversial issues. Both sides clamored for their version of reform. Add to this religious unrest severe economic distress and an embarrassing defeat in a war with Scotland, and Somerset was in over his head—which he lost 1552.

Masterminding Somerset's demise was the Duke of Northumberland, John Dudley. Capitalizing on Somerset's mistakes, Dudley manipulated his way into power. Dudley confiscated church property in the name of Protestant reform, thereby making himself a very wealthy man. Unfortunately for Dudley, King Edward VI's health was failing. Dudley feared that Mary, Edward's Catholic sister, would take over the throne and revert his real estate back to the Catholic Church. In a preemptive strike, Dudley convinced King Edward VI to bestow bastard status to his sisters, Mary and Elizabeth. Edward's cousin, Lady Jane Grey, was then selected as successor.

Poor Edward VI died of consumption in July of 1553 at the age of sixteen. Lady Jane Grey, a reluctant pawn, was Queen of England for nine days. Dudley set out to capture Princess Mary to keep her from claiming the throne, only to end up in Mary's clutches. He promptly converted to Catholicism hoping it would save his neck. It didn't. Mary had him beheaded in August of 1553, a month after Edward passed away. The unfortunate Lady Jane Grey was also executed the following year. Mary Tudor took the throne at the age of 37, utterly devoted to restoring England to the hands of Roman Catholicism.

For five years Queen Mary I tried every trick in the book to reinstate Catholicism—she had Parliament repeal her father's Act of Supremacy, restored the Latin Mass throughout the country, and reinstated Catholic bishops. She was even married to a Catholic—and a foreigner besides—Philip of Spain. Everyone was in an uproar. Before Mary completed her five-year reign she had burned over three hundred Protestants at the stake (including Cranmer, the author of the Book of Common Prayer), earning herself the name Bloody Mary. Her subjects were more relieved than grief stricken when she died in 1558.

> **How many Anglicans does it take to change a lightbulb?**
>
> Five. One to screw in the new bulb and four to found an organization for the preservation of the old bulb.

Fortunately for England, her twenty-five year old sister, Elizabeth, followed her to the throne. Intelligent, politically shrewd, and practical, Queen Elizabeth I was able to gain the support of her subjects by instituting a moderate Protestantism. For the majority of the English, who were Protestant and disinterested in bowing to Rome, Anglicanism was the religion of choice. To appease adamant Catholics, Elizabeth declared that their worship could be considered a Mass. Extremists on both sides were dissatisfied, but the mainstream accepted the compromise. The common people adored Queen Elizabeth, calling her "Good Queen Bess," but the Queen was no softy. When Anglican clergy took their doctrinal vows, they also vowed allegiance to their Queen.

The American Revolution and a Name Change

The Anglican Church was officially brought to America in 1578 when Sir Francis Drake planted a cross in California in the name of Queen Elizabeth I. It took a few more years for colonists to arrive and set up Anglican congregations, but the Church of England was one of the firsts to be represented on American shores.

Many of the people who immigrated to America were fed up with their European pasts, but not everyone who came from England was at odds with their monarch or their state religion. In the early colonial days, Anglicanism was seen as a very acceptable, even respectable, church affiliation. In fact, the Church of England counts some of the most influential American movers-and-shakers among its ranks—George Washington, Thomas Jefferson, and Patrick Henry, to name a few.

However, as colonists became more rebellious against their English rulers, Anglicanism fell out of favor. The American Revolution put a huge wrinkle in the growth of the Anglican Church, since membership was correlated with being a traitor to freedom. How do you fight against England for independence while simultaneously vowing allegiance to England? By the end of the war, the structure of the Anglican Church was in shambles, with many clergy looking elsewhere for work. A rag-tag band of ministers who wanted to be both Anglican and Americans gathered together in 1783 in Annapolis, Maryland. They set up a new church with nearly all the same beliefs and practices, only without political ties to England. It's the only denomination that resulted from a "split of countries not a split of the church." This new denomination was named the Protestant Episcopal Church—Protestant to denote its distinction from Roman Catholicism and Episcopal to illustrate its form of church government. Now we refer to this body simply as the Episcopal Church.

As can be expected, a number of schisms have occurred over the years since the founding of the Episcopal Church. The first split of note occurred in 1873 when Bishop George D. Cummins felt the church was becoming too ornamental and ritualistic. Taking his faction in a more evangelical direction, Cummins helped found the Reformed Episcopal Church (REC). While the REC retained many aspects of the Episcopal Church, it differs in at least three significant ways:

- The REC does not believe that the presence of Christ resides in the eucharistic elements. Rather, the Lord's Supper is symbolic of Christ.
- Regeneration is possible without baptism, which is seen as an expression of salvation.
- Since all Christians are seen as part of the "priesthood," the term "priest" is not reserved for clergy.

The next wave of dissention occurred more recently. In 1962, the Southern Episcopal Church was formed in response to what they saw as a trend of liberalism in the Episcopal Church. Based in Nashville, Tennessee, the Southern Episcopal Church claims to cling to "an unchanging faith in a changing world."

Another faction took a stand in 1977, again in reaction to what was perceived as the growth of liberalism within the Episcopal Church. In particular, this group disagreed with the ordination of women and new revisions made to the prayer book. Blending Catholic and Episcopal beliefs, the Anglican Catholic Church (ACC) renewed a commitment to the first seven ecumenical councils of the traditional church. The

How to Speak Episcolianese

Parish: a local church

Diocese: a geographical area containing a number of parishes or missions

Rector: the priest who leads a parish

Vicar: the priest who leads a mission

Vestry: the council who makes decisions for a parish

Vestments: special outfits people wear in the services

Cassock: an black gown usually worn under a surplice

Surplice: an gown that is white and gathered and often worn over the cassock

Alb: a white tunic with sleeves that cover the body from neck to ankles

Stole: a narrow band of colored fabric that deacons wear over one shoulder (priests and bishops wear it over both shoulders)

Chasuble: a circular garment a bishop or priest may wear under the alb and stole

Dalmatic: a deacon's chasuble that has sleeves

Mitre: headgear worn by bishops

ACC uses the 1928 version of the Book of Common Prayer exclusively and does not ordain women.

The last schism I'm going to include occurred as recently as 1992—the formation of the International Communion of the Charismatic Episcopal Church. The Communion integrates the active use of spiritual gifts into traditional liturgical worship. In the first decade of its existence, the Communion has expanded into twenty or more countries, with two hundred thousand members worldwide.

What Makes a Church Episcopal?

Two major threads tie Episcopalians of various factions together —the episcopalian church structure and the Book of Common Prayer. The word "episcopal" means "oversight," indicating that there is leadership at the top. Like a federal union, each individual church (parish) belongs to a larger governing area (diocese) overseen by an elected bishop. The diocese are overseen by a specially elected bishop, usually called the presiding bishop.

The Book of Common Prayer, originally penned in 1549 in England, was revised for American Episcopalians in 1789 and has since been revised more than once, resulting in controversy and schism. This book contains the prayers, liturgies, historical documents, church calendar, catechism, and lectionary.

Episcopal Church

As was the case for all churches that were around in the 1800s, the controversy over slavery was a serious threat to church unity. The various threads in the fabric of Episcopal faith proved extremely strong when the issue divided most other Christian affiliations. The Episcopal Church was the only major denomination that did not split over the Civil War. Both sides prayed publicly for the other, and once a truce was declared, the Episcopal Church quickly mended fences.

Today the Episcopal Church offers a wide umbrella under which Christians can gather. Within the denomination, you'll find theological conservatives and liberals, Democrats and Republicans, gay and straight, and a sampling from every ethnic group. While most Protestant churches give minimal or no credence to tradition or human reason, Episcopalians are more like Roman Catholics in what sources inform their faith.

An Episcopalian is either a Roman Catholic who flunked Latin or a Presbyterian whose stocks paid off.

Scripture is revered as the Word of God in two ways: first, God inspired the human authors in telling the story of God's relationship with us and,

169

Just the **FACTS**

Episcopal Church

Kind of Church:	Protestant/Anglican/Eclectic
Worship Style:	Liturgical
Church Structure:	Episcopal
Trinity Affinity:	Father
Clout Continuum:	1st Place: Anglican tradition
	2nd Place: Personal experience through sacraments
	3rd Place: Scripture
Founded in USA:	1789
Members in USA:	2,333,000
Churches in USA:	7,300
Headquarters:	815 Second Ave.
	New York NY 10017
Phone:	800-334-7626
Web site:	www.episcopalchurch.org

second, God still speaks through the Bible today. True understanding of Scripture comes through the church with the aid of the Holy Spirit. While the Bible is authoritative, it is interpreted with the aid of tradition, human reason, personal experience, and a lot of discussion.

Like the Orthodox and Roman Catholic Churches, seven sacraments are honored. These are:

- Baptism: The sacrament of baptism is necessary for children and adults for regeneration, and can be performed through pouring, sprinkling, or immersion. Your baptism will be recognized in the Episcopal Church if the church in which you were baptized believes in the Trinity.

- Confirmation: Adults are confirmed through the laying on of hands by a bishop.

- Reconciliation (confession and absolution): Episcopal priests do not regularly hear confessions from individual members as do Roman Catholic priests. This sacrament is, under normal circumstances, experienced collectively during the worship service.

- Anointing of the sick: Prayer and anointing of oil is available.

- Marriage: Members do not have to be "married in the church" for a marriage to be acknowledged.

- Ordination: In addition to the Apostles' and Nicene Creeds, clergy state upon ordination "I do believe the Holy Scriptures of the Old and New Testaments to be the Word of God, and to contain all things necessary to salvation; and I do solemnly engage to conform to the doctrine, discipline, and worship of the Episcopal Church."

- Eucharist: Without going into theological detail, the Episcopal Church believes that Christ's presence resides in the elements of the Lord's Supper—not quite as defined as the Roman Catholic tradition and not as "symbolic" as most Protestants.

To summarize Episcopalian basic beliefs, their web site states: "Episcopalians believe in a Trinitarian God (the Father, the Son, and the Holy Spirit) who created us, redeems us, and never lets us go. This means that God is the source of all life, that through the life, death, and resurrection of Jesus Christ, our sins are forgiven and our lives are brought into closer union with God. It also means that God's love is present in the world and with us always. We believe in the church as

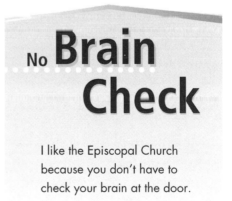

No **Brain Check**

I like the Episcopal Church because you don't have to check your brain at the door.

—a poster from the 1970s

the body of Christ, one that is holy, catholic (or universal), and apostolic, continuing the teaching of Jesus through the apostles to this day. The Nicene Creed and the Apostles' Creed, found in the Book of Common Prayer and often recited in our liturgy, outline our beliefs."

Because tradition plays such a significant role in the Episcopal Church, women were not ordained as deaconesses until 1970 or into the priesthood until 1976. The first woman elected to the office of bishop was Rev. Barbara C. Harris in 1988. Today it's quite common to see women in the priesthood.

Now that everyone's gotten over that revolution thing back in the late 1700s, the Episcopal Church has reestablished a relationship with the Church of England and more than thirty other Anglican churches all over the world. They share common traditions, history, and use of the Book of Common Prayer.

Many Christians feel at home in the Episcopal Church because it offers such a variety of perspectives. Some congregations are very formal and conservative, while others are more flamboyant and cause-oriented, but all Episcopal Churches share a common devotion to their liturgy and worship style. Discussion is encouraged, and members usually pride themselves on being intellectually informed and open-minded. For a high church experience with an English-American twist, check out the Episcopalians. You may find a very good fit.

What to Expect When You Visit

All Episcopalian services are liturgical, but not all are considered to be formal. To be on the safe side for your first visit, I'd recommend men wear a jacket and tie and women wear a skirt, dress, or nice pantsuit. However, you may want to call ahead if you're visiting a church in a more informal part of the country, or if it is especially hot. You may find a wide array of more casual clothing is acceptable.

Since the service is structured, it's more difficult to slip in unnoticed if you arrive late. Try to be early, but if you get caught in traffic, ask an usher when and where to sit. Some churches will provide you with a printed liturgical program, and it's easy to follow along. Others will use a hymnal and the Book of Common Prayer and assume you know what you're doing. When I've visited the latter, I have gotten lost flipping back and forth through the pages. By the time I find the place, the rest of the group is off on another section. If this happens to you, just relax and let yourself experience the worship rather than get uptight about participating. Basically, as long as you stand and sit with the group, no one will notice that you don't know the words.

Some congregations are stricter about participating in the Lord's Supper than others. I've been to Episcopal churches that welcome everyone—you don't even have to be a Christian to join in. Others expect you to be a member of the Episcopal Church, and in the middle are those congregations who request that only baptized believers (of any denomination) partake in Eucharist. Check out the bulletin to see if they have a stated policy. You can always ask an usher, who will be glad to let you know what is appropriate.

One thing that seems important to Episcopalians is that no one be expected to do anything against their conscience or beliefs. So if there are prayers or songs or any other activities that conflict with your convictions, quietly refrain from participating. Otherwise, expect a worshipful experience that will nurture your spirit.

More Episcopal Churches

Anglican Catholic Church
www.anglicancatholic.org

International Communion of the Charismatic Episcopal Church
www.diochi.org

Reformed Episcopal Church
www.recus.org

Southern Episcopal Church
www.angelfire.com/biz/southern

Further Info

- John N. Wall, *A Dictionary for Episcopalians,* illustrated by Philippa J. Anderson (Cowley, 2000)

- David L. Holmes, *Brief History of the Episcopal Church* (Trinity, 1993)

- Richard H. Schmidt, *Glorious Companions: Five Centuries of Anglican Spirituality* (Eerdmans, 2002)

eight

Reformed Churches

Next to Martin Luther, it's safe to say that John Calvin (1509–1564) was the most influential Protestant-era reformer. Even though there is no denomination named after Calvin (as the Lutheran church is named after Martin Luther), his doctrine was the foundation for the Puritan, Congregationalist, and Baptist movements in England, the Presbyterian Church in Scotland, the Huguenots in France, and the Reformed Church throughout Europe, especially in Holland and Germany. Luther may get more credit for the Reformation in general, but Calvin's influence can be seen far beyond religion, most notably in the impact he had on the emergence of democracy and the United States. His theology arguably provided some basis for the development of capitalism, the emergence of what is now called the Protestant or Puritan work ethic, and the idea of "covenant," which proved to be foundational to democracy. According to Richard Hooker from Washington State University, "at the heart of the way Americans think and act, you'll find this fierce and imposing reformer."

Swingin' with Zwingli

The town was abuzz when Ulrich Zwingli, a feisty and strong-willed priest in Zurich, Switzerland, preached directly from the Bible, chapter by chapter. We may take this for granted today, but church teaching in the early 1500s was largely based on commentaries, not directly from Scripture. Huge crowds showed up for Zwingli's sermons. They were not only hearing about what the Scriptures said but also coming to believe that only Scripture should be authoritative in the life of the church.

Under Zwingli's influence, the Zurich church council banned teaching that was not founded on the Scriptures, thereby breaking ties with Rome in 1523. All of the priests in the Swiss canton were ordered to go with the Protestant flow. They destroyed the church organs, removed religious images from the churches, turned monasteries into hospitals, and revised the mass altogether, doing away with the sacrament of the Eucharist. Instead, Communion was shared as a "commemorative feast." Allowing priests to marry was par for the Protestant course, but Zwingli didn't wait until it was "legal." He lived with a woman for two years before the rules were changed and he could legalize the union in 1524. Clearly, this guy did what he wanted when he wanted. Zwingli didn't stop at reforming the church, he also impacted the city life of Zurich. Along with a Christian magistrate, Zwingli ruled Zurich as a theocracy (as John Calvin did a few years later in Geneva).

Even though Zwingli developed his beliefs prior to coming into contact with Luther, the two reformers had many things in common. They both

A Brief History of Reformed Churches

How did this Frenchman get so influential?

First of all, John Calvin was extremely bright. His father, Gérard, recognized his son's aptitude for logic and verbal persuasion and encouraged John to follow in his footsteps and go into law. Obediently, John went to law school but was more attracted to the intellectual swirl of humanism and the emerging Protestant movement. His readings of Erasmus, Luther, and others fueled his interest in theology and was the cat-

believed in the authority of Scripture and justification by faith, and rejected the selling of indulgences or the need for confession to a priest. They both had "theses," Luther posted ninety-five in 1517 and Zwingli presented sixty-seven in 1523. Even though Zwingli had a shorter list, his were much more radical than Luther's.

It's no surprise that before too long Luther and Zwingli locked doctrinal horns. Zwingli saw communion as a call to reflect on Jesus, whereas Luther still maintained a metaphysical change in the elements. They tried to iron out their differences in 1529 at the Marburg Colloquy, but no deal was made and they went their separate Protestant ways.

Zwingli tried to convert all Swiss cantons to Protestantism. One of his "evangelistic" tactics was to impose a trade embargo on the Catholic cantons. That didn't go over well and triggered a civil war. In 1531, while serving as chaplain and standard-bearer for his forces, Zwingli was wounded in battle and later killed by enemy forces. Today, Switzerland remains divided, with six Protestant cantons and five Catholic.

After Zwingli was killed, his son-in-law was formally recognized as carrying on Zwingli's work. But in fact, John Calvin stepped into Zwingli's reformation shoes and guided the movement away from Zwingli's view of the Lord's Supper. From 1531, the Swiss reformation took on a distinctly Calvinistic bent.

alyst for a "sudden conversion" occurring some time between 1532–1534. Reflecting on his conversion later in life, he wrote that "God at last turned my course in another direction by the secret rein of his providence." He focused his fine mind on theology rather than legal arguments.

In 1536, when he was only twenty-seven, John Calvin wrote an essay called *The Institutes of Christian Religion* for French King Francis I in the hopes of showing that Protestants posed no political threat. John had been in and out of prison for his beliefs, fled a few times for his life, and was invested in the king embracing Protestantism. King Francis I remained unconvinced. Young John may have felt his efforts had failed, but he had successfully penned the basics for a theological framework that would rock the world—Reformed theology, sometimes called Calvinism. Calvin expanded the *Institutes* over the years, but the essentials were in place.

Not His Finest Moment

I think its safe to say that John Calvin was a tad controlling. But Calvin hit an all time low in his dealings with Michael Servetus.

Michael Servetus (1511–1553) was a skilled physician and theologian from Spain. He rubbed shoulders with many of the leading Protestant reformers, including Calvin, but didn't go along with the Trinitarian view of God. Had he quietly disagreed, perhaps I'd not be writing about him now. But he published his ideas and his Protestants foes were especially aware of the power of the written word. After one escape from prison, Servetus was spotted and captured while on his way to Italy. Servetus was placed on trial in Geneva. Calvin, playing a key but behind-the-scenes role in this drama, heavily influenced the outcome. Servetus was burned at the stake on October 27, 1553.

But a lot of people are smart and they don't have a number of denominations built on their ideas. Had Calvin simply been blessed with a keen mind capable of constructing logical theological categories, he may not have played such a significant role in history. I believe a second reason for his influence can be attributed to a less-than-desirable personality trait. Simply stated: John Calvin was controlling.

I've yet to find anyone, even Calvin's staunchest supporters, who accuses him of being a live-and-let-live kind of guy. Calvin enthusiastically imposed his view onto other people's lives. Even though he never held a public office, he nevertheless gained control of the unruly citizens of Geneva in 1541 (he had been thrown out in 1538 for being too pushy). From then on, it was his way or the highway—literally. He even tossed out Protestant groups who disagreed with him, such as the more radical Anabaptists.

Some say he went a bit overboard (I might agree) when he tried to orchestrate nearly every aspect of daily life. He had no trouble having a city magistrate enforce "Christian" behavior, banning plays, and trying to get the taverns in town to distribute religious literature and have group psalm-sings over their ale.

On the upside, Calvin improved many aspects of city life including developing an effective sewage system, the development of quality health and hospital care, mandating rails on upper stories to protect children from falling, and setting up educational opportunities for children and adults. Most notably, Calvin founded a training school for Reformed theologians, which eventually became the University of Geneva.

Third, I think Calvin can also thank the Catholics for his success. The persecution of major Protestant leaders was so intense that many fled for their lives—some to the safety of Geneva. They came to Geneva united in their opposition to Roman Catholicism, but not necessarily embracing a shared view of Protestantism. Once in Geneva, however, they were schooled in Reformed theology, and naturally bonded to

Calvin and each other under adversity. By the time they left for their homelands, most believed that preaching Calvinism was synonymous with preaching Christianity.

"Reformed" reformers spread across Western Europe, the British Isles, and soon to the New World. Queen Mary of England (Henry VIII's Catholic daughter) wanted to restore England to the way it was before her father broke with Rome. Bloody Mary was brutal in her treatment of Protestant heretics. While in Geneva, some of these exiled Protestants completed the first translation of the Bible into English. When Mary died after a mere five years on the throne, the English Protestants returned with a newly translated Bible and a strong Calvinistic bent.

Five years before he died, Calvin published his final version of *The Institutes of Christian Religion* in 1559. During his life he expanded the first version of six sections into seventy-nine comprehensive chapters. Calvin's theology flows from an awe of God. Benjamin B. Warfield wrote that a Calvinist is someone "who has seen God, and who, having seen God in His glory, is filled on the one hand, with a sense of his own unworthiness to stand in God's sight as a creature, and much more as a sinner, and on the other hand, with adoring wonder that nevertheless this God is a God who receives sinners." Not a bad place to start. Calvin's *Institutes* have been heralded, by supporters and dissenters alike, as a masterpiece of spiritual insight.

Like the Orthodox Church, Reformed Churches tended to organize along national lines—particularly in Holland, Germany, Bohemia, Poland, and Hungary. A majority of Reformed immigrants were either Dutch or German, bringing this brand of Calvinism to the States with an ethnic twist. They set up separate affiliations, merged, split, and merged again. Regardless of the national influences, however, Reformed Christians have several key beliefs in common.

What Makes a Church Reformed?

Today, most Reformed Churches hold three confessions of faith as standards of doctrine and practice:

- The Belgic Confession. Written in 1561 by Guido de Bres, a Dutch Reformed pastor from the Netherlands. De Bres tried to persuade Philip II of Spain that the Reformed faith was not heretical. The King of Spain was unswayed and continued his persecution. In 1567, de Bres was martyred for his Reformed beliefs.

- The Heidelberg Catechism: Written in 1563 by Zacharius Ursinus and Caspar Olevianus. The catechism was intended to mediate between Lutheran and Reformed theology. The Heidelberg Catechism is clearly Reformed and is still used today in many Reformed Churches.

- The Canons of Dort: Written in 1618 in response to the theological battle over predestination, this statement outlines the five points of Calvinism. If Calvin were alive I wonder what he would think of how his views are presented today. While he was undoubtedly a man given to theological categories, it's possible he might question those who boiled down his seventy-nine chapters into five points.

These five points were developed in Holland as a defense against the five points of Arminianism, a doctrine the Calvinists saw as a heresy. To clarify doctrine, the Synod of Dort was convened for seven months, from November 1618 to May 1619. Representatives from the Reformed Churches in the Netherlands, England, Scotland, Germany, and Switzerland sat on the Synod. The deck was stacked against the Arminians, with the Synod being less of a theological discussion and more of a hearing.

The most significant and lasting outcome of the Synod was the declaration of the five points of Calvinism. Here's a simplified version:

- Total Depravity:
  Humanity is totally unable to save itself.
- Unconditional Election:
  God's electing purpose is not conditioned by anything in humanity.
- Limited Atonement:
  Christ's atoning death is sufficient to save all of humanity, but efficient only for the elect.
- Irresistible Grace:
  The gift of faith, sovereignly given by God's Holy Spirit, cannot be resisted by the elect.
- Perseverance of the Saints:
  Those who are regenerated and justified will persevere in the faith.

As you may have noticed, the first letters of the five points spell TULIP—a catchy way to remember the five points of Calvinism (sort of poetic for Dutch Calvinists, don't you think? Get it? Dutch? Tulips?). The Arminians were set packing, and Calvinism gained a stronghold in the Netherlands.

Reformed Church in America

While Arminian and Calvinist Christians were arguing in Holland, many Dutch Christians decided to head for the New World. As early as 1614, Reformed Christians were meeting informally in what is now the state of New York. The Reformed Church in America traces its for-

Just the FACTS

Reformed Church in America

Kind of Church: Protestant/Calvinist/Mainline
Worship Style: Traditional
Trinity Affinity: Father
Clout Continuum: 1st Place: Scripture
2nd Place: Reformed tradition
3rd Place: Personal experience
Founded in USA: 1628
Members in USA: 300,000
Churches in USA: 950
Headquarters: 475 Riverside Dr., 18th Floor
New York NY 10115
Phone: 212-870-2954
Web site: www.rca.org

mal roots to a Sunday in April 1628 when fifty or so Dutch immigrants gathered to share the Lord's Supper in the loft of a mill in the small town of New Amsterdam. This congregation is still intact today, known as the Collegiate Reformed Church in New York City, "the oldest evangelical church in North America with a continuous ministry."

As the Dutch were Americanized, they wanted independence from the church structure in Holland. In 1792, the Reformed Protestant Dutch Church was founded and then incorporated in 1819. The name was changed to the Reformed Church in America (RCA) in 1867.

Today the Reformed Church in America defines itself as a "mainline church that also has clear evangelical sensitivities." Along with other Reformed denominations, the RCA holds the Belgic Confession, the Heidelberg Catechism, and the Canons of Dort as standard for faith. In addition, the RCA embraces the Apostles' Creed, the Athanasian Creed, and the Nicene Creed. In 2001, the General Synod the Reformed Church accepted the Belhar Confession from the Uniting Reformed Church of Southern Africa.

Their web site states:

"We in the Reformed Church in America believe God created humans perfect and free to make choices. They chose to disobey their Creator. Turning away from God, humanity fell into sin. All of the suffering and evil in the world is because of this sin.

"Even though we have turned away from God, God still loves all people and wants our lives to be full of joy and peace. Right from the beginning, God had a plan to make this happen.

"God's plan was to send Jesus, who lived a life of perfect obedience to God and who died to pay the price for all people's sins. God raised Jesus back to life. He is in heaven now, but he has promised to return to earth someday. When he comes again, he will resurrect all believers and take them to be with him in heaven.

"Believers are people who accept that Jesus Christ is God's Son, who believe that Jesus died for their sins and rose from the dead, and who do their best to follow his teachings and example. Together they form the church, which is called Christ's body on earth, and which has a responsibility to continue Christ's work.

"Living the Christian life is not always easy, but believers receive guidance from the Bible and from the teachings and example of Christ; and they receive encouragement and power from God's Holy Spirit."

RCA church government is presbyterian in structure. The local congregation has a certain amount of autonomy, but is ultimately accountable to a group of delegates of elders and pastors from a specific area. Classes are grouped together into regional synods. At this point, the RCA is comprised of forty-six classis and eight regional synods. At the top is the General Synod made up of representatives from the classis. The General Synod meets annually to oversee the entire denomination. The General Synod Council (GSC) serves as the board of directors and administrates daily functioning of the RCA. It is comprised of one representative from the forty-six classis, thirteen at-large members, and a member from the five racial-ethnic councils. The racial-ethnic councils focus on the concerns of African-Americans, Hispanics, Native American Indians, and Pacific and Asian-Americans. GSC is organized into six committees: congregational services; evangelism and church development services; finance services; ministry and personnel services; mission services; and policy, planning, and administration services.

How many Calvinists does it take to change a lightbulb?

None. God will change the bulb when it's predestined to be changed.

In 1972, women in the Reformed Church in America were allowed to serve as deacons and elders. Today, about 26 percent of those holding these offices are women. In addition, the ordination of women was approved in 1979, making it possible for women to preach and serve the sacraments. According to their 1999 records, nearly half of the theological students enrolled at the two RCA seminaries were women.

The RCA is a member of:

- World Alliance of Reformed Churches
- World Council of Churches
- National Council of Churches of Christ in the USA

The RCA is also in dialogue with:

- The Evangelical Lutheran Church in America
- The United Church of Christ
- Presbyterian Church (USA)

I especially enjoyed visiting the RCA web site because of the humor section. The church seems to have a sense of humor about itself that I find refreshing. This is not to imply they're not serious about their faith, just that the church has been around long enough to have a little perspective. The RCA views itself as mainline—if you see yourself as a moderate in most areas, the RCA may be a good fit for you.

Christian Reformed Church in North America

In 1848, a secessionist pastor named Albertus Van Raalte brought his family and small congregation to Michigan due to persecution and famine spreading through the Netherlands. The colony they established, named Holland, Michigan, "held onto Calvinist doctrine, practical piety, and a strong commitment to living all of life to the glory of God." Life was especially harsh due to disease, lack of experience, and severe weather. In desperation, the group reached out to the established Dutch Reformed Church thriving in New York (now the RCA), and a merger resulted in 1850.

Seven years later, about one hundred and thirty families split off from the RCA due primarily to a clash between American and Dutch culture. The Dutch felt Americanized believers lacked piety, rejected the use of hymns for more traditional psalm-singing in worship, and opposed the American practice of opening communion to all believers, not just Dutch Reformed members. This split resulted in establishment of the Christian Reformed Church in 1857.

Just the **FACTS**

Christian Reformed Church in North America

Kind of Church: Protestant/Calvinist/Moderately Conservative
Worship Style: Traditional
Trinity Affinity: Father
Clout Continuum: 1st Place: Scripture
2nd Place: Personal experience
3rd Place: Reformed tradition
Founded in USA: 1857
Members in USA: 300,000
Churches in USA: 1,000
Headquarters: 2850 Kalamazoo Avenue SE
Grand Rapids MI 49560
Phone: 616-224-0744
Web site: www.crcna.org

Due to it's strong Dutch identity, the CRC has had a bit of a struggle assimilating into mainstream American culture. Some felt their religious roots could only be expressed in Dutch language and custom. Others embraced the broader English-speaking American ways and issues. The tension between purity and progress showed itself in a dispute over the doctrine of common grace—that grace in some degree is extended to all of humanity, not exclusively the "elect." The conservative faction, lead by Herman Hoeksema was forced to leave the CRC, resulting in the establishment of the Protestant Reformed Churches in America in 1926.

Along with most Protestant churches, the CRC embraces three historical creeds: The Nicene Creed, the Apostles' Creed and the Athanasian Creed. In addition, the CRC shares three confessions in

Just the FACTS

Protestant Reformed Churches in America

Kind of Church: Protestant/Calvinist/Conservative
Worship Style: Traditional
Trinity Affinity: Father
Clout Continuum: 1st Place: Scripture
2nd Place: Reformed tradition
3rd Place: Personal experience
Founded in USA: 1926
Members in USA: 6,730
Churches in USA: 27
Headquarters: 4949 Ivanrest Ave.
Grandville MI 49418
Phone: 616-531-1490
Web site: www.prca.org (unofficial)

common with other Reformed churches: the Belgic Confession, the Heidelberg Catechism and the Canons of Dort.

While creeds and confessions may be seen to clarify doctrine, the CRC asserts that the Bible is "uniquely, verbally and fully inspired by the Holy Spirit and that it is the supreme and final authority in all matters on which it speaks. . . . This inspiration is organic, extending to the ideas and the words of Scripture, and is so unique that Scripture alone is the Word of God. The human authors of Scripture were moved by the Holy Spirit so that their writing, reflecting their own personalities, language, and style, communicates infallibly God's self-revelation. Belief in the inspiration of Scripture, required by Scripture itself and by our Lord and his apostles, is indispensable to our Christian faith. The infallibility of Scripture is inferred from inspiration, and the inspiration of Scripture secures its infallibility."

Drawing from Scripture, the CRC has outlined five specific teachings it holds as distinctive. These are:

Our God Reigns

The CRC asserts that "nothing in this world happens outside of God's will. Our Creator is in control of all things. No forces in heaven, earth, or hell can frustrate what God promises to do for us (Ps. 2). That does not mean that everything that happens is God's will. We do many things God does not want. Our disobedience sets into motion many disastrous events that are our own doing. In spite of that, we may still exercise our human freedom. But our actions and decisions are under our heavenly Father's restraining, providing care. Nothing we do can spoil God's wondrous plan for us (Rom. 8:28). This gives us the confidence to do our Lord's work in this world. Our Provider's loving, guiding hand will sustain us in good times and in hard times as well."

Partners with God

The relationship we have with God is called a "covenant" in which we become partners with God. God fulfills "his promises if we accept them with a repentant, believing heart (Heb. 8.6)." The partnership is celebrated through the Lord's Supper and baptism.

Jesus is Lord

The CRC teaches that "Jesus is not only our crucified Savior. He is also our Lord. He not only rose from the dead but he also ascended into heaven. From there he now rules the whole world (Eph. 1:22). He will not only rescue our souls from hell but also raise us from the dead and give us eternal life. There's more. When he returns, Jesus will restore this spoiled creation. He will make it truly good and glorifying to God."

God Gives Us Assurance

Believers can be sure of belonging to God and will inherit eternal life because of God's faithfulness. "No one can tear us from Jesus' hand (John 10:27–29), not even our own failings or the weakness of our faith (Luke 22:31–32). This teaching does not make us complacent about living our lives in God's service. It fills us daily with deep gratitude and an earnest desire to live as God's joyful, obedient children (Rom. 8:12–17)."

God is With Us

The CRC believes that God speaks through a variety of ways such as the preaching and teaching of God's Word and through baptism and the Lord's Supper. The Lord's Supper is a "reminder of Jesus' sacrifice. Jesus is present with us through the Holy Spirit in our hearts (John 14:15–18). Christ, our host, strengthens our faith as we participate, remember, and believe."

Organizationally, the church is comprised of thirty classis in the U.S. and twelve in Canada, for a total of forty-two. Unlike the RCA, there are no regional synods. The General Synod is comprised of two clergy and two elders from each classis, meeting annually. To oversee ministries, eight boards and agencies have been developed. The CRC ministries include:

- The Back to God Hour: A radio and television ministry available internationally in French, English, Arabic, Chinese, Russian, Spanish, and other languages.
- Christian Reformed Home Missions: Responsible for supporting existing CRC churches and setting up new churches throughout Canada and the United States.

- Abuse Prevention: A resource and support ministry to prevent abuse and combat its effects.
- Chaplaincy: Ministry in specialized settings such as the military, hospitals, prisons, industry, drug and alcohol rehabilitation centers, universities, and pastoral counseling centers.

All People That On Earth Do Dwell

John Calvin and his early followers believed that metric psalms were the only type of hymn that should be used in worship. This hymn was written by William Kethe, a Scot who fled from persecution by Queen Mary and found sanctuary in Calvin's Geneva. Kethe helped to translate the Bible into English as well as write and compile a hymnal of metrical psalms. This hymn is the earliest one written in English that is still sung today.

1
All people that on earth do dwell,
    Sing to the Lord with cheerful voice;
Him serve with fear, his praise forth tell,
    Come ye before him, and rejoice.

2
The Lord, ye know, is God indeed;
    Without our aid he did us make;
We are his folk, he doth us feed,
    And for his sheep he doth us take.

3
O enter then his gates with praise,
    Approach with joy his courts unto;
Praise, laud, and bless his name always,
    For it is seemly so to do.

4
For why? the Lord our God is good;
    His mercy is for ever sure;
His truth at all time firmly stood,
    And shall from age to age endure.

5
To Father, Son, and Holy Ghost,
    The God whom heaven and earth
    adore,
From men and from the angel-host
    Be praise and glory evermore.

- Disability Concerns: Assists CRC churches to respond to the needs of persons with disabilities within the congregation and the community.
- The Office of Social Justice and Hunger Action: To raise awareness and promote action on issues of justice and world hunger.
- The Ministry of Race Relations: To create and provide programs to eliminate racism and to reconcile people from many different races and ethnic groups.
- Christian Reformed World Missions: Sponsors more than three hundred missionaries who live and work in about thirty countries in Africa, Latin America, and Asia.
- Christian Reformed World Relief Committee: Equips local deacons in their work, brings relief in times of disaster, and establishes long-term projects in Canada, the United States, and about twenty-seven other countries around the world.

The CRC sponsors Calvin College, a four-year liberal arts college, and Calvin Theological Seminary, where CRC ministers are trained. Both are located in Grand Rapids, Michigan.

The role of women in church leadership has been a hotly contested issue. I'm very impressed with the honesty and openness of their web site where their conflicts over this and other issues are presented. Supporters of both sides base their arguments in a shared view of Scripture but fail to persuade the other side. A compromise was made in 1996 allowing individual churches to ordain women as elders and for classis (regions) to decide if the churches within their jurisdiction can ordain women as ministers of the Word. At this point, eighteen of the forty-two classis have opened the offices of elder, minister, and evangelist to women in their congregations. This was too much for some, with approximately forty thousand members leaving the CRC.

Not claiming to have a corner on the truth market, the CRC sees itself as "one small part of Christ's church on earth. It recognizes as fellow-Christians all people who accept the teachings of the Bible as they are summarized so beautifully in the Apostles' Creed. This includes believers from many denominations such as Roman Catholic, Orthodox, Lutheran, Baptist, Presbyterian, and Pentecostal. We may disagree with these believers on some practices or teachings. But we recognize them as sisters and brothers in Christ if they believe in God the Father, Son, and Holy Spirit, and if they confess that Jesus died for their sins, rose from the dead, and ascended into heaven.

"On the way to achieving unity, major differences in the perception of biblical truth must be overcome. God must be trusted to teach all of us as we engage in ecumenical dialogue and thereby to unite us through a more common understanding of his truth. In the search for unity the biblical message must not be compromised, but the presumption of possessing the truth in all of its fullness must also be guarded against. Churches must seek to heal past wounds by overcoming differences with those who are closest to them. The Christian Reformed Church in North America gives high priority to relations with other Reformed churches and after that to churches of other traditions such as non-Reformed Protestant churches, the Roman Catholic Church, and Orthodox churches."

The CRC is historically a conservative denomination that is currently in transition toward a more moderate stance on issues of social justice, the ordination of women, and issues of faith. Within its membership, you'll find sincere advocates for both sides of most issues and a great deal of discussion going on. If you want a church that is determined to retain its connection to its Calvinistic roots, along with a high view of Scripture, but is also grappling with social changes in this country, the CRC may be the church for you.

What to Expect When You Visit

The first time you visit an RCA or a CRC congregation, I'd recommend dressing in a more respectful manner just to be on the safe side. Even though some congregations are fine with more casual clothing, you'll fit in with a basic jacket and tie for men and dress, skirt or nice pantsuit for women. Sleeveless tops and open-toed shoes are acceptable for women (unless you're in Michigan in the winter . . .).

A particular congregation may vary its services if it so chooses, and some are incorporating contemporary worship into their services, but RCS and CRC services tend to follow a fixed structure that reflects the values inherent in Calvinist theology. A worship service usually contains three sections:

- The Approach to God: Congregants confess their sin and unworthiness to God and ask for forgiveness through Christ.
- The Word of God: The Word is communicated to participants through the reading of Scripture, hearing the sermon, and participating in the Lord's Supper. Affirming correct doctrine is highly regarded, so it is no surprise that the sermon is often a main event. Holy Communion is usually included in Sunday worship— through which Christ is spiritually but not physically present.
- The Response to God's Word: Prayers of intercession and gratitude are offered to God by the congregants.

Christians of any background are welcome to participate in the entire service, including Communion. If you do not claim to be a Christian, then please refrain from sharing the Lord's Supper and from joining in the recitation of the Apostle's Creed.

The congregation will sit and stand together at prescribed times. If you're physically able, it's a good idea to follow along. RCA and CRC churches don't tend to kneel like more liturgical churches. But if you happen upon one that does, feel free to kneel or remain seated. Most churches will provide you with a bulletin with any specific instructions. As is always the case, if you're unsure about what to do or where to go, just ask an usher. That's why they're there.

More Reformed Churches

Hungarian Reformed Church in America
   www.calvinsynod.org

Netherlands Reformed Congregations in North America
   home.earthlink.net (unofficial)

Reformed Church in the United States
   www.rcus.org

Further Info

- David N. Steele and Curtis C. Thomas, *Five Points of Calvinism* (Presbyterian and Reformed, 1989)

- John Calvin, *The Institute of Christian Religion*, edited by Tony Lane and Hilary Osborne (Baker, 1987)

- Jean-Jacques Bauswein and Lukas Vischer, *The Reformed Family Worldwide: A Survey of Reformed Churches, Theological Schools, and International Organizations* (Eerdmans, 1998)

- Paul Smith, *The Westminster Confession: Enjoying God Forever (Foundations of the Faith)* (Moody Press, 1998)

nine

Presbyterian
Churches

John Knox, the founder of Presbyterianism, was bold and brash and quite fortunate to have died in his bed in 1572 rather than going up in martyr's flames, considering that he offended so many people who had the power to do him in. Short in stature but thunderous in voice, the red-haired Scotsman squared off with anyone, commoner and royal alike, using pulpits in Germany, Switzerland, England, and Scotland to articulate his views. John's voluminous writings were sprinkled with adjectives like "bloody," "beastly," "rotten," and "stinking" when referring to his adversaries. He blasted the Catholic Church as "the synagogue of Satan" and referred to the Mass as a "superstitious and idolatrous substitute for the sacrament of the Lord's Supper." He could think on his feet under the most stressful of situations, certain to get in the last well-chosen, unrelenting word. Empowered by his faith and enraged by losing so many friends to the sword and flames of persecution, Knox bowed to no one but his God.

Under Knox's influence, Scotland not only threw off a medieval mindset to embrace the Reformation but also moved beyond it. Knox was heavily influenced by Martin Luther, and became a student and personal friend of John Calvin's. But Knox found these reformers a tad reserved in their political application of theology. He became the first Protestant reformer to cross the line between resisting governmental rule for the sake of one's faith and actively revolting against it. The church structure Knox implemented became more than just a nice way to organize a denomination; it became a model for future democratic governments. The seed that ultimately bore fruit in the American Revolution two hundred years later was certainly cultivated, if not planted, by this radical Scottish peasant, priest, bodyguard, galley slave, preacher, reformer, and revolutionary.

John the Covenanter

John Knox made several "covenants" or agreements with fellow Scottish Protestants to stay true to their Protestant convictions, thereby becoming one of the founders of the Covenanter Movement. Previously, people were a part of the church by merit of being born into a "Christian" country, being baptized, and participating in the sacraments of the Roman Catholic Church, but Protestants believed personal faith was the basis for being a part of the universal church. Groups of believers voluntarily joined associations to encourage, strengthen, and hold each other accountable. These covenants were made with the knowledge that they were putting their lives on the line due to rampant persecution.

Brief History of Presbyterianism

Called one of the "ruffians of the Reformation," no one would mistake Knox for a pacifist. Along with his Bible, he was known to tote a large two-edged sword that took both hands to wield. Although it's never been proven that he personally assaulted anyone, he most certainly condoned a number of displays of violence perpetrated by Protestants. This is not to say Knox was an anarchist or crazed maniac. I believe he can be best understood as a Scotsman first, and then as a Protestant.

Knox's Scotland was wild and untamable, comprised of people whose ancestors had been able to stop the Roman Empire in its tracks. Let's say the Scots were not a compliant group. England, although full of its own brand of violence and intrigue, produced Protestants who rebelled against religious tyranny yet continued to submit to political authority "even to the flames of martyrdom." The Scots, however, reacted quite differently to this kind of oppression.

The first Scottish martyr was a Protestant nobleman and teacher named Patrick Hamilton, who was condemned as a heretic by the Bishop of St. Andrews in 1528. Hamilton's death was more of a roasting than a burning. The winds on that cold February day made it difficult to keep the fire going. After the executioners started and restarted the flames for six agonizing hours, Hamilton finally died. The cruelty of his death only increased the attractiveness of the Protestant cause, making the demand for illegal Protestant writings from Europe all that more popular.

The second Scottish martyr was George Wishart, a Protestant preacher who, after a Catholic priest tried to assassinate him, hired a young John Knox as a bodyguard. Even though Knox was himself a Catholic priest at the time, he was sympathetic to the Protestant perspective. Wishart's supporters urged him to lay low and stop preaching, but Wishart refused. Knowing there would be consequences to this decision, George released John from his duty, not wanting him to become a martyr as well. John asked to stay, but George told him "Nay, return to your home and God bless you. One is sufficient for a sacrifice." Cardinal Beaton, the nephew of the bishop who killed Hamilton, had Wishart arrested, tried, and burned as a heretic in 1546. John Knox's personal grief galvanized his shift to Protestantism.

Two martyrs were two too many for the Scots. A band of Scottish Protestants broke into the cardinal's castle of St. Andrews, stabbed him to death, and threw his body out the window. They then took over the castle, where Knox and other Protestants seeking asylum joined them. Some say Knox contributed to the assassination plot. Others say he was guilty only by association. Regardless of the role he played, when the French, called in to defend Catholic territory, captured the castle, John was inside with the Protestant assassins.

Everyone was rounded up and John ended up a French galley slave for nineteen months. After enduring floggings and various attempts to get him to recant his Protestant ways, Knox became even more committed to the Reformation. After his release, John preached in England for the next five years under the protection of the Protestant King Edward (Henry VIII's son). While in England, he contributed to the formulation of the Thirty-nine Articles of the Church of England. When King Edward died in 1553 and his Catholic half-sister, Mary Tudor, came to power, John and many other Protestants fled to the continent. Like others, Knox spent time in Geneva studying under Calvin and coming to embrace Reformed theology.

During the next thirteen years in exile, John Knox "became the driving force behind the Scottish Reformation, the most radical in all Europe." He may have been out of sight, but he was not out of the loop. His published writings, personal letters, and spirited sermons inspired Scottish Protestants to denounce the rule of Mary of Guise, King James V's widow.

He Had a Way with Women

John Knox's most notorious book, *The First Blast of the Trumpet against the Monstrous Regiment of Women*, was published while he was still in exile. Knox was fed up with violent women rulers (who all seemed to be Catholics named Mary)—Bloody Mary, who was the Queen of England; Mary of Guise, who ruled Scotland and made his life miserable; and Mary, Queen of Scots. Knox was ultimately instrumental in diminishing Mary of Guise's power and running her daughter, Mary Queen of Scots, out of Scotland.

On the list of "Queens Who Have No Use For John Knox," you can add Queen Elizabeth I of England. Even though she shared John's disdain for Mary Queen of Scots, Elizabeth wasn't waving any flags for Knox either. Queen Elizabeth, who was Protestant, was not named Mary and was supposedly on the same side with Knox, took personal offense at John's diatribe against "the monstrous regiment of women." As a consequence, she gave Knox a hard time when he needed anything from England. Later in life, Knox, in a rare moment of checking his words, admitted the first blast was "blown out of season."

On a brighter note, John fared quite well with women in his personal life. He married Marjorie Bowes around the year 1553, with whom he raised two sons. John Calvin referred to Marjorie as Knox's "most sweet wife." After seven years of marriage, Marjorie died in 1560.

Four years later, Knox married Margaret Stewart of Ochiltre, the daughter of a duke. This was a bit scandalous at the time for a couple of reasons. First, he was a commoner and she was of royal blood. Second, Knox was 50 and Margaret was 17. Upon news of the marriage, Mary Queen of Scots threw a temper tantrum. I don't think Calvin had a tantrum, but he did think the age difference was a bit much. But Knox didn't care who approved or who didn't. He'd always done what he wanted, and who can blame him for spending his last eight years with a young Scottish lass?

Knox returned to Scotland in 1559 allied with the party of Reformers, called the Congregation, which had considerable power by that time. John spearheaded a petition to Parliament that altered not only religious practice but also initiated social reform and a redistribution of wealth. This petition, The Confession of Faith Professed and Believed by the Protestants within the Realm of Scotland, was ratified by the Scottish Parliament in 1560 and remained the official Scottish creed for two hundred years. The Roman Catholic Church was out and Protestantism was the official religion of Scotland.

John's next task was to contribute to the First Book of Discipline, the plan for church government. The liturgy in Knox's Book of Common Prayer was adopted by churches throughout the country. Within the Book of Discipline, Knox also laid out an elaborate educational scheme, from elementary to university level. John was on a roll.

However, a young but powerful Mary (daughter of the Scottish King James V and Mary of Guise and the rightful heir to the Scottish throne) showed up and put a crimp in the works. Mary, thoroughly Catholic, and John, thoroughly not, stood in each other's way of getting what they wanted. The verbal duels between them are legendary. I only wish someone had caught them on tape. Knox stood nose to nose (literally) with the Queen in five personal meetings in which they only succeeded in infuriating each other. Mary tried to persuade him with her considerable charm, death threats, and sobbing. He boldly criticized her personal life, which included various extramarital affairs, plotting to assassinate her second husband (who had murdered her lover), and then marrying the man who murdered her second husband. More importantly, Knox denounced her royal right to rule. No one, let alone a mere commoner, talked to a sovereign this way

After five or six years of power plays, a couple of hearings for treason, a few uprisings, Protestants being exiled and pardoned, several assassinations, and a lot of yelling back and forth, Mary Queen of Scots lost control of Scotland. She fled to England in 1568. Her infant son, James VI, was crowned King of Scotland and the Protestants gained even more political ground. Knox lived four more years after Mary left town, dying of natural causes in 1572.

Presbyterianism Takes Hold

Andrew Melville took over the Protestant cause after Knox died. Melville, the principal of the University of Glasgow and later of St. Mary's College at St. Andrew's in Edinburgh, was no shrinking vio-

James and the Family Tree

Having fled to England in 1568, Mary Queen of Scots was imprisoned by Queen Elizabeth. Elizabeth hoped confinement would keep Mary out of trouble. It didn't work. From her cell, Mary plotted to assassinate Queen Elizabeth, was found out, and beheaded. Meanwhile, Mary's son, James VI, was being raised in Scotland and, once old enough, took his rightful place on the throne. Having no heirs of her own, Queen Elizabeth advocated for James VI to follow in her footsteps (not wanting to bring too much attention to the fact that his mother had tried to kill her and she, in turn, had his mother beheaded). Upon Elizabeth's death in 1603, James VI of Scotland was crowned James I of England.

James was also the first monarch to rule both England and Scotland. Wales was brought into the mix and Great Britain was launched. (They're still having trouble getting the Irish to fully participate, but that's another story.) This particular James is the James of the "King James Bible" with all the "thee's" and "thou's" in it. Many Protestants still use this version of the Bible today.

let but was quite refined in comparison to his sword-wielding predecessor. A brilliant educator and reformer, Melville replaced the church's bishops with presbyteries, giving more influence to the congregation. Politically, Melville advocated for a church that was free of state interference.

In 1578, Andrew published *The Second Book of Discipline,* which got him into a lot of trouble. Plus he'd composed a satiric poem that annoyed King James VI of Scotland (who was simultaneously King James I of England). As his mother, Mary Queen of Scots, had called Knox to face her, James VI summoned Melville for a similar discussion. It didn't go well, and Melville ended up in the Tower of London for a few years. After his release, Melville taught theology in France where he lived out the rest of his life, but he had already fulfilled his vision. The Presbyterian form of worship had taken root and would not be undercut no matter how hard the Anglicans or the Catholics tried to interfere.

The following years were full of political maneuverings between Protestants and Catholics, the Church of England and the Church of Scotland, the new King Charles I and Parliament, and just about anyone and everyone else. The overriding schism was between the king and the English Parliament. Both sides wanted control. King Charles I rejected Scottish Presbyterianism and tried to force the church in Scotland to use the Anglican Book of Common Prayer. That didn't go over well. The English Parliament, lead by Oliver Cromwell, called together a group of biblical scholars and spiritual leaders to compose a document that would hopefully bring the struggle to resolution. They were also trying to gain the support of Scottish Presbyterians in their attempt to overpower the king. From 1643 to1648, Scottish and English theologians labored to write what is now called the Westminster Confession. Meanwhile, Parliament was busy imprisoning, trying, and finally beheading Charles I in 1649. Having overthrown the monarchy, Oliver Cromwell became the leader of the newly founded commonwealth.

All of this politicking resulted in a watershed statement of faith for Presbyterians. Instructed to eliminate anything that was Arminian or Catholic, the authors constructed a confession that is essentially Calvinistic in doctrine and presbyterian in church structure. In addition, the Longer and Shorter Catechisms were written. The Westminster Confession of Faith was first adopted for use by the Church of Scotland in 1647. The Scottish Parliament ratified the Westminster Confession in 1649. Even though this statement was developed under the direction of the English Parliament, the Church of England never adopted it. Today, Presbyterian and Episcopal churches reflect this difference in theological and structural traditions.

Presbyterians in America

I'm not including all of the factions of the Presbyterian Church in the States because it's too cumbersome. Even with my simplified version, it's easy to get confused, especially since it seems that each new group used a lot of the same names but in a different order. If I drew the chart accurately, it would look more like a plate of spaghetti than a timeline, so all of you church history students, just relax. It ain't exact. And the rest of you, hang on . . .

Beginning in the mid-1600s through the mid-1800s, thousands of Presbyterians poured into America to escape political, economic, and religious pressures in Scotland. Local Presbyterian churches were set up throughout the colonies, with a number of associations formed over the years. The first was founded in Philadelphia in 1706 and called the Presbyterian General Synod. This association was the forerunner of a major branch of American Presbyterianism—the Presbyterian

Church in the USA (PCUSA). For the sake of clarity, from here on I'll refer to this group as the PCUSA, even though it's had various name modifications over time.

The PCUSA has experienced four major periods of upheaval, resulting in splits, mergers, more splits, and more mergers: the First Great Awakening in the 1700s, the Second Great Awakening in the early 1800s, slavery and the Civil War in the mid-1800s, and the conservative vs. liberal debate in the 1900s.

The First Great Awakening

Presbyterians played major roles in the formation of the American way of life. One avenue of influence came through education. Princeton University began as a "log school" started in the 1720s by Rev. William Tennent, a Presbyterian minister. This young institution produced a number of well-known and influential preachers of its day, including Rev. John Edwards and two of Tennent's own sons, William Jr. and Gilbert.

These ministers joined forces with George Whitefield, an English evangelist who influenced the revivals taking place in England under the preaching of John Wesley and those in America called the First Great Awakening in the early 1700s. These revivals were highly emotional and focused on personal conversion experiences. The hoopla was a bit disconcerting for your typical Presbyterian, who equated Christianity with adherence to Calvinistic doctrinal creeds such the Westminster Confession. A controversy arose between the "Old Side" and the "New Side" (not very creative names, if you ask me). The Old Side Presbyterians rejected the emotionalism while the New Side embraced the revivals.

One of the most outspoken members of the New Side was the president of Princeton, Rev. John Witherspoon. Witherspoon was a major mover and shaker in American politics—a member of the Continental Congress and eventually the only clergy to sign the Declaration of Independence. Some give Witherspoon some credit for getting the

Stand Up! Stand Up for Jesus

A tragedy in the summer of 1858 inspired George Duffield to write this hymn. Duffield, a Presbyterian minister, was helping a well-known evangelist, Dudley Atkins Tyng, during a success series of revivals in Philadelphia that drew thousands of people. One day, after a service, Tyng took a walk through the fields of his nearly farm. He patted one of his mules that was hooked up to corn husking machinery. The sleeve of his preaching robe got caught in the machine and, horribly, his arm was ripped from his body. He lay in the field bleeding for so long that by the time anyone found him, he was near death.

Duffield was with him when he died. Moments before, Tyng whispered to Duffield, "Tell them to stand up for Jesus." Duffield went home and wrote the hymn, which he shared in his sermon the next Sunday. It's stirring words were immediately embraced and it is said that soldiers on both sides of the Civil War sang the song in battle.

1

Stand up!—Stand up for Jesus!
  Ye soldiers of the Cross;
Lift high his royal banner,
  It must not suffer loss.
From victory unto victory
  His army he shall lead,
Till every foe is vanquished,
  And Christ is Lord indeed.

2

Stand up!—Stand up for Jesus!
  The solemn watchword hear,
If while ye sleep he suffers,
  Away with shame and fear,
Where'er ye meet with evil,
  Within you or without,
Charge for the God of battles,
  And put the foe to rout.

Presbyterians to stop bickering and unite behind the American Revolution, which may not have been all that hard since many of them were Irish and Scottish immigrants who were fed up with the English anyway.

Second Great Awakening

After the American Revolution, the PCUSA grew expansively into the frontier. In spite of tension remaining between the Old and the New sides, things went along pretty well until the early 1800s when the Second Great Awakening stirred things up again. As the revivals spread across the frontier, some churches found the restraints of the PCUSA unhelpful. Several factions left or were tossed out, and some reunited later after everyone had calmed down.

3
Stand up!—Stand up for Jesus!
  The trumpet call obey,
Forth to the mighty conflict
  In this his glorious day.
Ye that are men now served him
  Against unnumbered foes;
Let courage rise with danger,
  And strength to strength oppose.

4
Stand up!—Stand up for Jesus!
  Stand in his strength along;
The arm of flesh will fail you,
  Ye dare not trust your own.

Put on the Gospel armor,
  Each piece put on with prayer;
Where duty calls or danger,
  Be never wanting there!

5
Stand up!—Stand up for Jesus!
  The strife will not be long;
This day the noise of battle,
  The next the victor's song.
To him that overcometh
  A crown of life shall be;
He with the King of Glory
  Shall reign eternally.

A major split occurred in 1810 when three Presbyterian ministers met in Dickson County, Tennessee. They formed the Cumberland Presbyterian Church (CPC). Their gripe was over the strict Calvinism of the Westminster Confession and the desire for more flexible ordination standards for those who ministered in the American frontier.

A CPC confession of faith was written four years later that drew to some extent from the Westminster Confession, but it differed in these points: "(1) There are no eternal reprobates; (2) Christ died for all humankind, not for the elect alone; (3) there is no infant damnation; and (4) the Spirit of God operates in the world coextensively with Christ's atonement, so 'as to leave all men inexcusable.' "

Slavery and the Civil War

Like so many other churches, the PCUSA divided over the issue of slavery, increasing the tension between the Old and New Sides. The

Cumberland Presbyterian Church in America

Originally called the Synod of Colored Cumberland Presbyterians, the CPCA was established in 1869 as an off-shoot from the Cumberland Presbyterian Church (CPA). Founded by minister and former slave, Moses T. Weir, the CPCA started with over twenty-thousand African-American pastors and laypeople. Doctrinally, the CPCA and the CPA are very similar. In 1984, representatives from both denominations contributed to the development of a revised Confession of Faith. For more information, check out their web site at www.Cumberland .org/cpca.

Just the FACTS

Cumberland Presbyterian Church

Kind of Church: Protestant/Calvinist/Conservative
Worship Style: Traditional
Trinity Affinity: Son
Clout Continuum: 1st Place: Scripture
2nd Place: Calvinist tradition
3rd Place: Personal experience
Founded in USA: 1810
Members in USA: 86,049
Churches in USA: 775
Headquarters: 1978 Union Ave.
Memphis TN 38104
Phone: 800-333-CPRC (2772)
Web site: www.cumberland.org

Old Side folks were more accepting of slavery while most in the New Side were adamantly against it. A few New Side churches in the south split to form the United Synod of the Presbyterian Church (USPC) in 1857. Once the Civil War was underway, forty-seven Old School presbyteries in the South broke off and founded the Presbyterian Church in the Confederate States of America (PCCSA) in 1861. After the war, both the New and Old Side groups in the south merged to become the Presbyterian Church in the United States (PCUS).

Conservative vs. Liberal Debate

The church pendulum swings between conservatives and liberals—the old purity vs. unity debate. Generally speaking, the more conservative camp held to inerrancy of Scripture and believed that, since personal sin is the source of evil in the world, the church should focus on spreading the message of salvation, not involve itself in "social" endeavors. On the other side were those who were more concerned about moving beyond arbitrary doctrinal boundaries and addressing social problems from an institutional rather than individual level. The conservatives feared that the liberals were watering down the gospel to the point where Jesus had no significance, and the liberals felt the conservatives were divisive and exclusionary. Presbyterian churches were among the debaters, with splits and mergers abounding.

Working toward unity, in 1907 the PCUSA welcomed back a large portion of the Cumberland Presbyterian Church that had split off in 1810. Most CPC churches entered the PCUSA fold, but a small group of congregations could not accept what they saw as compromises. They have remained under the CPC name. A relatively small but enthusiastic church, the CPC has an inviting web site that you may want to check out.

The next group to merge with the PCUSA was the United Presbyterian Church of North America (UPCNA). Way back in 1858 two other groups of Presbyterians, the Associate Presbyterian Church (APC) and the Associate Reformed Presbyterian Church (ARPC), merged to create the UPCNA. Even though this denomination held to many of the beliefs stated in the Westminster Confession, the UPCNA no longer held to a strict Calvinistic doctrine, having modified their statement of beliefs in 1925. In particular, the UPCNA rejected the idea of infant damnation, asserted that salvation was available to everyone and welcomed anyone who professed a belief in Christ to participate in the sacraments. These views were compatible with those held by PCUSA and their merger was complete in 1958.

At the same time, the Presbyterian Church in the United States (PCUS) (remember them? . . . they were the southern branch) was also considering merging with PCUSA. The conservative branch opposed changes in the PCUS including the denomination's affiliation with ecumenical associations such as the World Council of Churches. Additionally, they opposed the proposed merging with the PCUSA, a denomination they viewed as too liberal regarding the ordination of women and their stand on Scripture. Before the merger took place, the conservatives formed the Presbyterian Church in America (PCA) in 1973. They were joined in 1982 by the Reformed Presbyterian Church, Evangelical Synod (RPCES), which had been formed in 1965 by merging the Evangelical Presbyterian Church (EPC) and the Reformed Presbyterian Church in North America, General Synod (RPCNA). The remaining PCUS church reunited with the PCUSA in 1983.

What Makes a Church Presbyterian?

No matter how far to the left or right they may roam, Presbyterian churches are fundamentally Reformed in doctrine and presbyterian in structure—a blend they owe to the two John's in their historical past—John Calvin and John Knox. From John Calvin, Presbyterians have inherited a majestic, albeit arbitrary at times, view of God. In keeping with Calvin's teachings, Presbyterian Churches affirm the Westminster Confession and catechisms as reference points, if not standards, for their faith.

While your average Presbyterian isn't known for colorful language, carrying large swords, or squaring off with political leaders (as was John Knox), most Presbyterians are ardently committed to the presbyterian form of church government. Presbyterian denominations may not see eye to eye on every point of doctrine, but they all have plenty of committees and procedures through which they debate these differences. John Knox may have pushed the religious envelope in his day, but now Presbyterians politely pass the envelope in accordance with order and procedure.

Just the **FACTS**

Presbyterian Church in America

Kind of Church: Protestant/Calvinist/Conservative Evangelical
Worship Style: Traditional
Trinity Affinity: Son
Clout Continuum: 1st Place: Scripture
2nd Place: Personal experience
3rd Place: Tradition
Founded in USA: 1973
Members in USA: 303,176
Churches in USA: 1,215
Headquarters: 1852 Century Place
Atlanta GA 30345-4305
Phone: 678-825-1000
Web site: www.pcanet.org

Presbyterian Church in America

As a more conservative denomination, the Westminster Confession of Faith and Catechisms are held as standards for PCA's Calvinist or Reformed doctrinal tradition. Since reformers based their doctrinal claims on Scripture alone, the PCA asserts that inspiration "is a special act of the Holy Spirit by which He guided the writers of the books of Scriptures (in their original autographs) so that their words should convey the thoughts He wished conveyed, bear a proper relation to the thoughts of other inspired books, and be kept free from error of fact, of doctrine, and of judgment—all of which were to be an infallible rule of faith and life." In keeping with this stance, the PCA believes that "infallibility" includes the idea of biblical inerrancy.

In addition to a more conservative theology, the PCA has taken a stand against the ordination of women. Doctrinally, the PCA affirms the five points of Calvinism. Their web site provides the following summary of faith:

1. The Bible is the inspired and inerrant Word of God, the only infallible rule of faith and practice.
2. There is one God, eternal and self-existing in three persons (Father, Son and Holy Spirit), who are to be equally loved, honored, and adored.
3. All mankind participated in Adam's fall from his original sinless state and is thus lost in sin and totally helpless.
4. The Sovereign God, for no other reason than His own unfathomable love and mercy, has chosen lost sinners from every nation to be redeemed by the quickening power of the Holy Spirit and through the atoning death and resurrection of His son, Jesus Christ.
5. Those sinners whom the Spirit quickens, come to believe in Christ as Savior by the Word of God, are born again, become sons of God, and will persevere to the end.
6. Justification is by faith and through it the undeserving sinner is clothed with the righteousness of Christ.
7. The goal of God's salvation in the life of the Christian is holiness, good works, and service for the glory of God.
8. At death the Christian's soul passes immediately into the presence of God and the unbeliever's soul is eternally separated from God unto condemnation.
9. Baptism is a sign of God's covenant and is properly administered to children of believers in their infancy as well as to those who come as adults to trust in Christ.

10. Jesus Christ will return to earth, visibly and bodily, at a time when He is not expected, to consummate history and the eternal plan of God.

11. The Gospel of God's salvation in Jesus Christ must be published to all the world as a witness before Jesus Christ returns.

Representative in nature, local PCA congregations elect a board of elders or presbyters. Congregations are combined by area into regional presbyteries, who in turn answer to the national General Assembly located in Atlanta, Georgia.

In order to carry out PCA's overall ministries, three program committees operate under the General Assembly. These are (1) mission to the world, (2) mission to North America, and (3) christian education and publication. In addition, the PCA has a conference center, Ridge Haven, located in North Carolina, Covenant College, a liberal arts college located at Lookout Mountain, Georgia, and Covenant Theological Seminary in St. Louis, Missouri.

The PCA is a good place for those who embrace Reformed theology and tend to be conservative in lifestyle and doctrine. If you feel want a church with strong convictions and the courage to stand up for those beliefs, the PCA may be a great place for you.

Presbyterian Church (USA)

The Presbyterian Church (USA), the largest Presbyterian denomination in the country, operates out of Louisville, Kentucky. In the mid-1900s, the PCUSA affirmed the Westminster Confession as being a historical reference point for American Presbyterians, but the denomination was in need of a revised, updated statement of faith. After eight years of work, the Confession of 1967 was ratified by the

Just the **FACTS**

Presbyterian Church (USA)

Kind of Church:	Protestant/Calvinist/Moderate
Worship Style:	Traditional
Trinity Affinity:	Father
Clout Continuum:	1st Place: Scripture
	2nd Place: Calvinistic tradition
	3rd Place: Personal experience
Founded in USA:	1983
Members in USA:	2,525,330
Churches in USA:	11,178
Headquarters:	100 Witherspoon St.
	Louisville KY 40202
Phone:	888-728-7228
Web site:	www.pcusa.org

General Assembly. Significantly shorter than the Westminster Confession, the Confession of 1967 generally reiterates the same doctrines in current language. The emphasis, however, has shifted slightly more toward God's love.

Having added this confession to its Book of Confessions, the PCUSA affirms the following:

The Nicene Creed

The Apostles Creed

The Scots Confession

The Heidelburg Confession

The Westminster Confession, Larger and Shorter Catechisms

Theological Declaration of Barmen

The Confession of 1967

All of these statements of faith are seen as based on Scripture and infallible but not necessarily inerrant. In addition, there is an expectation that "God alone is lord of the conscience, and it is up to each individual to understand what these principles mean in his or her life."

The PCUSA emphasizes "God's supremacy over everything and humanity's chief purpose as being to glorify and enjoy God forever." Basic beliefs include:

- The election of the people of God for service as well as for salvation;
- Covenant life marked by a disciplined concern for order in the church according to the Word of God;
- A faithful stewardship that shuns ostentation and seeks proper use of the gifts of God's creation;
- The recognition of the human tendency to idolatry and tyranny, which calls the people of God to work for the transformation of society by seeking justice and living in obedience to the Word of God.

The PCUSA differs from the PCA in that women have been ordained to ministry since 1956. The web sites states, "One of the places where the church has had the opportunity to live up to its proclamations for the equality of all persons is in the status that it gives women in its own life and work."

In addition, the PCUSA has focused on social concerns in addition to personal piety in the statement that "neither the Church as the body of Christ, nor Christians as individuals, can be neutral or indifferent toward evil in the world." This entails not only encouraging and training members in daily obedience to God but also "corporately to reveal God's grace in places of suffering and need, to resist the forces that tyrannize, and to support the forces that restore the dignity of all men as the children of God, for only so is the gospel most fully proclaimed."

The PCUSA is an ever-changing denomination that retains a core belief in Christ while being open to change. The umbrella of the PCUSA is broader than many Presbyterian churches. Since the PCUSA has come about through a number of mergers, you'll find an ecumenical outlook in this denomination. If unity is important to you, you may find a comfortable spot somewhere in the PCUSA family.

What to Expect When You Visit

Most Presbyterian churches are traditional in worship, although some have included contemporary worship services to their programs. Expect a more traditional service on Sunday morning than if you visit an evening gathering. Men will probably feel like they fit in with a jacket and tie while women will be appropriate in a dress, skirt, or pantsuit.

It's best to come on time, or even a few minutes early, so you can be seated before the service begins. You can expect the congregation to stand for singing or prayer, but there will be much less movement than in most liturgical services. You're apt to find a Bible and a hymnal in the pew ahead of you to use during the service. Presbyterians do not share the Lord's Supper every Sunday. If you do visit a service where Communion is shared, check the bulletin for any statement about participation. In general, membership in the church is not required to participate, although professing to be a Christian may be seen as important. In less conservative congregations the decision will be left solely up to you.

More Presbyterian Churches

Associate Reformed Presbyterian Church
   www.arpsynod.org

Evangelical Presbyterian Church
   www.epc.org

Korean-American Presbyterian Church
   www.kapc.org

Orthodox Presbyterian Church
   www.opc.org

Reformed Presbyterian Church of North America
   www.reformedpresbyterian.org

Further Info

- James H. Smulie, *A Brief History of the Presbyterians* (Geneva, 1996)

- Ted. V. Foote and P. Alex Thornburg, *Being Presbyterian in the Bible Belt: A Theological Survival Guide for Youth, Parents, and Other Confused Presbyterians* (Presbyterian Publishing, 2000)

- Dean W. Chapman, *How to Worship as a Presbyterian* (Geneva, 2001)

ten

Congregational and Restoration Churches

When King Henry VIII severed ties with the Roman Catholic Church and set up the Church of England, he seemed satisfied with making himself the head of the state church, granting himself a divorce the Catholics would not, and marrying Anne Boleyn. There were those, however, who felt the church needed more radical alterations than Henry's marital status. They wanted the church to be purified. They became known as the Puritans.

Having been strongly influenced by John Calvin's theology, the Puritans had a few suggestions—such as reforming how the church worshiped, how the church was governed, and how the church did just about everything else. At first the Puritans attempted to change things from the inside, but that proved futile, so some of them began

When I Survey the
Wondrous Cross

Along with Charles Wesley, Isaac Watts could share the title of world's greatest hymn writer. The son of a Congregational pastor in England, Watts was only sixteen when he complained to his father that the songs sung in church were "dull and profitless." At that time, worship music was defined by Calvinist tradition that restricted worship music to metrical psalms. His father responded, "Then write something better." And he did. By the time he died at the age of seventy-four, he had written nearly seven hundred hymns, many of which are still sung in today's traditional churches.

When I Survey the Wondrous Cross was written as a communion hymn, published in 1707. The fourth verse is usually omitted from most hymnals for being "too gory," but I grew up singing this song and still love it.

1.
When I survey the wondrous Cross,
   Where the young Prince of Glory
   died,
My richest gain I count but loss,
   And pour contempt on all my pride.

2.
Forbid it, Lord, that I should boast
   Save in the death of Christ my God;
All the vain things that charm me most,
   I sacrifice them to his blood.

3.
See from his head, his hands, his feet,
   Sorrow and love flow mingled down:
Did e'er such love and sorrow meet,
   Or thorns compose so rich a crown?

4.
His dying crimson, like a robe,
   Spreads o'er his body on the Tree;
Then am I dead to all the globe,
   And all the globe is dead to me.

5.
Were the whole realm of nature mine,
   That were a present far too small;
Love so amazing, so divine,
   Demands my soul, my life, my all.

meeting in private homes for prayer and Bible study. This was scandalous at the time; well, it was more than that—it was against the law to meet without bishops or priests. But that didn't stop them from gathering solely on the covenant made with each other. Neither the civil or religious authorities were pleased with this development. You were expected to be subject to the king alone, which meant you *had* to belong to the Church of England.

A Brief History of Congregational and Restoration Churches

One of these "separatist" groups, led by John Robinson, met in the home of William Brewster, the postmaster in a village called Scrooby. After observing that a number of people who came into disfavor with the king lost contact with their heads, the little group took off for Holland and, in 1620, set sail on the Mayflower for America.

This group of a hundred or so people created a bond so strong it withstood the stresses of immigrating to Holland and then to the New World. Before they set foot on American soil, they transferred the idea of making a covenant with each other from their spiritual community to their political community. The Mayflower Compact was the first of its kind—a written contract in which people agree to form a political entity and to be governed by that entity. This was HUGE!

We Did Church Our Way—Congregational Churches

Only about half the group survived that first winter in Plymouth, but their legacy lives on. These particular Puritans, now referred to as the Pilgrims of Plymouth, contributed to the foundation of a self-governing society. More Puritans immigrated to America, and nine years later, in 1629, the Massachusetts Bay Colony was established. Consequently, more self-governing churches were set up, calling themselves Congregationalists. Some twenty years later, the Plymouth Pilgrims and the Massachusetts Bay Colony Puritans affirmed their commonality in the Cambridge Platform of 1648. The Congregational Church resulted from this merger.

United in vision but independent in structure, the ideals of the Congregational churches fit naturally with the American spirit of individualism. A series of revivals swept the colonies during the 1730s and 1740s called the First Great Awakening (the Second Great Awakening came in the late 1700s and early 1800s). Congregationalists were at the forefront of the movement, most notably Congregationalist preacher and writer, Jonathan Edwards.

Since self-governance was a cornerstone of faith for Congregationalists, it is not surprising that many Congregational churches actively supported the American Revolution. The simple idea of covenantal community contributed to the American passion for democracy and the birth of the United States in 1776.

Don't Fence Me In—Restoration Movement

In the years immediately following the American Revolution, large numbers of people moved westward filling the frontier with Baptists, Methodists, Presbyterians, Congregationalists, and many other variations on the Christian theme. In general, denominationalism ran against the grain of life on the frontier. Let's face it, if you're trying to survive a rough winter out in the woods, you don't care if your neighbor is a Baptist or a Methodist or a Presbyterian. You just want help. The necessity of working together caused settlers to focus more on commonalities among Christians than delineating differences—an attitude that challenged the divisiveness of denominational distinctions.

Within this context, another wave of revivals swept through America in the late 1700s and early 1800s called the Second Great Awakening. Realizing how denominations separated Christians, preachers worked to restore the church to unity—like that experienced by the New Testament church. Emphasis was placed on the individual's need for personal conversion rather than adherence to specific doctrinal creeds or membership in a particular denomination.

Without centralized coordination, several different movements spontaneously sprung up with similar concerns and goals that eventually became known as the Restoration Movement. I'm going to focus on two of these groups, one starting in Kentucky and the other in Pennsylvania. Both were initiated by Presbyterian ministers, Barton W. Stone and Thomas Campbell, who were fed up with rigid denominational creeds that served to divide rather than unite Christians in community.

Barton W. Stone invited Christians of all denominations to his Presbyterian church in Kentucky. To Stone's surprise, somewhere between twenty to thirty thousand Presbyterians, Methodists, Baptists, and others showed up to participate in what came to be known as the Cane Ridge Revival of 1801. Barton and friends denounced historic creeds and declared the Bible to be the sole authority for faith and practice. Discarding all denominational labels, Stone adopted the term "Christian," aiming to be inclusive of all believers.

Over in Pennsylvania, a father and son team were guiding a similar protest against denominational exclusiveness. Thomas Campbell, originally from Scotland, left the Presbyterian clergy after coming under fire for serving communion to non-Presbyterians. He insisted that "the church of Christ upon earth is essentially, intentionally, and constitutionally one." His son, Alexander, joined the movement and with associates, the Campbell's founded the Christian Association in 1808 with

Sharon's Story

I knew I wanted to go back to church, but had no idea where to go. So I visited a church that was down the street from where I live. At first I really enjoyed attending. The congregation was warm and accepting, I enjoyed the openness of the expression, dialogue, openmindedness. I'd grown up in a really rigid church and was tired of that sort of thing.

After a while, however, I heard people say derogatory statements toward "born-agains." I was stunned, because I saw myself as having a personal relationship with God and would put myself in that category. Slowly, I recognized a general bias against any form of conservatism. It was odd, really, to be in a church that overtly said, "We're open to all" but to discover that what they really meant is that "We're open to all except conservatives." I didn't realize I was a conservative until I felt criticized by the church. I thought, "Well, my conservative Christian belief is unpopular here!"

In one of the denominational publications, a church leader confronted this issue in an interesting way. He said that, even though the vision of denomination focused on inclusiveness, the membership nationwide was dropping. He challenged the church to regain its original evangelistic fervor and to fulfill the Great Commission of Jesus Christ: "Go, therefore, and make disciples of all nations, baptizing them in the name of the Father, and of the Son, and of the Holy Spirit." I agreed with this guy. The church had lost the central message of Christ.

I read that the denomination is actually considering merging with the Unitarians. They don't believe that Jesus was divine, and certainly don't affirm the doctrine of the Trinity. I realized then that, even though I liked the people at the church, I needed to find a place that is more theologically compatible with my beliefs.

this motto: Where the Scriptures speak, we speak; where the Scriptures are silent, we are silent. The Campbell movement adopted the name "Disciples of Christ," intending to be inclusive of all believers.

Eventually, the Christian group and the Disciples of Christ joined forces, referred to as the Stone-Campbell Movement. By 1832, the Christian Church and the Disciples of Christ merged into one church.

Some Splits and Mergers

While the Restoration was bringing Christian groups together, the Congregational churches were splintering. The essential glue that held Congregationalists together was their form of church government— the autonomy of the local congregation. Their anticreedal bias made it difficult to define, let alone enforce, any overarching theology or orthodoxy. Congregationalists polarized into two camps—Trinitarians and Unitarians.

Unitarianism asserts that the doctrine of the Trinity developed over time and was not a belief of the early church. Rather, they believe that there is only one God and deny the divine essence of Jesus. In 1825 the American Unitarian Association was formed and was primarily made up of older Congregational churches from New England. The group merged with Universalists in 1961 to form the Unitarian Universalist Association. In my opinion, by denying the divinity of Christ, the Unitarians-Universalists moved themselves outside of Christendom. So, that's all I'll say about them . . .

Trinitarian Congregationalists continued to grow in number and developed informal relationships with other congregations. The first official association was founded in 1871, called the National Council of the Congregational Christian Churches (NCCCC). The NCCCC met twice a year and served in an advisory capacity.

The NCCCC merged with the Evangelical Protestant Church of North America in 1925 to form the Evangelical Protestant Conference of Congregational Churches (EPCCC). Six years later the EPCCC and the Christian Church joined forces, renaming themselves the Congregational Christian Churches (CCC) in 1931.

In 1948, the Conservative Congregational Christian Conference was formed to promote a conservative evangelical perspective while the CCC was negotiating with the Evangelical and Reformed Church (ERC) for another merger. But the more conservative Congregationalists didn't like that. The congregations that refused to cooperate with the proposed merger founded the National Association of Congregational Christian Churches in 1955. The remaining churches in the CCC finalized the merger with the ERC in 1957, to become the United Church of Christ.

What Makes a Church Congregational or Restoration?

Even though the Congregational and Restoration movements initiated from different branches of the Christian tree, their common beliefs eventually brought them together. Congregational and Restoration churches share the following convictions:

Denominations divide rather than unite Christians

The churches that have emerged from the Congregational and Restoration movements disdain the idea that Christians would be required to join a denomination in order to participate in the life of the church. They tend to draw and redraw the Christian circle large enough to make room for as many believers as possible. You'll find some exceptions among more conservative congregations who value purity of doctrine over inclusiveness.

Individuals are responsible solely to God

Agreeing with Luther's belief that a person is saved through faith in Christ alone, these churches tend to shy away from overt doctrinal creeds and give an individual a great deal of leeway in personal beliefs.

The local congregation is the basic unit of the church

Rejecting a centralized denominational authority, Congregational and Restoration churches view the local church as an autonomous unit. In keeping with their antidenominational agenda, individual Congregational churches, to this day, affiliate voluntarily in "conferences"—associations that have essentially no power over member congregations. The Christian Church (Disciples of Christ) was congregational in church structure for the first hundred years of its existence. While the local congregation is still the fundamental unit of the church, they have since added regional and general levels of organization (shifting to a more presbyterian format).

While you can find exceptions, Congregational and Restoration churches value the autonomy of the local church and placing more importance of a person's spiritual experience with Christ than on creedal dogma.

National Association of Congregational Christian Churches

The National Association of Congregational Christian Churches is a "voluntary association of free churches, each church having one vote in the affairs of the association." Funded solely by voluntary contributions, member congregations pay no dues to belong, nor does membership in any way infringe on their local autonomy. The association

Just the **FACTS**

National Association of Congregational Christian Churches

Kind of Church: Protestant/Calvinist/Moderate
Worship Style: Traditional
Trinity Affinity: Son
Clout Continuum: 1st Place: Scripture
2nd Place: Personal experience
3rd Place: Tradition
Founded in USA: 1955
Members in USA: 70,000
Churches in USA: 433
Headquarters: P.O. Box 288
Oak Creek WI 53154-0620
Phone: 800-262-1620
Web site: www.naccc.org

is set up so that local congregations can consult with one another about common concerns—both spiritual and organizational.

Their web site has an interesting way of putting their mission: "The National Association of Congregational Christian Churches is a body purposely designed to have no power. It is designed this way so that local churches may enjoy the benefits of national fellowship without the slightest compromise of their freedom."

Since the churches affiliated with the NACCC are autonomous, you will probably find a spectrum of beliefs and concerns. If being a part of an empowered local congregation appeals to you, the NACCC can help you locate churches in your area. Just give them a call or check out their web site.

Conservative Congregational Christian Conference

The Conservative Congregational Christian Conference is distinctive among Congregational and Christian associations in that it defines itself as a denomination that is theologically conservative. Among the doctrines the CCCC affirm are:

The autonomy of the local church

The CCCC is made up of churches from Congregational, Christian, Evangelical, and Reformed traditions, which share a strong commitment to the freedom of each local congregation while enjoying the benefits of national affiliation.

The Full Divine Inspiration and Authority of the Bible

The CCCC asserts that "Christians, equally committed to the authority of the Holy Scriptures, may disagree on . . ." issues of doctrine and practice. Any position that sacrifice Biblical authority is not acceptable. The web site states, "We affirm that persons who are firmly committed to the authority of God's Word, though they differ in their interpretations of the Word . . . are welcome to hold their convictions with clear conscience within our fellowship."

Christ is the Head of the Church

The CCCC believes that "Jesus Christ alone is the head of the Church and Lord of the conscience. He directs His Church through Scripture, speaking in this manner to officers and individual members."

Just the **FACTS**

Conservative Congregational Christian Congerence

Kind of Church: Protestant/Calvinist/Conservative
Worship Style: Traditional
Trinity Affinity: Son
Clout Continuum: 1st Place: Scripture
2nd Place: Personal experience
3rd Place: Tradition
Founded in USA: 1948
Members in USA: 66,262
Churches in USA: 260
Headquarters: 7582 Currell Blvd., Suite 108
St. Paul MN 55125
Phone: 651-739-1474
Web site: www.ccccusa.org

The Importance of Maintaining Unity without Denying Diversity

No church within the denomination is required to teach or practice a particular viewpoint that is against the conviction of that particular assembly. Ultimately, the CCCC urges its members to "relate to one another in a spirit of love and unity. Members are not asked to compromise their own convictions, but are asked to respect the rights of others, who are also devoted to the Head of the Church and to His Word, to hold their own convictions as well."

The website has a number of position papers so you can see what lines they draw in the sand and what issues are viewed with more flexibility. In a nutshell, they leave the ordination of women and divorced persons to the discretion of each congregation, encourage building relationships among congregations of differing racial groups, and take a conservative position on homosexuality and abortion.

If you're looking for a more theologically conservative church that is committed to the autonomy of the local congregation, a CCCC church may be a good fit. To find a church in your area, check out their web site for a church directory.

Christian Church (Disciples of Christ)

The Christian Church (Disciples of Christ) was created by merging (you guessed it) the Christian Church and the Disciples of Christ. I guess they were able to agree on the merger, but not on a new name. (I would have suggested the Christian Disciples of Christ, but no one asked me.) They resolved the dilemma by sticking the two names together—perhaps not the most creative solution, but at least no one felt left out.

And leaving people out was the opposite of what these two groups from the American frontier wanted to do. While the beliefs the Christian Church and the Disciples of Christ held in common were important, perhaps the biggest attraction to one another is what they didn't believe—they did not (and still do not) believe in formal creeds.

Since faith in Christ is what brings Christians together, the groups took a stand against trusting in and fighting over creedal and doctrinal statements. Ironically, because these folks rejected formal creeds, they left or were forced to leave other existing denominations such as the Presbyterians and Baptists. They divided to avoid division. (You have to admit, human beings are entertaining.) The goal was to bring people together, and today the Christian Church (Disciples of Christ) tries to create unity and is one of the largest denominations founded on American soil.

Just the **FACTS**

Christian Church (Disciples of Christ)

Kind of Church: Protestant/Restoration/Liberal
Worship Style: Traditional
Trinity Affinity: Father
Clout Continuum: 1st Place: Restoration tradition
2nd Place: Scripture
3rd Place: Personal experience
Founded in USA: 1832
Members in USA: 823,018 (figure includes Canada)
Churches in USA: 3,781 (figure includes Canada)
Headquarters: P.O. Box 1986
Indianapolis IN 46206
Phone: 317-713-2496
Web site: www.disciples.org

In 1832, a formal handshake between Stone and Campbell in Lexington, Kentucky, marked the merger of the Christians and the Disciples of Christ into a "brotherhood." Over the years, their passion for unity could not keep some from within their ranks from splintering off—seen as too liberal by some and too conservative by others. Some may leave the fold, but the Christian Church (Disciples of Christ) has a commitment to inclusiveness that runs deep as it continues to build bridges among various Christian traditions. This church:

- contributed to the founding of the National and World Councils of Churches;
- has declared that "a relationship of full communion" had been established with the United Church of Christ;

- has engaged in theological discussions with the Roman Catholic Church, the Russian Orthodox Church, and the World Alliance of Reformed Churches.

Emphasis is placed on discarding the unnecessary while retaining the essentials of the Christian faith. Each congregation owns its own property and controls its own budget and ministries. Pastors are called

Bob's Story

I'd been a member of a rather conservative Congregational church for nearly thirty years. In the past five years or so, I've felt more and more out of place there. I noticed a tendency to not only be conservative theologically, which I basically agree with, but also in their actions, their politics, in dress and speech. Establishing a foundation for faith, I think, is a good thing. But if that attitude solidifies into a mindset where you're more interested in maintaining the status quo than speaking the truth, it becomes a problem. So I visited a different Congregational church that was also on the conservative side.

To be honest, I think a lot of us don't seek a church because it matches up with some preconceived ideas of theology we have in mind. Rather, we look for a place where we are loved and we can love and we can fit in. I think most of us can be flexible if what a church teaches doesn't grossly conflict with your beliefs on things like the mode of baptism, church government style, or many other things. What is important is experiencing genuine love.

After attending there a while I realized I didn't feel the acceptance I needed. It came to a head for me after attending there for several months. I was at a church event when a man I'd recently met came up to the group I was talking with. He made a political joke, clearly assuming that everyone there was Republican. Personally, I am conservative in some issues and more liberal in others, but I don't vote a party line. I thought it was remark-

to serve by each congregation. As might be expected with so much emphasis on inclusiveness, both men and women are ordained as pastors. Nearly 23 percent of the clergy are women. Of the 3,781 congregations, 397 are predominately African American, 80 congregations are predominately Hispanic, and 58 congregations are predominately Asian American.

able that, not knowing me, he assumed my political affiliation simply because I was attending the church. It felt like he had no interest in getting to me as a person, but simply lumped me into a category.

I wanted a place where people were willing to engage in dialogue, with an open heart to people of differing opinions. There's a difference between believing something and being closed to any dialogue on the subject. I decided that this second church wasn't a good fit.

There's a Disciples of Christ church near my house, so I thought I'd give them a try. Immediately I was invited to various events they had during the summer. I was attracted to a series of movie-night discussions in which they showed films—provocative, thought-provoking movies—and then followed up with significant guided discussion. I liked the intellectual approach, the fact that they were willing to discuss and be open to ideas and receive different ideas from different sources including the media. I like being in a church where people are open to take a look at issues from a variety of standpoints, but still not lose the basic foundation in Scripture as a Christian.

I checked out the denominational web site and liked what I read. Basically, the CC(DOC) is opposed to creeds, since they have been used to exclude people from the church. All a person needs to do to become a member is to answer yes to the question, "Do you believe that Jesus is the Christ, the Son of the living God, and do you accept Him as your personal Savior?" I like that. The Disciples of Christ church has eclectic dimensions that I find extremely attractive. I have found a new church home.

Some congregations see themselves as more liberal and others more conservative, but share in the following:

- Confess that "Jesus is the Christ, the Son of the living God, and proclaim him Lord and Savior of the world";
- Baptize believers by immersion in the name of the Trinity;
- Share the Lord's Supper on a weekly basis, primarily as a symbolic way of remembering Christ.

Their web site is especially user friendly, written in most part in normal English sans the traditional religious jargon. If you're looking for

Prayer

While no formal creed is authoritative in the Christian Church (Disciples of Christ), the following prayer captures the gist of their beliefs:

"As members of the Christian Church, we confess that Jesus is the Christ, the Son of the living God, and proclaim him Lord and Savior of the world. In Christ's name and by his grace we accept our mission of witness and service to all people. We rejoice in God, maker of heaven and earth, and in the covenant of love which binds us to God and to one another. Through baptism into Christ we enter into newness of life and are made one with the whole people of God. In the communion of the Holy Spirit we are joined together in discipleship and in obedience to Christ. At the table of the Lord we celebrate with thanksgiving the saving acts and presence of Christ. Within the universal church we receive the gift of ministry and the light of scripture. In the bonds of Christian faith we yield ourselves to God that we may serve the One whose kingdom has no end. Blessing, glory and honor be to God forever. Amen."

a church that is trying to undo several hundred years of Protestant protesting, you'll feel very much at home in this denomination.

Churches of Christ

The Churches of Christ trace their roots back to the New Testament church established in 30 A.D., valuing the restoration of Christ's original and unified church. On a more practical level, this denomination was founded in 1906 after a disagreement with the Christian Church (Disciples of Christ). So much for unity. Perhaps it is the thought that counts.

The Churches of Christ shares the same disdain for creeds and sectarian interference as does the Christian Church (Disciples of Christ). These two groups continue to hold to similar beliefs, such as sharing the Lord's Supper each Sunday, espousing a "believer's baptism" by immersion, and seeing the Bible as the only basis for faith and practice. But today these two groups differ in significant ways, with the Churches of Christ placing an importance on the following:

No centralized governing body

Churches of Christ are bound together by a common faith in Christ as revealed in the Bible. Like the Christian Church (Disciples of Christ), each congregation is an independent entity that calls its own pastors. However, the Churches of God have no central headquarters with no overriding organizational structure—at all. They do have a web site, but I couldn't find a mailing address anywhere.

In spite of this lack of formalized organization, Churches of Christ members have created over forty educational institutions, seventy-five homes for abandoned children and the elderly, and approximately forty periodicals. Radio and television programs, often sponsored by spe-

Just the **FACTS**

Churches of Christ

Kind of Church:	Protestant/Calvinist/Conservative
Worship Style:	Traditional (more conservative congregations do not use musical instruments)
Trinity Affinity:	Son
Clout Continuum:	1st Place: Scripture
	2nd Place: Personal experience
	3rd Place: Tradition
Founded in USA:	1906
Members in USA:	2,000,000
Churches in USA:	15,000
Headquarters:	None
Web site:	www.church-of-christ.org
Phone:	None

cific congregations or individuals, are aired on hundreds of stations in fourteen languages. Their web site offers links to churches in Spanish, Italian, French, German, Swiss, Dutch, Vietnamese, Brazilian, and Hungarian. Not bad for a group that can't be called up on the phone.

I respect the way they have translated their beliefs into action. They believe the original church was organized around local congregations. Other groups agree with this idea but go right ahead and organize denominations anyway. The Church of Christ is more consistent in living out their beliefs, in my opinion, than any other in this regard.

Scripture is infallible and the sole authority

Whenever there are disagreements in the Churches of Christ, a "reference to the scriptures is made in settling every religious question. A pronouncement from the scripture is considered the final word." As a consequence of denouncing creeds, no one is required to adhere to manuals, disciplines, or confessions of faith of any kind.

Worship is modeled after the early church

If it's not in the Bible, then these folks aren't going to do it. Since there were no pipe organs, pianos, or electric guitars in the apostolic church, more conservative Churches of Christ do not use instruments and sing acappella. Some are loosening up a bit. In addition, they shy away from using candles, incense, or any gizmo or gadget other Christian traditions may have created.

A Churches of Christ congregation may be the best place for you if you value simplicity and purity. Some feel that building bridges with other denominations and associations has been too costly in terms of biblical fundamentals. If that's how you feel, you may want to check out the Churches of Christ.

The **Tie** That
Binds

In the Churches of Christ, "there are no conventions, annual meetings, or official publications. The 'tie that binds' is a common loyalty to the principles of the restoration of New Testament Christianity."

United Church of Christ

Mergers, mergers, and more mergers—that's how the United Church of Christ came into existence back in 1957. In the early 1700s, German immigrants flooded into Pennsylvania, nearly half of them affiliated with the Reformed Church. The first German Reformed synod was organized in Philadelphia in 1747 (interestingly supported by the Reformed Church in Holland). In 1793, this group was ready to be self-supporting and adopted the name German Reformed Church. In 1869, they dropped "German" from the name to become the Reformed Church in the United States.

The Reformed Church in the United States merged with the Evangelical Synod in 1934, taking the name Evangelical and Reformed Church. Meanwhile, the Congregationalists merged with some of the Christian Church communities in 1931 under the name Congregational Christian Churches. They all joined forces in 1957 to become the United Church of Christ. The blending of these four major traditions—Congregational, Christian, Evangelical, and Reformed—has resulted in an association that emphasizes commonality and diversity.

Statements of faith, such as the Apostles' Creed, the Nicene Creed, the Heidelberg Catechism, the Evangelical Catechism, the Augsburg Confession, the Cambridge Platform, and the Kansas City Statement of Faith are seen as testimonies rather than tests of faith. Even though a UCC Statement of Faith was adopted in 1959, individual members or congregations of the church are not bound to this document in a formalized manner. The UCC, as a centralized body, has no authority to "impose any doctrine of form or worship on its members."

How many in the Churches of Christ does it take to change a lightbulb?

Where is the scriptural authority for a lightbulb?

The UCC Statement of Faith asserts:

"We believe in God, the Eternal Spirit, Father of our Lord Jesus Christ and our Father, and to his deeds we testify:

He calls the worlds into being, creates man in his own image and sets before him the ways of life and death.

He seeks in holy love to save all people from aimlessness and sin.

Just the FACTS

United Church of Christ

Kind of Church: Protestant/Calvinist/Liberal
Worship Style: Traditional
Trinity Affinity: Father
Clout Continuum: 1st Place: Tradition
2nd Place: Scripture
3rd Place: Personal experience
Founded in USA: 1957
Members in USA: 1,401,682
Churches in USA: 5,961
Headquarters: 700 Prospect Ave.
Cleveland OH 44115-1000
Phone: 216-736-2100
Web site: www.ucc.org

He judges men and nations by his righteous will declared through prophets and apostles.

In Jesus Christ, the man of Nazareth, our crucified and risen Lord, he has come to us and shared our common lot, conquering sin and death and reconciling the world to himself.

He bestows upon us his Holy Spirit, creating and renewing the church of Jesus Christ, binding in covenant faithful people of all ages, tongues, and races.

He calls us into his church to accept the cost and joy of discipleship, to be his servants in the service of men, to proclaim the gospel to all the world and resist the powers of evil, to share in Christ's baptism and eat at his table, to join him in his passion and victory.

He promises to all who trust him forgiveness of sins and fullness of grace, courage in the struggle for justice and peace, his presence in trial and rejoicing, and eternal life in his kingdom which has no end.

Blessing and honor, glory and power be unto him.
Amen."

Since "covenant" is big with these folks, each congregation is a "covenanted ministry" of the United Church of Christ, self-governing and voluntarily working cooperatively with other churches in the association. Their web site states, "Christ alone is Head of the church. We seek a balance between freedom of conscience and accountability to the apostolic faith. The UCC therefore receives the historic creeds and confessions of our ancestors as testimonies, but not tests of the faith."

The United Church of Christ is a church of firsts—in 1785, they ordained the first African American, Lemuel Haynes. The first woman

Ecumenical Movement

Derived from the Greek term *oikoumene*, ecumenical can be translated as "the whole inhabited world." Mentioned fifteen times in the New Testament, ecumenical is primarily used as a geographical term. Over the years, ecumenical has taken on an organizational usage, to mean the bringing together of various Christian groupings. For example, the major councils that met from the fourth century on were called ecumenical councils, drawing representation from the major Christian centers of the day. Significant declarations of doctrine, such as the Apostles' Creed, the Nicene Creed, and the Athanasian Creed, were results of ecumenical councils.

Today, the term is most often associated with interdenominational efforts to bring unity to the splintered world of Christendom. The ecumenical movement endeavors to restore unity in the church. Perhaps the most prominent organization associated with the ecumenical movement today is the World Council of Churches.

to be ordained was Antoinette Brown in 1853. And the UCC was the first denomination to ordain an openly gay person to ministry, William R. Johnson, in 1972.

Finding common ground with other believers and Christian organizations, the UCC has welcomed Christian groups comprised of Christian American Indians, African Americans, Asian Americans, Pacific Islanders, Volga Germans, Armenians, and Hispanic Americans. More inclusive than most, the UCC also invites gay and lesbian Christians into their congregations. As they say, "... the United Church of Christ celebrates and continues a broad variety of traditions in its common life."

How many United Church of Christ members does it take to change a lightbulb?

How dare you be so intolerant! So what if the lightbulb has chosen an alternative light style?

Ordained ministers from the UCC and the Christian Church (Disciples of Christ) may serve in either denomination. The UCC is affiliated with the following interfaith and ecumenical organizations:

- Churches Uniting in Christ
- National Council of Churches
- World Alliance of Reformed Churches
- World Council of Churches

In addition, the UCC has established relationships with the following "ecumenical partners":

- African Methodist Episcopal Church
- African Methodist Episcopal Zion Church
- Alliance of Baptists

- Christian Church (Disciples of Christ)
- Christian Methodist Episcopal Church
- Episcopal Church
- Evangelical Lutheran Church in America
- Evangelische Kirche der Union
- International Council of Community Churches
- United Methodist Church

The UCC is a church that welcomes diversity while building unity among believers of a variety of traditions. If you're more conservative, you may feel that some of the essentials have been traded off to blend traditions (keep an eye out for a watering down of the divinity and centrality of Christ). However, if you're looking for a church that is trying to relate to the current culture, is concerned with overcoming arbitrary denomination barriers, and that includes a wide range of Christian traditions, then the UCC may be the right fit for you.

What to Expect When You Visit

Congregational and Restoration worship services tend to be traditional in style. Some include contemporary worship, while others are holding fast to their uncomplicated traditions. As a general rule, men should wear a jacket and tie and women a casual dress or skirt to Sunday worship.

Since most Congregational and Restoration churches have, at this point in history, blended to some extent four Protestant traditions into its service style, you may find more variety in worship. Generally speaking, services are comprised of:

- A Call to Worship: The minister may lead the congregation in responsive reading. Traditional worship music and singing of hymns usually come next. Scriptures will be read, either by one individual or collectively.
- The Sermon: Usually the focal point of a service, the pastor will preach a sermon around twenty minutes in length.
- Closing Prayers: The minister and congregation will offer up prayers that often includes the group reciting the Lord's Prayer.
- Benediction: The pastor "sends forth" the congregation into the world (and off to lunch) by pronouncing a benediction, concluding the service.

More Congregational and Restoration Churches

Christadelphians
www.christadelphia.org

Christian Churches and Churches of Christ
www.cwv.net/christ'n (unofficial)

Church of God and Saints of Christ
www.churchofgod1896.org

International Council of Community Churches
www.akcache.com/community/iccc.html

Further Info

- Richard L. Hamm, *2020 Vision for the Christian Church (Disciples of Christ)* (Chalice, 2001)

- John Von Rohr, *The Shaping of American Congregationalism: 1620-1957* (Pilgrim, 1992)

- Leonard Allen, *The Transforming of a Tradition: Churches of Christ in the New Millennium*, edited by Lynn Anderson (New Leaf, 2001)

eleven

Baptist
Churches

King Henry VIII got the Protestant ball rolling through England when he created the Church of England. But the ball didn't stop there. It gathered momentum from the Protestant reliance on Scripture and crashed through the confines of Henry's state religion, taking a distinctly Puritan direction. After collecting a more personalized experience of salvation and a stronger emphasis on the priesthood of all believers, the ball bounced over the English Channel, off of the Dutch Mennonites, and back to London. This brand of Protestantism picked up beliefs in the separation of church and state, the autonomy of the local congregation, and baptism of believers by immersion. The Baptists were on a roll.

A Brief History of Baptists

Since the Baptist tradition sort of ping-ponged its way into existence, there is some controversy over exactly when and how the Baptists began (some adamantly say the Mennonites played no role, but I like to think so). It's generally accepted that a congregation of English Puritans fled persecution to Holland under the leadership of John Smyth. There they met up with the Mennonites. John was convinced by the Mennonites that baptism was intended for believers who have professed faith in Christ. Even though everyone in the congregation had been baptized as infants as either Catholics or Anglicans, John and his congregation were baptized in a believer's baptism in 1609. The little band may have been absorbed into the Mennonite Church except for a strong desire on the congregation's part to retain their English identity. To become Mennonite, in their minds, was to become Dutch. So, once it was safe, the congregation moved back to London, calling themselves Baptists.

The first formal Baptist churches were set up in England in the early 1600s. They hardly got started before there were two factions—General Baptists and Particular Baptists. Setting up their first church in 1611, the General Baptists were Arminian in doctrine, asserting that atonement was *generally* available to everyone. Baptists who were more copasetic with Calvin's doctrine of predestination became known as Particular Baptists because they believed that salvation was limited to *particular* individuals. The first congregation of Particular Baptists was set up in England in 1638. Controversies and conflict over practice and doctrine continued, resulting in variations of the Baptist theme.

Along with many others seeking religious freedom, Baptists immigrated to the colonies where their churches flourished. The first Baptist congregation in the New World was founded in Providence, Rhode Island, around 1639, by Roger Williams, a Puritan immigrant from England. Williams's fervor for freedom of faith and expression of personal conviction got him into trouble with the Puritan leadership who liked to keep things under their control. So Williams did what any self-respecting Puritan would do—he became a Baptist. So did a lot of others. Religious freedom beat in the heart of colonialists, making them

Baptism

Jesus had a cousin, but not your typical cousin. He was more like that colorful relative everyone likes to tell stories about at Thanksgiving. You might say he had an alternative lifestyle—he lived out in the desert, wore a camel hair robe with a leather belt, and somehow survived on a diet of grasshoppers and honey (not a popular combo in any culture). His profession? Prophet. His nickname? John the Baptist.

Not a lot of families can boast of having a prophet in their midst (but then few families can claim having the Son of God in the family tree, for that matter). John's mission in life was to let everyone know that the Messiah promised by preceding prophets would be here any day now. He caused quite a stir in Israel, drawing huge crowds out to the desert to hear him preach and to be baptized in the Jordan River. He claimed, "After me comes One who is mightier than I, and I am not even fit to stoop down and untie the thong of His sandals. I baptize you with water; but He will baptize you with the Holy Spirit" (Mark 1:7–8).

One day while John was preaching, Jesus walked up to his cousin and asked to be baptized. As Jesus came up from the water, the Holy Spirit in the form of a dove landed on his shoulder and everyone heard a voice say, "This is my beloved Son, in whom I am well pleased" (Matt. 3:17). Jesus' baptism was his first public appearance as the Messiah.

Even though Jesus never baptized anyone, the fact that he was baptized set an example to be followed. Christian groups through the ages have argued over what baptism means, whether babies or adults ought to be baptized and how. But most all agree on the fact that baptism, in some form, should be practiced. If it was good enough for Jesus, it's good enough for his followers.

ripe for conversion to this form of Protestantism. Baptists of all varieties contributed to the success of the American Revolution and the development of the First Amendment.

Crossing Racial Lines

In addition to converting white Americans to Baptist beliefs, African Americans—both free and slave—were drawn to these same ideals. It can be argued that slave owners, especially Baptists in the South, helped sow the seeds of slavery's destruction through the conversion of their slaves. Slaves often accompanied their masters to church, sitting in the gallery, hearing a gospel of freedom. The first Baptist church solely for slaves was founded around 1773 with permission of a Georgian plantation owner. Many other black congregations sprang up throughout the South. Slaves, like Nat Turner who led a rebellion in 1831, figured if their masters were entitled to freedom and justice, so were they. It didn't take long for Southerners to pass laws forbidding slaves to worship together, but that didn't stop such gatherings from happening. Christian slaves met secretly, strengthening their passion and hope for freedom.

Today, all kinds of Americans are well represented in Baptist churches. In fact, nearly 20 percent of all Americans identify themselves as Baptist of one variety or another (not 20 percent of Christians in America, 20 percent of *Americans*—that's impressive). The majority of Baptist churches in the U.S. are Calvinistic in doctrine, some extremely so. A smaller percentage continue in the General Baptists tradition, being heavily influenced by the teachings of Jacob Arminius. The Free Will Baptists fall into this category. In spite of these historical and doctrinal differences, most Baptists hold a number of beliefs in common.

What Makes a Church Baptist?

The local congregation is autonomous

Baptists believe that Scripture teaches that the true church takes the form of local congregations. Denominational authority, since it limits the autonomy of separate congregations, is seen as unbiblical.

The local congregation is a community of believers

Baptists hold to a spiritual unity of all Christians, whether they are Baptist or not. Being a member of an organization does not make you a Christian. Rather, being a Christian makes you a part of the universal church, and therefore eligible for becoming part of a local congregational community.

God is approached through Christ

In keeping with the Protestant tradition, Baptists believe that the Bible teaches that we come into a relationship with God through faith in Jesus Christ.

The Bible is the inspired Word of God

Baptists hold the Bible as the sole authority of truth for the believer. Some congregations take the stand of biblical inerrancy, while others believe the Scriptures are trustworthy specifically in matters of faith and practice.

Baptism is a symbol of personal faith

Baptists believe that baptism is a symbolic expression of something that has already happened between you and God, not the context in which transformation occurs. Once a person has become a Christian, baptism is an important part of expressing one's faith. As a consequence, infant baptism is not practiced and is seen as unbiblical.

The Lord's Supper is restricted to believers

Some churches require membership before receiving communion. Others require nothing at all, welcoming anyone, regardless of beliefs, to share the Lord's table. Baptists land somewhere in the middle, claiming that communion is a symbolic experience reserved for believers. You needn't be Baptist to receive communion at a Baptist church, but you are expected to be a Christian.

Like baptism, communion is not considered a sacrament, but an ordinance. Many Baptist groups were involved with the temperance movement of the early 1900s, so expect grape juice instead of wine. The elements are seen as symbolic of the body and blood of Jesus.

The priesthood of all believers

Baptists believe in ordaining individuals into full-time ministry and give great respect to their pastors. However, Baptists believe that every Christian has privilege before God and reject the role of clergy as mediators between us and God.

American Baptist Churches in the U.S.A.

While Baptist congregations had no intention of forfeiting any local autonomy, many saw the advantages of bonding together for the sake of evangelism and missions. In 1814, Baptists founded a convention originally called (take a deep breath) the General Missionary Convention of

Just the **FACTS**

American Baptist Church in the U.S.A.

Kind of Church: Protestant/Calvinist/Moderate
Church Structure: Congregational
Worship Style: Traditional
Trinity Affinity: Son
Clout Continuum: 1st Place: Scripture
2nd Place: Personal experience
3rd Place: American Baptist tradition
Founded in USA: 1814/1845
Members in USA: 1,436,909
Churches in USA: 5,756
Headquarters: P.O. Box 851
Valley Forge PA 19482
Phone: 800-ABC-3USA
Web site: www.abc-usa.org

the Baptist Denomination in the United States of America for Foreign Missions (the GMCOTBDITUSAFM?). Wisely, someone began referring to the organization as the Triennial Convention, and the first national Baptist organization in the U.S. was born. Things went along relatively nicely until the issue of slavery became a dividing line.

The bond to culture proved stronger than commitment to a united Baptist community. Fierce arguments broke out between Baptists living in the north and south over slavery. Preachers from both sides used their public platforms to passionately defend their political positions with Scripture and rhetoric. Baptist abolitionists as well as slave owners believed their oppositional causes were holy, blessed by God. In 1845, after the Boston-based missions board refused to commission slave owners as missionaries, the southern churches withdrew

Just the **FACTS**

National Association of Free Will Baptists

Type of Church: Protestant/Conservative/Arminian-Wesleyan
Worship Style: Traditional
Trinity Affinity: Son
Clout Continuum: 1st Place: Scripture
2nd Place: Personal experience
3rd Place: Tradition
Founded in USA: 1935
Members in USA: 206,000
Churches in USA: 2470
Headquarters: P.O. Box 5002, Antioch TN 37011
Phone: 615-731-6812 / 877-767-7659
Web site: www.nafwb.org

from the Triennial Convention and established the Southern Baptist Convention.

The Triennial Convention persevered without the southern constituency and has undergone a variety of reorganizations. The name was changed in 1907 to the Northern Baptist Convention and again in 1950 to the American Baptist Convention (ABC). American Baptist churches tend to take moderate stances on doctrinal as well as political issues. While Calvinistic in tradition, the ABC is not as strict as the Southern Baptists and accepts Free Will Baptists, who are Arminian, into full fellowship.

According to ABC web site, " . . . the Bible, composed of the Old and New Testaments, is the divinely inspired Word of God, the final written authority and trustworthy for faith and practice. It is to be interpreted responsibly under the guidance of the Holy Spirit within the community of faith. The primary purpose of the Bible is to point to Jesus Christ, the living Lord of the Church."

This view of biblical interpretation provides the latitude to see themes and patterns in Scripture rather than rely on specific verses to support their doctrinal or social justice stances. Many of the abolitionists in the 1800s were women who saw the securing of women's rights on par with racial equality. It is no surprise, then, that ordination of women is generally accepted among American Baptist congregations.

The Preamble of American Baptist Statement on Ordained Ministry, 1989, states "The New Testament provides no single pattern for leadership in the church, since it is composed of separate texts addressed originally to particular churches and situations. These texts reflect a variety of leadership patterns which have contributed to Baptist understandings of ordained ministry. . . . Both women and men were leaders in the early Church. Although the names of men are more familiar, the New Testament provides us with the names of ten women who were leaders in the ministry of the earliest churches, including Phoebe, Priscilla and Lydia (Romans 16:1–16; Philippians 4:2–3; Acts 16:13–15, 40.)" As of May 2001, women made up approximately 13 percent of American Baptist clergy.

In 1967, the General Board Committee on Christian Unity was established, actively pursuing ecumenical relationships. The 1988 report from Ecumenical Relations Review Commission states, "God's people must refuse to break fellowship with any within our ranks. More than that, we must move toward one another embracing the gift of our unity in Christ which is indeed the fruition of his presence and spirit."

In keeping with this goal, the ABC is a member of

- The National Council of the Churches of Christ, U.S.A. (NCCC)
- The World Council of Churches (WCC)

- The Baptist World Alliance (BWA)

Has observer status with

- The National Association of Evangelicals (NAE)
- Church of the Brethren (COB)
- Consultation of Church Union (COCU

They also have an official relationship with the Progressive National Baptist Convention.

If you're looking for a church that is open to dialogue, concerned with social justice issues, and is building bridges rather than drawing lines, an ABC church may be a good fit for you.

Southern Baptist Convention

It would be unfair if, after reading the preceding section, you assumed that today's Southern Baptist Convention endorses racism or is a small, exclusionary, geographically limited group. SBC churches are found in every state in the union, putting the term "Southern" in an antiquated light. Having grown from approximately 352,000 members at its inception in 1845 to nearly 16 million at the turn of the millennium, Southern Baptists are by far the largest Baptist association in the country. People of all racial and ethnic backgrounds, and African Americans in particular, are making Southern Baptist

How many Southern Baptists does it take to change a lightbulb?

One to change the bulb, and 16 million to boycott the maker of the old bulb for bringing darkness into the church.

Just the FACTS

Southern Baptist Convention

Kind of Church:	Protestant/Calvinist/Conservative Evangelical
Church Structure:	Congregational
Worship Style:	Traditional
Trinity Affinity:	Son
Clout Continuum:	1st place: Scripture
	2nd place: Personal salvation experience
	3rd place: Baptist tradition
Founded in USA:	1814/1845
Members in USA:	5,000,000
Churches in USA:	40,000
Headquarters:	901 Commerce St., Suite 750, Nashville TN 37203
Phone:	615-244-2355
Web site:	www.sbc.net

churches their spiritual homes. Internationally, services are conducted in 110 languages and dialects.

I suspect that the Southern Baptist Convention has grown so rapidly and remains a force to be reckoned with because of the tenacious way SBC churches hold to their core beliefs. Southern Baptists stand their ground, unwilling to bow to pressures of political correctness. It can be argued that the SBC provides a point of reference for many in a society of lightening-speed change, relativism, terrorism, and uncertainty. Their 2000 summary of faith states, "In an age increasingly hostile to Christian truth, our challenge is to express the truth as revealed in Scripture, and to bear witness to Jesus Christ, who is 'the Way, the Truth, and the Life.'"

While many other denominations share this same conviction regarding Christ, few have the edge or spirit of mission that Southern Baptists exude. Building from a belief in the inerrancy of Scripture, Southern Baptist churches tend to be conservative, doctrinally as well as politically. Their 1999 statement of faith affirms that Southern Baptists "cherish and defend religious liberty, and deny the right of any secular or religious authority to impose a confession of faith upon a church or body of churches. We honor the principles of soul competency and the priesthood of believers, affirming together both our liberty in Christ and our accountability to each other under the Word of God."

Political hot buttons for many of the churches in the SBC are the separation of church and state, abortion, family values, and homosexuality. Southern Baptists see such stands more as spiritual directives than political bias. Adrian Rogers, chairman of the Baptist Faith and Message Study Committee, writes "Each generation of Christians bears the responsibility of guarding the treasury of truth that has been entrusted to us [2 Timothy 1:14]. Facing a new century, Southern Baptists must meet the demands and duties of the present hour."

Consequently, Southern Baptists "are not embarrassed to state before the world that these are doctrines we hold precious and as essential to the Baptist tradition of faith and practice." These Chris-

Speak Up!

Baptists are one of the most vocal churches in America. Whether you agree with their positions or not, you have to hand it to them—they exercise their right to free speech. And why not? Baptists played an instrumental role in advocating for free speech and the adoption of the First Amendment. Today's Baptists are exercising the rights their spiritual ancestors fought for.

tians don't shy away from political activism, ridicule, or television cameras. It's not what they believe that intrigues me, personally, but how they express what they believe—intensely, passionately, and urgently. I don't agree with the SBC on every issue, but I do admire their zeal. You may find both the content of their beliefs and the way they express them a perfect fit for you.

National Baptist Conventions

Today there are three conventions with "National Baptist" in their names: the National Baptist Convention of the United States (NBC-USA), the National Baptist Convention of America (NBCA) and the Progressive National Baptist Convention (PNBC). I ask you, why can't each new group come up with a clearly different name? Nevertheless, here is how they came to be.

A number of smaller conventions combined in 1895 to form The National Baptist Convention of the United States of America. Unity lasted for around twenty years, during which time this organization published Sunday school materials, founded colleges, and engaged in missions primarily in Africa and the Caribbean. The convention broke in two in 1915 over disagreements regarding a charter of incorporation and the control of the publishing house resulting in the National Baptist Convention USA (NBC-USA) and the National Baptist Convention of America (NBCA). Later, in the 1960s, the PNBC broke off from the NBC USA.

National Baptist Convention USA

The National Baptist Convention USA weighs in as the largest African-American coalition in the United States with over eight mil-

Just the **FACTS**

National Baptist Convention USA

Kind of church:	Protestant/Calvinist/Moderate
Church Structure:	Congregational
Worship Style:	Loudly and rhythmically Traditional
Trinity Affinity:	Son
Clout Continuum:	1st place: Personal experience
	2nd place: Scripture
	3rd place: Tradition
Founded:	1895/1915
Members in USA:	8,500,000
Churches:	Not available
Headquarters:	1700 Baptist World Center Dr.
	Nashville TN 37207
Phone:	615-228-6292
Web site:	www.nationalbaptist.com

lion members. Headquartered in Nashville, Tennessee, since 1990, the Convention's mission is to "promote foreign missions, encourage and support Christian education, publish and distribute Sunday School and religious literature, and engage in other Christian endeavors that may be required to advance the work of Christ throughout the world."

At their 97th Congress, the Convention developed V.I.S.A.—Vision, Integrity, Structure, and Accountability. According to their web site, they are committed to cultivating the following qualities in their association:

- Vision:
  Focusing on doing Christ's work in the world.
- Integrity:
  Designing all operations and finance programs to meet the high standards of Christ.

Just the **FACTS**

National Baptist Convention of America

Type of Church: Protestant/Calvinist
Worship Style: Traditional
Trinity Affinity: Son
Clout Continuum: 1st Place: Scripture
2nd Place: Personal experience
3rd Place: Tradition
Founded in USA: 1895/1915
Members in USA: 3,500,000
Churches in USA: 11,000
Headquarters: 1320 Pierre Avenue
Shreveport, Louisiana 71103
Phone: 318-221-2629 or 318-221-3701
Web site: www.nbcamerica.org

- Structure:
  Creating the proper infrastructure to carry out Christ's mission in a manner that includes the total body.

- Accountability:
  Holding the Convention accountable to its members.

Extensively involved in missions and education, the NBC-USA supports a number of colleges and seminaries. Even though the Convention shied away from political activism during the Civil Rights movement of the 1960s, the NBC-USA has become more involved in voter registration drives and other activities of social impact.

The National Baptist Convention USA welcomes anyone of any racial background, but it is primarily comprised of African-American members. If you feel most comfortable in that milieu, contact their web site for a congregation close to you.

National Baptist Convention of America

According to their web site, the NBCA's mission statement "encapsulates the ministry objectives including the teaching, evangelical, missionary, benevolence, and stewardship ministries, scholarly and Christian publication, religious liberty, doctrinal authenticity, social justice and economic development." Today, they draw the majority of their membership from Mississippi, Texas, Louisiana, Floriday, and California.

Progressive National Baptist Convention

During the Civil Rights movement of the 1960s, Joseph H. Jackson led the Convention away from political activism. His motto was "from protest to production," urging a practice of "racial uplift" rather than racial justice. Jackson's approach didn't sit well with a number of his constituents, especially those actively advocating for political reform, such as Martin Luther King Jr. In 1961 these activists broke away to form the Progressive National Baptist Convention, an organization that has since played a highly visible, openly influential role in American politics.

According to their web site, the PNBC is "an association of Baptist churches throughout the world—is commited to the mandate of making disciples for Christ. The convention is founded on the precepts of fellowship, service, progress and peace, and seeks to affirm the 'priesthood of all believers.'" Their mission statement directs their efforts to "equip,

Just the **FACTS**

Progressive National Baptist Convention

Type of Church:	Protestant/Calvinist/Progressive
Worship Style:	Traditional
Trinity Affinity:	Son
Clout Continuum:	1st Place: Scripture
	2nd Place: Personal experience
	3rd Place: Tradition
Founded in USA:	1961
Members in USA:	2,500,000
Churches in USA:	2,000
Headquarters:	601 50th Street NE
	Washington DC 20019
Phone:	202-396-0558
Web site:	www.pnbc.org

enable, empower constituents to change systems, structures, and attitudes through mission to meet the needs of people."

Each year the PNBC sponsors The Annual Session of the Convention and the Congress of Christian Education, from Tuesday through Griday the week following the first Sunday in August. The Mid-Winter Adjouned Session of the Convention is held annually on Tuesday through Friday following the third Sunday in January. To locate a church that is a member of the PNBC, contact their web site.

What to Expect When You Visit

Generally speaking, American Baptist Churches are less demonstrative than churches in the Southern Baptist Convention or the

National Baptist Convention USA. But Baptists have a tradition of speaking up and telling it like they see it no matter what crowd they're in. Services usually start off with prayer and congregational singing. A soloist or a group may sing a "special" number as the congregation listens. Since the sermon is the main event, the preaching portion of the service may last a minimum of twenty minutes, and in some churches much longer.

While there are exceptions, Baptist preaching tends to be boisterous and emphatic—whether in predominantly white or predominantly African-American congregations. In some churches, congregation participation is encouraged—when you hear something you agree with, you're welcome to join in with an "Amen!" or "Praise God!" (just make sure other people are doing this before you start yelling).

Don't mistake enthusiasm for informality. Most Baptists show their respect for God by dressing up on Sunday mornings. You'll find exceptions in certain parts of the country, but generally it's wise to make your first visit in a jacket and tie (if you're a man) and a dress or skirt outfit that covers your shoulders (if you're a woman). It's also a good idea to keep your skirt length close to the knee.

Holy Communion is served on special occasions. Baptist churches have a tradition of using grape juice instead of wine in the Lord's Supper, since some take strong stands against the use of alcohol. Check the bulletin for any printed policy the church may have about participation. Some congregations offer the Lord's Supper only to members of the local body while others invite anyone who confesses to be a "born again." There are some churches that welcome anyone, regardless of faith, to take part. As with any church you visit, if you have any questions, ask an usher for guidance.

More Baptist Churches and Conventions

Baptist General Conference
   www.bgc.bethel.edu

Cooperative Baptist Fellowship
   www.cbfonline.org

General Association of General Baptist Churches
   www.angelfire.org

General Association of Regular Baptist Churches
   www.garbc.org

National Missionary Baptist Convention of America
   www.natl-missionarybaptist.com

National Primitive Baptist Convention, USA
   www.natlprimbaptconv.org

North American Baptist Conference
   www.nabconference.org

Separate Baptists in Christ
   www.scparatebaptist.org

Further Info

- James T. Draper Jr. and Kenneth Keathley, *Biblical Authority: The Critical Issue for the Body of Christ* (Broadman and Holman, 2001)

- Tom J. Nettles and Russell Moore, eds., *Why I Am a Baptist* (Broadman and Holman, 2001)

- Evelyn Brooks Higginbotham, *Righteous Discontent: The Women's Movement in the Black Baptist Church 1880-1920* (Harvard University Press, 1993)

Traditional Churches

In the Arminian-Wesleyan tradition

twelve

Methodist and Holiness Churches

It all started in 1729, when John Wesley, Charles (his younger brother), and a couple of friends at Oxford started meeting together. This wasn't your typical hanging-out-with-chips-and-salsa kind of meeting. They were serious. John, having been ordained the year before, regularly led the group in Communion. The whole gang fasted two days a week. But just acting spiritual didn't cut it. The group visited people in debtor's prison, paid off their debts, taught folks how to read and find work, and generally helped those who needed it. Word got out and the group grew. Those who felt it was a tad much nicknamed them "The Holy Club," "The Bible Moths," and "The Methodists" (because they were so methodical in their activities). Fortunately, the latter name was the one that stuck.

A Brief History of Methodism

In 1735, John and Charles left Oxford for a missionary venture in the colony of Georgia. While the experience was a dismal failure (Charles returned in 1736 and John in 1738), they had the fortune of meeting some Christians called the Moravians. Once back in England, they attended Moravian services and were challenged to read Martin Luther's writings. Within days of one another, Charles and John had life-changing spiritual experiences. John's intellectual and rather obsessive faith was transformed into a personal relationship with God. Charles said that he was "finally at peace with God."

Both in their early thirties, John and Charles dedicated the rest of their lives to telling people about their experience with Christ. Charles was a gifted orator and poet who wrote over seventy-five hundred hymns by the time he died in 1788. He was so respected in his day that George Frederic Handel even wrote melodies for some of his lyrics (wow!). Perhaps his most well-known creation is "Hark, the Herald Angels Sing," which has now become a standard Christmas carol sung by many denominations (and is occasionally heard overhead in department stores).

Meanwhile, John threw himself into his new calling with fervor, enthusiasm, and discipline. He preached anywhere and everywhere he could gain access to a pulpit. Unfortunately, John and his message were a bit over the edge for your average Anglican at the time. After a number of church doors were slammed in his face, George Whitefield, a well-known evangelist and former member of the Holy Club, encouraged him to take his message outside the church. And John did, literally. He preached in town squares, road sides, and out in the fields—anywhere he could gather a crowd, sometimes thousands of people at a time. It is estimated that John averaged four thousand miles annually, mostly on horseback, and preached over forty thousand sermons in his lifetime.

Just the FACTS

The Moravian Church in America

Kind of Church: Pre-Protestant
Worship Style: Free-Form
Trinity Affinity: Father
Clout Continuum: 1st Place: Scripture
2nd Place: Moravian tradition
3rd Place: Personal experience
Founded in USA: 1735
Members in USA: 50,000 (figure includes Canada)
Churches in USA: 160 (figure includes Canada)
Headquarters: P.O. Box 1245
Bethlehem PA 18016
Phone: 610-867-0593
Web site: www.moravian.org

John repeatedly tried to bring his ministry under the auspices of the Anglican Church, but when the bishop in London refused to ordain ministers in John's societies, he started ordaining them himself. Charles didn't support this, and the two brothers had a falling out. But John would not be deterred. He continued to train preachers and leaders to spread the Methodist message throughout England and to the colonies.

The Method of Methodism

John accompanied his message with a specific plan of action—to organize people into small groups or societies where members supported each other and were held accountable to live out their faith.

The **Moravian** Church in America

John Wesley and his brother Charles both experienced spiritual conversion while worshiping with members of the Moravian church, a rare breed among Protestant denominations. When the Reformation was launched in 1517 by Martin Luther, the Moravian Church was already sixty years old. Taking its name from the area of Moravia, in what is now the Czech Republic, the church was launched by John Hus, rector of Prague University, who preached against the abuses of the Roman Catholic Church. Citing the Bible as his authority, and not the pope, Hus taught his followers to pray directly to God without the priests as intermediaries and to worship through a simple "liturgy accompanied by music, education, missions, and fellowship of believers."

Today's Moravian Church may be small but nevertheless a viable part of mainstream Protestantism. Moravians believe that Jesus is Lord and Savior and salvation comes by his grace, through repentance for sins and faith in him. Seeing themselves as one of the many subgroups within Christianity, they adhere to the principle of "in essentials unity, in nonessentials liberty, and in all things love. Essentials relate to the life, death, and resurrection of Jesus Christ, the Holy Trinity, the universal nature of sin, and the Bible as the sole standard for all our Christian beliefs."

Music plays a major part in Moravian worship. Chorales and hymns as well as trombone choirs and brass bands contribute to weekly worship and special festivals of the church. The Moravian's lovefeast service consists of singing with the sharing of food.

Over the years, the Moravians have developed a number of meaningful rituals and traditions that are unique to their tradition. These include the Moravian Christmas Candle service that began in 1747 in Germany, in which children light candles tied with a red ribbon representing "his kindling of blood-red flame in each believing heart thereby." Moravians also have created and distributed the annual Moravian Daily Texts for the last two hundred and fifty years. Today, more than 1.5 million believers each year around the world receive the booklet of Scriptures and hymns.

In an attempt to be inclusive, the Moravian Church welcomes people who consider themselves to be liberal, moderate, and conservative in their politics. They emphasize the unity of the church as an expression of God's love for everyone. For more information, contact their web site.

They were somewhat like recovery groups are today, where people meet, talk, and tell the truth about their lives. Societies usually met in private homes, and were "the church" to Wesley—functioning as the church, doing what a church ought to be doing.

The small group format is commonly used in churches of all denominations today for Sunday School, youth groups, women's associations, and prayer groups. It is easy to take this approach for granted. But before the Reformation, Christians had, by and large, met in larger congregational groups for the purpose of worship and receiving communion. Meeting in small groups to talk about one's personal spirituality was rare. Wesley's emphasis on small group accountability and support was heavily influenced by Jakob Philip Spencer, who initiated the Pietist movement in Germany in the late 1600s. Spencer is credited with promoting the idea of pastors meeting with smaller subgroups of the congregation for Bible study, prayer, and support. He believed that the church was less about preaching doctrine than it was about creating a context for spiritual transformation and a "religion of the heart."

The importance John attributed to a person's willingness to meet for Christian "fellowship" can't be overstated. In his personal journal, he wrote on May 26, 1759: "I found the little society which I had joined

As John Would Say . . .

"Think and let think."

"Once in seven years I burn all my sermons; for it is a shame if I cannot write better sermons now than I did seven years ago."

"When I was young I was sure of everything; in a few years, having been mistaken a thousand times, I was not half so sure of most things as I was before; at present, I am hardly sure of anything but what God has revealed to me."

here two years since had soon split in pieces. In the afternoon, I met several of the members of the praying societies: and showed them what Christian fellowship was, and what need they had of it. About forty of them met me on Sunday, 27, in Mr. Gillies's kirk, immediately after the evening service. I left them determined to meet Mr. Gillies weekly, at the same time and place. If this be done, I shall try to see Glasgow again: If not, I can employ my time better."

John had no intentions of wasting his time on anything or anyone who didn't take faith seriously. He nurtured his groups personally, as well as trained local leadership to provide pastoral care to Methodist believers. In 1743, John published rules for the Methodist societies to provide structure and direction. Wesley included both men and women into leadership as the network grew throughout England and to the New World.

Methodist Societies

John Wesley created six disciplines or rules that society members were expected to follow:

- " To meet once a week, at least;
- To come together at the hour appointed;
- To begin exactly at the hour, with singing or prayer;
- To speak each of us in order, freely and plainly, the true state of our souls, with the faults we have committed in thought or deed and the temptations we have felt since our last meeting;
- To end every meeting with prayer suited to the state of each person;
- To desire some person among us to speak his own state first, and then to ask the rest, in order, as many and as searching questions as may be, concerning their state, sins, and temptations." [bullets added]

What Makes a Church Methodist or Holiness?

A number of traditions influenced John Wesley's theology. Martin Luther's view of justification by faith served as a catalyst for John's personal salvation experience. Doctrinally, John Wesley followed in the tradition of Jacob Arminius, a Dutch theologian who was a contemporary of John Calvin's, but who put more emphasis on human free will.

Prevenient Grace

At the heart of Wesley's teaching was a palpable experience with love—God's love for us and grace to all who had faith in Christ alone. Wesley believed that God reaches out to everyone offering a valid opportunity to accept or reject a personal relationship through Jesus. Methodists refer to this as "prevenient" or anticipatory grace based on God's initiation toward us.

Justification

Human beings are sinful by nature and need to repent and be converted. While a person may reject God, our ability to accept is an exercise of our free will empowered by God's grace. If we choose to accept God's offer, God attributes us the righteousness of Christ (justification).

Wesley on Slavery

"Is it lawful to abuse mankind, that the avarice, the vanity, or the passion of a few may be gratified? No! There is such a thing as justice, to which the most sacred regard is due. It ought to be inviolably observed. Have not these unhappy men a better right to their liberty and to their happiness, than our American merchants have to the profits which they make by torturing their kind? Let therefore our colonies be ruined, but let us not render so many men miserable."

Sanctification

The Holy Spirit begins to change us from the inside out (regeneration or sanctification). Wesley saw sanctification as a growing and purifying process that takes place between conversion and death. Since Wesley believed that perfection is an act of God's grace, he acknowledged an instantaneous element to sanctification. However, since "sanctification was the infinite and dynamic love of God at work in a finite believer," perfection was seen as a process, not a static state.

Lifestyle Focus

Calvinist theology tends to direct the focus on whether or not you have been chosen by God as one of the elect. Since there is nothing you can do to earn salvation, personal behavior or choices carry no spiritual significance. However, you cannot assume to be among the elect and flagrantly sin, so lifestyle issues are important as a demonstration of election but not a part of salvation or regeneration.

Wesleyan theology has a different emphasis. Since you and I can choose whether or not to accept or reject Christ, what we do and the choices we make become highly significant. Accepting Christ is the first step but not the goal of a Wesleyan Christian who "works out" his or her salvation while being sanctified into a closer image of Christ. (This belief can be compared, to some extent, with the Orthodox view of "theosis," wherein we become more and more like God.)

Because a Wesleyan Christian participates with God as an empowered partner, how one lives takes on a greater importance. Wesley tirelessly advocated for the poor, argued against slavery, and fought against a variety of social ills. It comes as no surprise to find Methodists in the forefront of a number of movements—including the Holiness, Temperance, Social Gospel, and Ecumenical Movements. Methodism also spawned groups like the Salvation Army that effectively wed spiritual truth with ministry to the poor and disenfranchised.

Methodism in America

Wesley had an opinion on everything, and he was decidedly English. He criticized the rebelliousness of the colonies and urged Methodists in America to work within the Church of England whenever possible. This became impossible after the Revolutionary War when there was no Church of England on American soil.

John wrote a new prayer book titled *The Sunday Service of the Methodists in North America* and sent several Methodist ministers to America, including a dynamic leader named Francis Asbury. Asbury was especially gifted at adapting Methodism to American culture. Circuit riders rode horseback throughout the frontier to preach at camp meeting revivals where often hundreds, if not thousands, would attend, sometimes for days on end. Even though Methodism was yet to be formalized into a separate denomination in England, by 1784 the movement was strong enough in the States to formally create the Methodist Episcopal Church in America.

Almost as soon as the denomination was formally established, subgroups started splitting off. Some split over church governance, like the Methodist Protestant Church, founded in 1830, because a large subgroup couldn't get lay representation in the church government.

A number of schisms occurred over the issues of racism and slavery. There was no mistaking John Wesley's opinion of slavery—he was adamantly against it. Insisting that "the African is in no respect inferior to the European," Wesley wrote and preached about its horrors. (I encour-

Just the **FACTS**

African Methodist Episcopal Church

Kind of Church: Protestant/Wesleyan/Progressive
Worship Style: Traditional/Contemporary
Trinity Affinity: Son
Clout Continuum: 1st Place: Scripture
2nd Place: Personal experience
3rd Place: Tradition
Founded in USA: 1814
Members in USA: 2,500,000
Churches: 6,200
Headquarters: 1134 11th Street NW
Washington DC 20001
Phone: 615-256-5882
Web site: www.amecnet.org

age you to read Wesley's *Thoughts About Slavery*. It's graphic, confrontational, and brave. Find it at http://docsouth.unc.edu/wesley/wesley.html.)
While there were many in the Methodist church who shared Wesley's view against slavery, racial inequality was rampant and served to splinter Methodism in America.

African Methodist Episcopal Church

Racial tension came to a head in 1787 at Philadelphia's St. George's Methodist Church. A group of white trustees, upset by seeing a black man kneeling in prayer in the "wrong" section, forcibly carried Absalom Jones to the back of the church. When this behavior was condoned by the congregational leadership, there was a mass exodus led by

Richard Allen. Allen, a former slave, had become a Christian while he was still in slavery and, once freed, began preaching to other freed slaves. Allen and his group set up their own congregation. Francis Asbury supported Allen's leadership and ordained him as the minister of the Bethel Church for Negro Methodists in Philadelphia in 1793. (By the way, Absalom Jones got tired of the Methodists in general and eventually became the first African American ordained as an Episcopal priest.)

Meanwhile, the whites in Methodist denominational leadership refused to let Allen and the congregation control the church property, as was standard in predominantly white churches. This resulted in a long court battle. By the time the Pennsylvania Supreme Court ruled in favor of Allen in 1816, he and the congregation were long gone. Two years earlier, Allen's congregation merged with five other predominantly black churches resulting in the African Methodist Episcopal Church. Once again, Allen had Asbury's blessing and was consecrated as AMEC's first Bishop in 1816.

African Methodist Episcopal Zion Church

Back in 1796, another group split off from John Street Methodist Church in New York over racial discrimination. They called themselves the Zion Church. Richard Allen tried to incorporate members of the Zion Church of New York into the AME, but the congregation wanted to set up a differenct alliance. In 1821, the Zion Church combined with five other African-American congregations throughout the northeast to form the African Methodist Episcopal Zion Church. Today, this denomination counts over three thousand churches among its membership.

Just the FACTS

African Methodist Episcopal Zion Church

Kind of Church:	Protestant/Wesleyan
Worship Style:	Traditional/Contemporary
Trinity Affinity:	Son
Clout Continuum:	1st Place: Scripture
	2nd Place: Personal experience
	3rd Place: Tradition
Founded in USA:	1821
Members in USA:	1,276,662
Churches in USA:	3,125 congregations
Headquarters:	Beth Shalom AME Zion Church
	1249 Bladensburg Rd. NE
	Washington DC 20002
Phone:	202-399-4357
Web site:	www.amezion.org

Christian Methodist Episcopal Church

The next year, in 1844, tension over slavery come to another tumultuous head. One of the five bishops, James O. Andrew, had acquired slaves through marriage. Even though it was against Georgia state law to free slaves, an example was made of Andrew. As long as he "could not or would not" free his slaves, he was suspended from office. By the next year, the Methodist Episcopal Church, South, formally separated.

Since much of the South was devastated by the Civil War, so was the Methodist Episcopal Church, South. Church buildings were destroyed and membership dropped by a third due, in part, to casualties among members and clergy. The Methodist Episcopal Church came through the war better than some denominations, but not thriving.

Amazing Grace

"Amazing Grace", first published in 1779, was written by an ex-slave trader named John Newton. His mother died when he was seven, and at eleven, John went to sea to become a sailor like his dad. By the time he was twenty-two, he had deserted the navy, been caught and flogged, and had taken command of a slave ship en route between West Africa, the West Indies, and Britain. While sailing across the Atlantic, Newton was dramatically converted through the combined influence of *The Imitation of Christ*, written in 1427 by Thomas à Kempis, a German Catholic priest, and surviving a terrible storm. As huge waves threatened to sink his ship, John and his crew fought the storm for twenty-six hours. He cried out loud for God's protection. Once the storm passed, Newton experienced a "great change," which prompted him to quit the slave trade and return to England.

After meeting John Wesley and George Whitefield, Newton turned to a life of ministry. He was ordained in 1774 in the Church of England, serving as curate at Olney in Buckinghamshire for sixteen years and as rector of St. Mary Woolnoth in London until his death in 1807. His lyrics, set to a Scottish folk melody, have stirred hearts for centuries. Certainly the words take on fresh meaning with the knowledge of Newton's participation in the evils of slavery.

1. Amazing grace! How sweet the sound
   That saved a wretch like me!
   I once was lost, but now am found,
   Was blind, but now I see.

2. 'Twas grace that taught my heart to fear,
   And grace my fears relieved;
   How precious did that grace appear
   The hour I first believed.

3. Through many dangers, toils, and snares
   I have already come;
   'Tis grace hath brought me safe thus far,
   And grace will lead me home.

4. The Lord has promised good to me,
   His word my hope secures;
   He will my shield and portion be
   As long as life endures.

Just the **FACTS**

Christian Methodist Episcopal Church

Kind of Church: Protestant/Wesleyan
Worship Style: Traditional/Contemporary
Trinity Affinity: Son
Clout Continuum: 1st Place: Scripture
2nd Place: Personal experience
3rd Place: Tradition
Founded in USA: 1870/1954
Members in USA: 784,114
Churches in USA: 3,069
Headquarters: 4466 Elvis Presley Blvd.
Memphis TN 38116
Phone: 205-929-1640
Web site: www.c-m-e.org

After the Civil War, about 145,000 of the 225,000 the freed slaves who had been members of the Methodist Episcopal Church, South, left to join either the African Methodist Episcopal Church or the African Methodist Episcopal Zion Church. By mutual agreement, the remaining eighty thousand African Americans broke with the Methodist Episcopal Church, South, in 1866 to become the Colored Methodist Episcopal Church. Their name was changed in 1954 to the Christian Methodist Episcopal Church.

United Methodist Church

The United Methodist Church is comprised of several Wesleyan groups. The first merger occurred at the beginning of the twentieth cen-

Arminianism vs. Calvinism

Jacobus Arminius was born in Holland in 1560 (four years before John Calvin died) during a time in history when Holland was being ripped apart by political and religious persecution. Soon after his birth, his father died, leaving him, two siblings, and their mother to struggle financially. His superb intellectual abilities came to the attention of wealthy patrons, and Jacobus's education was sponsored by several individuals and eventually by the municipal authorities in Amsterdam.

When he was fifteen and studying at the University at Marburg, Germany, Arminius received word that his hometown had been destroyed by a Spanish invasion. He quickly returned to Holland to discover that his entire family had been slaughtered. In grief, he walked the entire way back to the university. That same year, Arminius returned to Holland to study at the University of Leyden, where he stayed for six years. Arminius then studied briefly in Geneva under Calvin's successor, Theodore Beza, who had taken Calvin's predestination a step further in what is called the supralapsarian view of predestination. This doctrine asserts that God first decided who would be saved and who would be damned and then permitted the fall of humanity in order for this decision to be fulfilled. It didn't take long for theologians to disagree. (When have they ever agreed on anything for any length of time?)

After a year at the University of Basel, Arminius returned to Geneva and studied there an additional three years, finally returning to Holland in 1587. He was licensed to preach and garnered such acclaim that he was called to pastor the Dutch church in Amsterdam. In 1588 he was ordained. He went on to teach at the University at Leyden. One would have expected him to live out his days preaching Reformed theology and ministering from the pulpit and in the classroom, but his life took an unexpected turn.

A scholarly layman named Coornhert disagreed with Calvinism, specifically rejecting the doctrine of predestination and punishing heretics by death (which could have resulted by his expressing his opinion). He published his

tury after years of negotiating. In 1939, the Methodist Episcopal Church, the Methodist Episcopal Church, South, and the Methodist Protestant Church recombined to become, simply, the Methodist Church.

While this was going on, another branch of Christendom was also consolidating—the Pietist or Brethren tradition. As mentioned previously, John Wesley's approach to small groups had been shaped by Jakob Philip Spencer, the German Pietist. Spencer also strongly influ-

ideas in 1589. As his pamphlet made the rounds, Coornhert's ideas gained popularity, which, of course, upset the Reformed crowd. Since Arminius was known for his intellect, training, and strict devotion to Calvinism, he was asked to write a rebuttal to Coornhert's pamphlet.

To his surprise, when he looked at the matter more closely, Arminius found he couldn't refute Coornfert's views. He carefully examined the Scriptures and writings of the early church and came up with the doctrine that today bears his name, Arminianism. When he first made this theological shift, he laid low. Why upset people who might want to burn him at the stake? But believing one thing and teaching another chafed his integrity, and by 1590 he was openly teaching his views.

His archrival was Franz Gomarus, a colleague at the University of Leyden. In 1602 when Francis Junius, professor of divinity at Leyden, died, the curators of the University invited Arminius to fill his chair. However, many Reformed ministers, especially those who were strict Calvinists, protested vehemently against this decision. The controversy, seasoned with acrimony and disrespect, moved beyond the university, splitting the Dutch church and impacting politics.

Arminuis died in 1609, but his death didn't put a damper on the fervor. His views were both expanded upon and simplified by his followers. In 1610, they launched the "five point" debate by presenting the Arminian Articles of Remonstrance. A "remonstrance" is a formal statement of opposition or disagreement, and Arminius's followers were referred to as Remonstrants. The five points of Arminianism were:

enced a German Reformed pastor, Philip Otterbein, and Martin Boehm, a Mennonite, whose work in America led to the formation of the Church of the United Brethren in 1800. Otterbein and Boehm were similar to Wesley in their views of spiritual experience and on social concerns, especially on the issue of slavery.

Three years after the Church of the United Brethren was set up, another denomination was organized in 1803 called the Evangelical

"God has decreed to save through Jesus Christ those of the fallen and sinful race who through the grace of the Holy Spirit believe in him, but leaves in sin the incorrigible and unbelieving." (In other words, predestination is said to be conditioned by God's foreknowledge of who would voluntarily respond to the gospel.)

"Christ died for all men (not just for the elect), but no one except the believer has remission of sin.

"Man can neither of himself nor of his free will do anything truly good until he is born again of God, in Christ, through the Holy Spirit.

"All good deeds or movements in the regenerate must be ascribed to the grace of God, but his grace is not irresistible.

"Those who are incorporated into Christ by a true faith have power given them through the assisting grace of the Holy Spirit to persevere in the faith. But it is possible for a believer to fall from grace."

The Synod voted unanimously to reject Arminianism and to punish anyone who didn't get with the Calvinist program. Over two hundred ministers were fired from their churches, and around eighty were thrown out of the country. Ministers who continued to preach an Arminian view were sentenced to life in prison.

The persecution of Arminians lasted until 1632 when the country government included them in the "tolerated" category. It took another century and a half for the Remonstrants to be established as a separate denomination.

Association. The founder was Jacob Albright, a former Lutheran who had joined a Methodist society/support group. These denominations cross-influenced each other, especially in the early years.

Fast forward to 1946. After twenty years of negotiation, the Church of the United Brethren merged with the Evangelical Association to become the Evangelical United Brethren Church. After more negotiations, in 1968, the Evangelical United Brethren Church merged with the Methodist Church to become the United Methodist Church. Since the various groups that make up today's United Methodists were strongly influenced by John Wesley's teaching from their inception, doctrine and practice remains Methodist in flavor.

Social justice issues were a major part of Wesley's focus, and you will find today's UMC abuzz with a variety of concerns. In keeping with that mindset, you'll find 17 percent of the ordained clergy to be women. The first Social Creed was adopted in 1908 by the Methodist Episcopal Church. Following in this tradition, the UMC has developed a number of social principles, which are "a call to all members of the United Methodist Church to a prayerful, studied dialogue of faith and practice."

These principles are based in the following doctrinal beliefs:

- Scripture "is the primary source and criterion for Christian doctrine. Through Scripture the living Christ meets us in the experience of redeeming grace."
- Reason is held in high regard. They believe that "any disciplined theological work calls for the careful use of reason. By reason we read and interpret Scripture. By reason we determine whether our Christian witness is clear. By reason we ask questions of faith and seek to understand God's action and will."

Just the **FACTS**

United Methodist Church

Kind of Church:	Protestant/Wesleyan/Moderate
Worship Style:	Traditional
Trinity Affinity:	Father
Clout Continuum:	1st Place: Wesleyan tradition
	2nd Place: Scripture
	3rd Place: Personal experience
Founded in USA:	1968
Members in USA:	8,333,770
Churches in USA:	35,609
Headquarters:	Information Services UMC
	P.O. Box 320, Nashville TN 37702
Phone:	800-251-8140
Web site:	www.umc.org

- Prevenient grace, defined as "the divine love that surrounds all humanity and precedes any and all of our conscious impulses," makes acceptance of God possible.

- The UMC believes that the process of justification, or conversion, may be "sudden and dramatic, or gradual and cumulative. It marks a new beginning, yet it is part of an ongoing process." In addition, their doctrine emphasizes that Christians can have assurance of their relationship with God when the Holy "bears witness with our spirit that we are children of God."

- Sanctification and perfection, mainstays in Wesleyan theology, is seen as a work of God in our lives "by which those who have been born again are cleansed from sin in their thoughts, words and acts, and are enabled to live in accordance with God's will, and to strive for holiness without which no one will see the Lord."

- Faith and good works hold a higher value in Methodism than in other Protestant denominations. Service to others and living in a way that pleases God does not save us, but is rather a demonstration of the relationship we already have with God.
- Nurture and mission of the church.

UMC Social Creed

We believe in God, Creator of the world; and in Jesus Christ, the Redeemer of creation. We believe in the Holy Spirit, through whom we acknowledge God's gifts, and we repent of our sin in misusing these gifts to idolatrous ends.

We affirm the natural world as God's handiwork and dedicate ourselves to its preservation, enhancement, and faithful use by humankind.

We joyfully receive for ourselves and others the blessings of community, sexuality, marriage, and the family.

We commit ourselves to the rights of men, women, children, youth, young adults, the aging, and people with disabilities; to improvement of the quality of life; and to the rights and dignity of racial, ethnic, and religious minorities.

We believe in the right and duty of persons to work for the glory of God and the good of themselves and others and in the protection of their welfare in so doing; in the rights to property as a trust from God, collective bargaining, and responsible consumption; and in the elimination of economic and social distress.

We dedicate ourselves to peace throughout the world, to the rule of justice and law among nations, and to individual freedom for all people of the world.

We believe in the present and final triumph of God's Word in human affairs and gladly accept our commission to manifest the life of the gospel in the world. Amen.

For Wesley "there is no religion but social religion, no holiness but social holiness." The UMC does not believe we grow as Christians in a vacuum, but in relationship with other believers. From this grounding, Christians then reach out to the world in global witness.

The United Methodist Church holds the unity of the church in high regard. If you're more comfortable with a Wesleyan theology than a Calvinistic one and have a heart for social justice, the UMC may be the church for you.

Wesleyan Church

The Holiness movement started in the mid-1800s. Advocates of holiness emphasized the importance of having a spiritual experience subsequent to salvation called sanctification. (Pentecostals, an offshoot of the Holiness movement, refer to this experience as being baptized in the Spirit.) Once sanctified, a person is set free of sin and able to live a holy, possibly even perfect, life.

Exactly what constituted "perfection" became the center of much discussion and controversy. Being perfect isn't easy, but if you are sanctified holy, you'd better behave yourself. To clarify the situation, many in the Holiness movement focused on

How many United Methodists does it take to change a lightbulb?

This statement was issued: "We choose not to make a statement either in favor of or against the need for a lightbulb. However, if in your own journey you have found that a lightbulb works for you, that is fine. You are invited to write a poem or compose a modern dance about your personal relationship with your lightbulb (or light source, or nondark resource), and present it next month at our annual lightbulb Sunday service, in which we will explore a number of lightbulb traditions, including incandescent, fluorescent, three-way, long-life, and tinted—all of which are equally valid paths to luminescence."

Just the **FACTS**

Wesleyan Church

Kind of Church: Protestant/Wesleyan
Worship Style: Traditional
Trinity Affinity: Son
Clout Continuum: 1st Place: Scripture
2nd Place: Personal experience
3rd Place: Wesleyan tradition
Founded in USA: 1843
Members in USA: 121,000
Churches in USA: 1,700
Headquarters: P.O. Box 50434
Indianapolis IN 46250
Phone: 816-333-7000
Web site: www.wesleyan.org

behavior, and took a strong stand against smoking, drinking, playing cards, joining secret societies, dancing, attending circuses, and other "worldly" entertainment. Women were expected to dress modestly, sans makeup or jewelry.

Through outside camp meetings and indoor, emotionally charged, spiritually vibrant gatherings, the Holiness movement gained momentum. Many were attracted to the movement out of concern that the Methodist church was overemphasizing social concerns to the neglect of spiritual well-being.

A number of Holiness churches sprang up throughout the country, loosely affiliated through personal relationships and identification with specific evangelists, speakers, and mentors. The first Holiness denomination to be founded was the Wesleyan Church, having separated from the Methodist Episcopal Church in 1843 over slavery. After the Civil War, Holiness became the denomination's guiding influence. According to their web site, "Wesleyans believe in one God, who is Father, Son and Holy Spirit, and the Savior of all men and women who put their faith in Him alone for eternal life. We velieve that hose who receive new life in Christ are called to be holy in character and conduct, and can only live this way by being filled with the Lord's Spirit. We believe in the Bible and seek to establish our faith and actions on its teachings. We believe God wills for people everywhere to know Him and that the purpose of the church is to tell the world about Christ through its worship, witness, and loving deeds." Today the church has approximately 121,356 members in 1,594 congregations.

Church of the Nazarene

The largest holiness denomination today is the Church of the Nazarene. The denomination's name was coined by Dr. Joseph P. Widney, the first dean of the School of Medicine at the University of Southern California. Widney's family was wealthy and influential in the early days of Los Angeles, contributing to such activities as founding of the University of Southern California and participating in the Flower Festival Society (the forerunner of Pasadena's Tournament of Roses). Joseph was a close friend of

What about Us Girls?

Those original Nazarene guys were ahead of their time by ordaining women from the get-go. Breaking with their mainline Methodist heritage, in their very first meeting they stated: "We recognize the equal rights of both men and women to all offices of the church including ministry." The founder, Phineas F. Bresee, was fond of saying, "Some of our best men are women."

Just the FACTS

Church of the Nazarene

Kind of Church: Protestant/Holiness/Conservative
Worship Style: Traditional (contemporary in some churches)
Trinity Affinity: Holy Spirit
Clout Continuum: 1st Place: Scripture
2nd Place: Personal experience
3rd Place: Tradition
Founded in USA: 1908
Members in USA: 643,568
Churches in USA: 5,101
Headquarters: 6401 The Paseo
Kansas City MO 64131
Phone: 816-333-7000
Web site: www.nazarene.org

Methodist minister Phineas F. Bresee, who came to Southern California in 1883.

By the late 1800s, relations were strained between the Methodist hierarchy and advocates of holiness. In 1895, Widney and Bresee launched the Church of the Nazarene. Widney proposed the name since Jesus, born in Nazareth, had been seen as lowly and insignificant because he was merely a Nazarene. Bresee embraced the name, as it captured a church in which rich and poor would find a spiritual home.

Bresee led the charge of "getting the glory down" in hand-clapping, hallelujah-shouting, and fiery sermons. Eventually Widney severed ties with the church to return to the Methodists. Some say he left because the services became too emotional for him, others cite doctrinal differences, still others argue that internal politics were to blame. For whatever reason, Bresee was left in charge and under his leadership the lone church rapidly turned into a denomination.

In 1907, the Association of Pentecostal Churches in America, primarily on the East Coast, merged with the Church of the Nazarene to become the Pentecostal Church of the Nazarene. The next year, a third group from the south, the Holiness Church of Christ, came on board. The denomination points this final merger in October 8, 1908, as its formal founding date. In 1919, the term "Pentecostal" was dropped from the name to distinguish between the Holiness movement and the Pentecostal movement.

The message of holiness continues to define the identity and mission of the Church of the Nazarene. Sanctification remains a cornerstone, also referred to as "Christian perfection," "perfect love," "heart purity," "the baptism of the Holy Spirit," "the fullness of the blessing," and "Christian Holiness." The web site states that "entire sanctification is that act of God, subsequent to regeneration, by which believers are made free from original sin, or depravity, and brought into a state of entire devotement to God, and the holy obedience of love made perfect. . . . We believe that there is a marked distinction between a pure heart and a mature character. The former is obtained in an instant, the result of entire sanctification; the latter is the result of growth in grace."

The church believes that the Scriptures were given to us "by

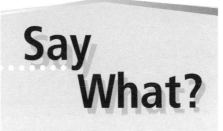

When I was a teenager, my family and I attended Bresee Church of the Nazarene in Pasadena, named after the denomination's founder. My friends and I referred to ourselves as "the holy Bresee-ers"—pronounced, of course, as "the holey brassieres."

plenary inspiration" and "contain all truth necessary to faith and Christian living." Like other Wesleyan denominations, Nazarenes believe in the Trinity, that atonement is available to everyone who has faith in Christ, and that believers are called to service to the poor and needy.

No church balances social and spiritual issues perfectly, and the Church of the Nazarene is no different. While there is a history of

Third Generation Nazarene

My grandfather was a Nazarene preacher who moved his family from the south to pastor a congregation in Southern California. He hired an especially handsome man as minister of worship. My mother, while visiting from college, batted her eyes in his direction and they were married seven months later. The rest, including my appearance on the planet, is history.

All in all, growing up in the Nazarene Church was a good thing. They got me memorizing Scripture as soon as I could read, and I have certificates and a framed picture of Jesus hammered out of copper to show for it. The Nazarenes are really into Bible quizzing—they even hold international competitions—so it's hard for those of us who grew up in its ranks not to emerge as amateur Bible scholars. By the time I graduated from a Nazarene college, I was thoroughly indoctrinated in the good news of Christ and the idiosyncrasies of my corner of Christendom.

On the downside, the Nazarene Church has been . . . well, how do I put this . . . it's been a bit legalistic, if not downright terrorizing. The Manual (to be said in a low, spiritual-sounding voice) outlines the denomination's doctrine and policy. It also lists out what you're not supposed to do, such as dancing, smoking, drinking, and going to movies. These activities were considered sin, and sinning Nazarene style means you go straight to hell, do not pass go, do not collect $200. I was twelve the first time I entered a

social concerns, the Nazarenes have placed more emphasis on salvation and sanctification than political activism. The government of the Church of the Nazarene is presbyterian. Six elected representatives serve on the Board of General Superintendents who administer the work of the church and serve as interpreters of the denomination's book of polity, the Manual of the Church of the Nazarene. If you are drawn to Wesleyan theology and feel comfortable in a conservative setting, the Church of the Nazarene may be a good place for you to visit.

What to Expect When You Visit

While both Methodist and Nazarene churches fall into the traditional worship category, Methodists include a bit more liturgy based on the English prayer book in their services. Worship services tend to begin with

movie theater, and then only by special parental decree to attend my non-Nazarene girlfriend's birthday party. I was wracked with guilt throughout the entire showing of *Mary Poppins*.

The good news is that the church is loosening up on things like dancing and going to movies, but I still get irritated when I run into the attitude that following Christ has more to do with what I do or don't do than in whom I believe (I'm with Luther on that one). Fortunately, the strong biblical training I received while growing up served me well when, as an adult, I reexamined my faith. Through life experience (and hanging around some Baptists), I've realized that God will never let me go, no matter how much I mess up.

Mostly Nazarenes are a friendly bunch. Just steer clear of the legalism, and you'll find a spiritual home that can nurture you in a personal, passionate relationship with God.

prayer, leading to singing of hymns or choruses, and Scripture reading. Like many Protestant churches, the sermon is the main event, and will usually last a minimum of twenty minutes. Communion is observed, but not every week. Expect bread or wafers and grape juice for the elements. Participation is open to all believers regardless of church affiliation.

Methodists tend to be less concerned with proper attire than the Nazarenes, but what you wear on your first visit depends on the area of the country you live in. On the East or West Coasts, the dress is more casual and a wider variety of fashion options are available. Women often wear pants, and younger people may even don jeans to these services. Churches in the Midwest and South tend to be more conservative. Hem lengths are eyed more often and sleeveless dresses are less acceptable in these areas. Men are always safe in a jacket and tie. But if you're in California, you can show up in just about anything.

More Methodist and Holiness Churches

Apostolic Christian Church of America
   www.apostolicchristian.org
Apostolic Overcoming Holy Church of God
   www.prairienet.org/stoah
Christian Methodist Episcopal Church
   www.c-m-e.org
Church of Christ (Holiness) USA
   www.cochusa.com/main.htm
Church of God (Holiness)
   www.kccbs.edu/cogh
Churches of Christ in Christian Union
   www.bright.net/~ccuhq

Evangelical Congregational Church
www.eccenter.com

Evangelical Methodist Church
www.emchurch.org

Free Methodist Church of North America
www.nafwb.org

Pillar of Fire
www.gospelcom.net/pof

Primitive Methodist Church, USA
www.primitivemethodistchurch.org

Southern Methodist Church
www.southernmethodistchurch.org

Further Info

- Kenneth J. Collins, *A Real Christian: The Life of John Wesley* (Abingdon, 1999)

- Hal Knight and Henry H. Knight III, *Eight Life-Enhancing Practices of United Methodists* (Abingdon, 2001)

- John R. Weinlick and Albert H. Frank, *The Moravian Church Through the Ages* (Moravian Church in America, 1989)

- Wes Tracy and Stan Ingersol, *What Is a Nazarene? Understanding Our Place in the Religious Community* (Beacon Hill Press, 1998)

thirteen

Pentecostal and Charismatic
Churches

Agnes Ozman, a young student Bethel Bible College in Topeka, Kansas, started it all on New Year's Day, 1901. At a gathering led by Charles F. Parham, a holiness evangelist and faith healer, she spoke a language no one could understand. Based on descriptions of similar happenings in Acts, it was believed that Agnes and those who had similar experiences were baptized in the Holy Spirit. The Pentecostal revival had begun.

A Brief History of the Pentecosal and Charismatic Movements

The Pentecostal movement was deeply influenced by Holiness revivals that stressed a "second blessing" called sanctification. To

Holiness preachers, sanctification was an experience a believer had after salvation, in which one's sinful nature was eradicated. Subsequently, a sanctified believer could lead a life of holiness or even perfection. The Pentecostals tweaked this doctrine by viewing this "second blessing" as the empowerment or indwelling of the Holy Spirit. To those in the Holiness movement, living a holy lifestyle was evidence

How Did Pentecostals Get Their Name?

Not long after Jesus' ascension into heaven, during the Jewish holy period called Pentecost, about one hundred and twenty of Jesus' followers, including Mary and other faithful women, met together in a large room. The room was suddenly filled with the sound of a violent wind and "tongues as of fire" appeared over the heads of everyone there. Each person was filled with the power of the Holy Spirit and began to talk in languages none of them knew how to speak.

Jerusalem was a multicultural city with people from all parts of the Roman Empire—people from Mesopotamia, Asia, Egypt, Libya, and Rome. The believers went outside and began telling people about Jesus in these different languages. People were amazed that this group of Jews was suddenly multilingual, and a large crowd gathered. Peter preached the first sermon as the crowd listened in awe, many of them converting on the spot. The believers, mockingly called "little Christs" or Christians, spread their miraculous story of Jesus throughout Jerusalem and then beyond the city gates.

Today's Pentecostals derived their name by harkening back to the Day of Pentecost when believers were given the gift of tongues as evidence of the presence of the Holy Spirit.

of being sanctified. In contrast, Pentecostal sanctification was evidenced by the presence of spiritual gifts, specifically the ability to speak in a language the speaker did not previously know.

Agnes got the charismatic tongues speaking in Kansas, and the movement spread quickly throughout the country. A mission on Azusa Street in Los Angeles became the icon for all things Pentecostal. At the helm was an African-American Holiness preacher named William J. Seymour who, in 1906, was originally invited to speak in Los Angeles at a Nazarene church. However, when Seymour insisted that the gift of tongues was the true test of being filled with the Spirit, he was shown the door.

Seymour soon found another venue for his preaching, and a revival started that some claim comprised of three services every day for nearly three-and-a-half years. Vinson Synan, in the introduction of *Azusa Street,* a first-hand account by Frank Bartleman, wrote, "Tongues-speaking was the central attraction, but healing of the sick was not far behind. The walls were soon covered with the crutches and canes of those who were miraculously healed. The gift of tongues was soon followed by the gift of interpretation. As time passed, Seymour and his followers claimed that all the gifts of the Spirit had been restored to the church."

There's rarely been a dull moment in the movement since—with emphasis placed on the term "movement." If you've ever been to a pentecostal service, you know what I mean—it's a visceral experience. It's usually very hands-on, so to speak: lots of hand clapping, hand waving, and laying on of hands. There's also singing that seems to lift you off your feet, crying and laughing and dancing, praying in groups, praying out loud, prayers in words that don't even make sense to those praying them—but somehow, in the midst of the hoopla, something important seems to be happening.

Tongues—A Dividing Line

Not everyone accepted the display of spiritual gifts. Few groups in recent history have garnered as much criticism, fear, or outright rejection as modern Pentecostals—and that's just the reaction from other Christians. To be fair, the energy bursting from these churches seems to demand a response of some sort—either get on board or get out of the way. And there have certainly been histrionics, theatrics, and a few con artists among the genuinely blessed and gifted.

The movement insisted that speaking in tongues was the true test of being baptized in the Spirit. Even though the Church of the Nazarene had an equally emotional and vivacious beginning with revival meetings galore, the denomination distanced itself from the movement over the "tongues" issue and soon removed the term "Pentecostal" from its original name. By 1928, fundamentalist churches formally "disfellowshiped" all Pentecostals from their ranks. Initially the vast majority of mainline Christians either knew little or nothing of the movement or dismissed it as another heresy among the "holy rollers." Not finding a welcome mat in front of established denominations, hundreds of new churches sprung up all over country with a distinctively Pentecostal identity.

Charismatic Renewal

The 1960s and 1970s were a time of tremendous change in America and in the Pentecostal movement. Denominational barriers were challenged as Pentecostalism spread among Christians who attended a variety of non-Pentecostal churches. More and more Catholics, Orthodox, and Protestants experienced the "baptism" of the Spirit and were becoming known as the Charismatic Renewal movement.

For the most part, charismatic Christians maintain the doctrinal stands of the church affiliation with the addition of a belief in full expression of Spiritual gifts. Some denominations have adamantly resisted the movement and removed clergy who participated in the movement. However, others have made room for their charismatic members, such as the Catholic and Episcopal churches.

Signs and Wonders

A "third wave" of Pentecostalism started in the late 1970s through the ministries of C. Peter Wagner of Fuller Theological Seminary and John Wimber, who founded VineyardUSA. After experiencing personal healing, Wagner embraced the expression of spiritual gifts, writing and speaking extensively on the subject. Wagner brought Wimber to Fuller to teach a class on "Signs and Wonders," focusing on divine healing. Due to controversy, the class was discontinued in 1985, but the movement continues.

What Makes a Church Pentecostal or Charismatic?

Theologically and organizationally, the Pentecostal movement traces its roots to Methodism and the teachings of John Wesley and are similar doctrinally in many respects to evangelicals, Holiness, and conservative Protestants. These similarities include belief in the divine inspiration of Scripture, the deity of Jesus, original sin, and the saving power of faith in Christ. Baptism, usually by immersion, and the Lord's Supper are practiced as ordinances, not sacraments.

However, Pentecostal denominations are distinctive in the way they perceive the role of the Holy Spirit and in the way they express their faith. Pentecostals and Charismatics generally see the baptism of the

Spirit as a second blessing, in which a believer receives an infilling or release of the Holy Spirit after a conversion experience. Spiritual baptism can be evidenced in a variety of ways, such as having a sense of personal peace, physical shaking or falling down, a release of emotion through crying or laughing, the emergence of specific gifts such as healing or prophecy, or experiencing "glossolalia"—speaking in tongues. Some churches teach that the gift of tongues is always evidenced when one is baptized in the Spirit, while others believe that this particular gift may be given, but not always. Since these churches teach that today's believer can receive and exercise the same spiritual gifts the apostles did in the early church, it is common to find "apostolic" in their current name or names that may have used in the past.

> **How many Assembly of God church members does it take to change a lightbulb?**
>
> Just one—he already has his hands in the air.

Assemblies of God

The General Council of the Assemblies of God (AG) was formed in 1914 when separate congregations, or assemblies, felt the need to build more formal ties to each other in order to cultivate doctrinal unity, share resources for missions efforts, and provide legal benefits of church charters. Each congregation is self-governing and self-supporting.

AG doctrine was outlined two years later when, in 1916, the Statement of Fundamental Truths was developed. Today, this statement stands "virtually unchanged and continues to provide a sound basis for the Fellowship, giving a firm position on vital doctrines." Sixteen doctrinal stands

Just the FACTS

Assemblies of God

Kind of Church: Protestant/Pentecostal
Worship Style: Contemporary
Trinity Affinity: Holy Spirit
Clout Continuum: 1st Place: Personal experience
2nd Place: Scripture
3rd Place: Tradition
Founded in USA: 1914
Members in USA: 2,577,560
Churches in USA: 12,084
Headquarters: The Assemblies of God
1445 North Boonville Ave.
Springfield MO 65802
Phone: 417-862-2781
Web site: www.ag.org

are described in the AG Statement, and can be read in their entirety by logging onto their web site. Some distinctive highlights include:

The Scriptures

According to the AG web site, "The Scriptures, both the Old and New Testaments, are verbally inspired of God and are the revelation of God to man, the infallible, authoritative rule of faith and conduct."

The Nature of God

The AG goes to great length to clarify their view of God and emphasize their understanding of the Trinity. This distinction is significant to this fellowship due to a doctrinal controversy within its ranks, resulting in the splitting off and creation of the United Pentecostal Church International. The United Pentecostal Church International does not hold to the traditional view of the Trinity. The AG asserts that "The one true God has revealed Himself as the eternally self-existent 'I AM,' the Creator of heaven and earth and the Redeemer of mankind. He has further revealed Himself as embodying the principles of relationship and association as Father, Son and Holy Ghost. . . . We therefore may speak with propriety of the Lord our God who is One Lord, as a trinity or as one Being of three persons, and still be absolutely scriptural."

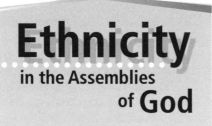

Ethnicity
in the Assemblies
of God

The ethnic makeup of AG congregations illustrates that the Pentecostal movement, while initiated by an African-American pastor, has drawn a variety of racial and ethnic groups. The following specifies AG churches by race:

White: 73%
Hispanic: 16%
Asian & Pacific Islander: 4%
Other: 4%
African American: 2%
Native American: 1%

Jesus Christ

In alignment with other conservative and evangelical denominations, the AG believes that "the Lord Jesus Christ is the eternal Son of God. The Scriptures declare His virgin birth, His sinless life, His miracles, His substitutionary work on the cross, His bodily resurrection from the dead, and His exaltation to the right hand of God."

Ordinances

Two ordinances are observed: baptism by immersion and a symbolic view of the Lord's Supper.

Baptism in the Holy Ghost

Perhaps the most important doctrinal distinctive for AG is their assertion that "The baptism of believers in the Holy Ghost is witnessed by the initial physical sign of speaking with other tongues as the Spirit of God gives them utterance."

Often more conservative denominations do not ordain women. However, the AG supports women in all aspects of ministry. Of the 32,310 certified, licensed, ordained, and specialized licensed AG clergy, 16.5 percent are women.

In an effort to strengthen the ties between AG churches and congregations of other denominational affiliation, the associations have been formed with:

- National Association of Evangelicals (NAE)
- The Pentecostal and Charismatic Churches of North America (PCCNA)
- The Pentecostal World Fellowship (PWF)
- The World Assemblies of God Fellowship (WAGF)

Assemblies of God traces its heritage to the beginnings of the American Pentecostal movement. If you want to worship in a congregation that makes room for the expression of spiritual gifts and has nearly ninety years of maturity, an Assemblies of God congregation may be for you.

International Church of the Foursquare Gospel

Los Angeles was the site of a second Pentecostal movement that hit full stride in the early 1920s. Exuberant and inspiring, thirty-something Aimee Semple McPherson preached to standing-room-only crowds at

Just the **FACTS**

International Church
of the Foursquare Gospel

Kind of Church:	Protestant/Charismatic/Conservative
Worship Style:	Contemporary
Trinity Affinity:	Holy Spirit
Clout Continuum:	1st Place: Personal experience
	2nd Place: Scripture
	3rd Place: Tradition
Founded in USA:	1923
Members in USA:	269,349
Churches in USA:	1,834
Headquarters:	1910 W. Sunset Blvd., Suite 400
	Los Angeles CA 90026
Phone:	213-989-4220
Web site:	www.foursquare.org

the 530-seat Angelus Temple in Los Angeles. Her message was eventually simplified into what she called the "Foursquare Gospel," which comprised of four major cornerstones of Christian doctrine: Christ as Savior, Baptizer with the Holy Spirit, Great Physician, and Soon-Coming King. The denomination that grew out of her work bears the same name as her message: the International Church of the Foursquare Gospel.

In a nutshell, Foursquare churches share their basic beliefs with Holiness and Pentecostal traditions.

- The Bible is held to be "true, immutable, steadfast and as unchangeable as its author, the Lord Jehovah."
- Baptism by immersion and the Lord's Supper are practiced as symbolic expressions of faith.

- Emphasis is placed on healing the sick through prayers of faith.
- The second coming of Christ is imminent.
- The Baptism of the Holy Spirit is evidenced by speaking in tongues.

As is true of most Holiness and Pentecostal groups, ordination is extended to women as well as men. Since the church was founded by a woman, this issue was resolved from day one. Today 30 percent of the ordained clergy are women.

One aspect of distinction that warrants mentioning is the Foursquare approach to evangelism. Their web site states, "it's the task to

The Foursquare Gospel

Jesus Christ as . . .
- The Savior of the world—"But He was wounded for our transgressions, He was bruised for our iniquities; the chastisement for our peace was upon Him . . ." Isaiah 53:5.
- The Baptizer with the Holy Spirit—"For John truly baptized with water, but you shall be baptized with the Holy Spirit . . . you shall receive power when the Holy Spirit has come upon you; and you shall be witnesses to Me in Jerusalem, and in all Judea and Samaria, and to the ends of the earth" Acts 1:5,8.
- The Great Physician—"He Himself took our infirmities and bore our sicknesses . . ." Matthew 8:17.
- The Soon-Coming King—"For the Lord Himself will descend from heaven with a shout . . . the dead in Christ will rise first. Then we who are alive and remain shall be caught up together with them in the clouds to meet the Lord in the air. And thus we shall always be with the Lord" 1 Thessalonians 4:16–1.

present Christ in the language, culture and understanding of the hearer, rather than of the speaker or church body. Jesus Christ is to be the incarnate Word to this age." Their focus on translating the gospel into language and concepts that communicate to various ethnic and age groups is expanding their outreach to a wide variety of people. They claim that in 1999 alone 815,365 adults and children "accepted Christ as their personal Savior" through the church's ministries. They now have churches in 107 countries, with nearly 38,000 ministers and lay leaders.

The Foursquare Church is affiliated with:

- The National Association of Evangelicals
- The American Bible Society
- Pentecostal/Charismatic Churches of North America
- Pentecostal World Conference
- Evangelical Fellowship of Missions Agencies

VineyardUSA

What do the Righteous Brothers and the Vineyard churches have in common? The same man was instrumental (get it? instrumental?) in getting these groups going—none other than musician, John Wimber.

It seems that most of the people who spearhead denominations are rather colorful, if not outrageous. John was of this ilk. He started out as a keyboardist for the Righteous Brothers, but then another musician invited him to a Quaker Bible study. *Christianity Today* described John as a "beer-guzzling, drug-abusing pop musician, who was converted at the age of 29 while chainsmoking his way through a Quaker-led Bible

Just the FACTS

VineyardUSA

Kind of Church: Protestant/Charismatic
Worship Style: Contemporary
Trinity Affinity: Holy Spirit
Clout Continuum: 1st Place: Personal experience
2nd Place: Scripture
3rd Place: Tradition
Founded in USA: 1977
Members in USA: 150,433
Churches in USA: 539
Headquarters: P.O. Box 2089, Stafford TX 77497
Phone: 281-313-8463
Web site: www.voa.org

study." John and his wife, Carol, became Christians and John left music for the ministry.

In 1982, after serving for several years in the Quaker church and then Calvary Chapel, John joined forces with Kenn Gulliksen, a prolific church planter affiliated with Calvary Chapel. Kenn coined the name "Vineyard," and John stepped into leadership. John was convinced that all the biblical gifts of the Spirit were available to Christians today. According to the Vineyard web site, the movement has "sought to hold in tension the biblical doctrines of the Christian faith with an ardent pursuit of the present day work of the Spirit of God."

Drawing from the evangelical tradition, the Vineyard teaches that the Bible is the final authority for faith and practice. In line with charismatic and Pentecostals beliefs, opportunity is given for the exercise of all of the spiritual gifts. John Wimber's musical background is evidenced in the worship services through a unique brand of worship music developed at the Vineyard. Churches of other denominations that include "contemporary worship" in their services often use Vineyard songs or a similar music style. CDs and tapes can be purchased through their web site.

Under John's leadership, the Vineyard grew rapidly, with a number of congregations springing up all over the world. Even though Wimber was thought by many to be "out there" in his teachings on healing, the gift of tongues, words of knowledge, and the like, John did not agree with the more extreme teachings of the Toronto Airport Vineyard. The disagreement resulted in conflict among congregants, and the Toronto group was "cut free."

Toward the end of his life, John suffered a heart attack, was diagnosed with cancer, had a stroke, and eventually died in 1997 of a mas-

The Righteous Brothers

In spite of the word "righteous" in their name, the Righteous Brothers have nothing to do with Christian denominations. I just thought I'd throw them in since they were mentioned in the Vineyard Church section. Bill Medley and Bobby Hatfield weren't brothers but they were righteous in the "blue-eyed soul" of the mid-1960s sort of way. Their biggest hits were "You've Lost That Lovin' Feeling" and "(You're My) Soul and Inspiration." In 1987, Bill sang "(I've Had) The Time of My Life" with Jennifer Warnes, a song that was wildly successful after being included in the movie *Dirty Dancing*. Another big hit for Bill and Bobby was "Unchained Melody," which was included in the soundtrack for *Ghost*.

Amazing Aimee

Hoping to introduce a calming influence on his teenage daughter, James Kennedy took Aimee to a Pentecostal tent revival near their farm in Ontario, Canada. James was concerned about his daughter's love of stage performance and dancing and cavorting and such—not at all acceptable activities for a young lady in the early 1900s. Up on the make-shift stage, a Scottish evangelist named Robert Semple fervently preached with a brogue and spoke in an unknown tongue. Seventeen-year-old Aimee was mesmerized.

Aimee had a life-changing spiritual experience at that tent meeting. Along with a new-found love for God, Aimee fell head over heels for twenty-seven-year-old Robert Semple. The attraction was mutual, and within a few months they married. The year was 1908.

Robert's call to evangelism was no hardship on Aimee, who gladly joined him on tour throughout England, Scotland, Ireland, Hong Kong, and other parts of China. Sadly, soon after their second wedding anniversary and right before the birth of their first child, Robert died of malaria in Hong Kong. Aimee survived her bout with the disease, but returned to the States a widow, with Roberta, her infant daughter.

While involved in evangelism in Chicago, Aimee met and married Harold McPherson, an accountant, in 1912. Harold soon found out that Aimee was not destined to be a traditional wife and mother. In one ear, she heard the voice of God telling her to preach. In the other was Harold saying no. After the birth of her second child and recovering from a life-threatening illness, Aimee opted for a life as a traveling evangelist and left Harold behind to iron his own shirts.

After a few years on the road, Aimee divorced Harold. She and her children landed in Los Angeles in 1918. Within five years, Aimee had attracted a large audience, raised the funds for the 5,500-seat Angelus Temple, and established what would become the Foursquare Gospel denomination. In addition, she founded a Bible college called Lighthouse of International

Foursquare Evangelism (referred to as L.I.F.E) and the Echo Park Evangelistic Association. Aimee matched her words with action, and during the Great Depression it is estimated that over a million-and-a-half people were fed through her ministries.

Her revival services were full-scale productions with elaborate sets (Charlie Chaplin gave her seating pointers), live musicians (Anthony Quinn played sax in her live band), colorful costumes, choirs, and special effects, including smoking dry ice and dramatic lighting. Her revivals were legendary for manifestations of the divine and healings were a mainstay. Although big on healing, Aimee distanced herself from other Pentecostal groups by downplaying manifestations of spiritual gifts such as speaking in tongues. As a consequence, her preaching appealed to those who generally saw Pentecostalism as peculiar or outside mainstream society.

Always on the cutting edge, Aimee recognized the potential in radio and was the first woman to attain a FCC radio license. In 1924, she bought her own radio station—KFSG short for Kall For Square Gospel, which was the only the third commissioned radio station in Los Angeles at the time, pioneering evangelism over the air waves. Her influence grew rapidly as her radio shows garnered a larger audience than could ever fit into the Angelus Temple. Press coverage, first local, then national, made her a focal point of intense loyalty or cruel criticism.

Her public image suffered greatly, beginning in 1926 through the end of her life in 1944. Aimee's personal life was a tabloid journalist's dream as she bounced from one fiasco to another. First, it was reported that she had been kidnapped and murdered. But when she resurfaced, the press uncovered witnesses (who later recanted, then recanted their recantations) who claimed her kidnapping was a cover for an affair she was having or perhaps the birth of a child. Before it was over, the Los Angeles District Attorney's office charged her and others with falsifying police reports and manufacturing evidence. Throughout the process of testifying before the grand jury and being featured in countless headlines across the nation's newspa-

sive brain hemorrhage at the age of 63. The Vineyard churches had difficulties organizationally in John's absence, but have since stabilized. They moved their headquarters from Southern California to Texas in 2000 and are going strong.

What to Expect When You Visit

While service structure may vary from denomination to denomination, it is common for Pentecostal churches to be more informal,

pers, Aimee insisted she was innocent. Finally, the charges were dropped in 1927.

But this was not the last time Aimee would tangle with the courts. Her next encounter with the legal system resulted from her third marriage to David Hutton, a vaudeville actor who sang at the Temple. In 1931, Aimee became Aimee Semple McPherson Hutton. Within days of the marriage announcement, a chorus girl named Hazel St. Pierre brought suit against David for breach of promise. Hazel won the suit. After David and Aimee divorced in 1934, she dropped his name from the list.

Allegations of legal and financial wrongdoing from within the organization resulted in several rounds of lawsuits—one initiated by an associate pastor and another by Aimee's own daughter. The strain of infighting and the loss of public esteem left Aimee physically drained and emotionally wrought. After turning over the Foursquare church to the leadership of her son, Rolf, she left Los Angeles on her final speaking tour. At the age of 53, Aimee died in Oakland, apparently from an accidental overdose of sleeping pills. Her ending may have an aura of tragedy, but I suspect Aimee would want us to remember her as a dynamic woman who lived her life on the edge, preached hope to the poor and despairing, and left the world with a thriving denomination.

less liturgical, and more spontaneous than other arms of Christendom. Opportunity to share one's spiritual gifts is often part of a service, with time for ministry through prayer, laying hands on those who are sick, and sharing visions and words of knowledge people have received from God.

Some congregations may be traditional in their selection of worship music, but many utilize contemporary songs accompanied by

The Jesus Movement

In the 1960s, when the counterculture was in full swing, the Jesus movement offered an alternative to sex, drugs, and rock and roll (well, not to rock and roll—they kept that part). Similar to the hippie movement at large, San Francisco's Haight Asbury district served as the spawning grounds for counterculture Christianity. Jesus Freaks were represented more heavily along the Pacific coast states, but here and there the movement made an impact in the Midwest and East Coast. In part, the movement was spontaneously initiated by Christian hippies who had a faith to share, but it was also fed and funded by churches and parachurch organizations, such as Calvary Chapel and Campus Crusade for Christ, who wanted to reach out to the counterculture youth. As a consequence, coffee houses, nightclubs, storefront missions, counterculture Bible studies, Christian communities, underground newspapers, and music festivals were everywhere.

With Nixon's political demise and the end of the Vietnam War, "the '60s" finally came to an end in the mid-1970s. The counterculture as a whole wound down, and so did the Jesus movement. Unless you personally participated in ocean baptisms, danced at Jesus Rock festivals like Explo '72, strummed your guitar at a Christian coffee house, or ever referred to yourself as a "Jesus Freak," the Jesus movement probably has no signifi-

electric guitars and drums. Expect the unexpected in Pentecostal services, in which personal expression is valued over a structured service.

In general, denominations that grew out of the early Pentecostal movement, such as the Assemblies of God and the Foursquare Church, are more traditional in dress—especially on a Sunday morning. Even if a particular congregation accepts casual dress, men will show respect by wearing a jacket and tie and women attend in a dress or skirt. On the other hand, if you attend a church that has been heavily influenced by the Charismatic movement, you'll be overdressed in a tie. Nice casual clothes are your safest bet if you're visiting a congregation that is affiliated with VineyardUSA, Calvary Chapel, or other more recently founded denominations.

cance to you. It seems to barely warrant a blip on the screens of Christian historians and scholars.

However, the Jesus movement left its mark on the American Christian culture as a whole in the music it left behind. Rock and roll is the language of youth. This is as true today as it was back in the 1960s. The Jesus movement made a crack in the wall of traditional worship and washed over the contemporary Christian music world like a tidal wave. Worship services in nearly every denomination have been influenced by the Jesus movement with the introduction of electric and acoustic guitars, drums, tambourines, and a solid rock beat. Traditionalists might bemoan the fact that this rowdy music was ever allowed inside the church doors, but to the younger set and those young at heart, music that moves the body and soul is at the center of life-changing worship. I include myself in this camp and agree with Larry Norman, an icon of the movement, when he sang, "Why should the devil have all the good music?"

More Pentecostal and Charismatic Churches

Assemblies of the Lord Jesus Christ
  www.aljc.org
Church of God (Cleveland, Tennessee)
  www.chog.org
Church of Our Lord Jesus Christ of the Apostolic Faith, Inc.
  www.apostolic-faith.org
Congregational Holiness Church
  www.ch.church.com
Full Gospel Fellowship of Churches and Ministers, International
  www.fgfcmi.org

Calvary Chapel

Chuck Smith, founder of Calvary Chapel in Costa Mesa, California, was a key mover and shaker in the Jesus movement. If you've ever seen pictures of people being baptized in the Pacific Ocean, most likely it was someone from Calvary Chapel. Starting out with twenty-five people in 1965, Chuck claims that an estimated twenty thousand individuals converted to Christianity in a two-year period in the mid-1970s, with over eight thousand baptisms performed.

According to Chuck, "Calvary Chapel has been formed as a fellowship of believers in the Lordship of Jesus Christ. Our supreme desire is to know Christ and be conformed to His image by the power of the Holy Spirit. We are not a denominational church, nor are we opposed to denominations as such, only to their over-emphasis of the doctrinal differences that have led to the division of the Body of Christ." Preach it, Chuck! If you want to learn more about Calvary Chapel, check out their web site at www.calvarychapel.com.

International Pentecostal Church of Christ
www.http.members.aol.com/hqipcc/

International Pentecostal Holiness Church
www.iphc.org

Pentecostal Church of God
www.pcg.org

Pentecostal Free Will Baptist Church, Inc.
www.pfwb.org

Further Info

- Eddie L. Hyatt, *2000 Years of Charismatic Christianity: A 21st Century Look at Church History from a Pentecostal/Charismatic Perspective* (Charisma House, 2002)

- Stanley M. Burgess and Ed M. Van Der Maas, eds., *New International Dictionary of Pentecostal and Charismatic Movements* (Zondervan, 2002)

- Stanley M. Horton, ed., *Systematic Theology: A Pentecostal Perspective* (Gospel, 1994)

Doin' the Stuff

Shortly after John Wimber became a Christian, he became a voracious Bible reader. The Scriptures excited him. Finally, after weeks of reading about life-transforming miracles in the Bible and attending boring church services, John asked one of the lay leaders, "When do we get to do the stuff?"

"What stuff?" asked the leader.

"You know, the stuff here in the Bible," said John. "You know, like stuff Jesus did—raising people from the dead, healing the blind and the paralyzed. You know, that stuff."

"Well, we don't do that anymore," the man said. "You don't? Well what do you do?" asked John.

"What we did this morning," replied the man.

In frustration, John responded: "For that I gave up drugs?"

fourteen

Mennonite
Churches

The Anabaptists had a way of alienating everyone. First off, they were Protestants, so the Roman Catholic Church wasn't fond of them. But even other Protestants were annoyed with the Anabaptists. For one thing, the Anabaptists weren't all that concerned with fighting over liturgy or the sacraments or even about proper doctrine like all the other Protestants were. Rather, they focused on Jesus' Sermon on the Mount from Matthew 5:1–7:29 as a blueprint for living, not just believing. This bugged Protestant theologian types who were tussling over matters the Anabaptists thought were peripheral.

It also didn't help public relation that the Anabaptists insisted that Luther, Zwingli, and Calvin did not take the Reformation far enough. The "moderate" Protestants didn't take kindly to this opposition—

after all, they were the ones who were protesting. How dare this group protest against them!

Another point of contention was the Anabaptists' view of baptism. The first Anabaptist congregation was formed in 1525 in Zurich. Three years earlier, Zwingli had been instrumental in the conversion of Conrad Grebel. Grebel's study of Scripture led him to see baptism not as a sacrament as much as a public testimony of one's personal faith. Even though most of the Anabaptists had been baptized as infants in the Roman Catholic Church, they decided to rebaptize each other as adult believers as a confession of faith. Consequently, they became known as the rebaptizers or Anabaptists. A couple of days after Grebel baptized the first adult in his congregation in 1525, the Zurich city

Do You Swear or Affirm?

Did you ever wonder why we're asked "Do you solemnly swear *or affirm* . . ." when making an important statement? Christian groups, like the Mennonites, took Jesus seriously when he said ". . . I say to you, make no oath at all, either by heaven, for it is the throne of God, or by the earth, for it is the footstool of His feet, or by Jerusalem, for it is the city of the great King. Nor shall you make an oath by your head, for you cannot make one hair white or black. But let your statement be , 'Yes, yes' or 'No, no'; and anything beyond these is of evil" (Matt. 5:34–37). To allow for religious freedom, the U.S. allows for affirming rather than swearing that a statement is true. In fact, one U.S. President, Franklin Pierce, 1853 to 1857, chose to be affirmed rather than sworn into office. Pierce was an Episcopalian, but nevertheless felt compelled to affirm.

council decreed that anyone who refused to baptize an infant eight days old or younger would be forced to leave the city.

Baptizing each other wasn't nearly as hard to handle as their assertion that the church should be separated from the state. This ran against the grain of most Protestant reformers who were working tirelessly to influence political attitudes and structure. Mainstream Protestantism was fundamentally a religious movement, but it was inextricably intertwined with politics. Radical Protestantism was not. The two camps argued their cases before the Zurich city council and the Anabaptists were sent packing.

John Calvin had the same trouble with them in Geneva. Calvin saw the Anabaptists as a threat to his vision of bringing Geneva's civil government under the control of the church and enforcing the rule of the church through civil government—and they were. The Anabaptists weren't about to let anyone tell them what to do. They were pacifists, but stubborn as can be, and they would rather die than submit to civil authority, no matter how much it dressed up in religious garb. So the Anabaptists got the boot from Geneva as well.

They had a hard time finding anywhere to hang their hats—in part because the Anabaptists were unwilling to take oaths, which were mandatory in legal and financial proceedings. In essence, they refused to play the political, legal, and religious game. The game players didn't like that.

The Anabaptists emerged as a countercultural movement that religious and governmental bodies saw as a threat. They were thrown out of cities, hunted down, and harshly persecuted from all sides. It's estimated that between 1531 and 1597 over fifteen hundred Mennonites were martyred, most by being burned at the stake. Those who stayed in Europe went into hiding and taught their beliefs to their children, afraid to go public. You have to give these people credit: with all they endured, they tenaciously held to a stand for nonviolence. That impresses me. It's only by God's grace that any of the Anabaptists survived at all.

A Brief History of Mennonite Churches

In 1534 the first Anabaptist congregation in Holland was formed. Two years later, a forty-year-old Catholic priest, Menno Simons, joined the church and their cause after his brother had been martyred for his Anabaptist faith. A devout student of Scripture, Menno's teachings emphasized the importance of Christian community, sharing of resources with other believers, providing support to widows, their children, and the poor, leading a simple lifestyle, and nonviolent peacemaking.

As Menno Used to Say

True evangelical faith cannot lie dormant.
- It clothes the naked.
- It feeds the hungry.
- It comforts the sorrowful.
- It shelters the destitute.
- It serves those that harm it.
- It binds up that which is wounded.
- It has become all things to all people.

Unfortunately, his theological and political enemies were quite willing to use physical force to try to put an end to this way of thinking. Menno spent many years on the road, having been declared a fugitive by Emperor Charles V. His travels put him in contact with many groups of Anabaptists, giving him opportunity to teach his views as he went.

I'm glad to report that Menno was never captured, and he died of natural causes in his sixties. Menno so shaped the theology as well as the growth of this movement that the Anabaptists became known as the Mennonites (which is why you won't find any churches called "Anabaptist" around your neighborhood today).

Mennonites in America

Quaker William Penn (1644–1718) was sympathetic to the Mennonite cause. In 1683 he offered them asylum in the colonies, and thirteen families fled to Pennsylvania. Subsequently, thousands of German, Swiss, French, and Russian Mennonites settled throughout Pennsylvania, Ohio, Virginia, Indiana, Illinois, and some western states.

Today there are a number of denominations that grew out of the Anabaptist movement in America, including the Mennonite Church, Old Order Amish, General Conference Mennonite, Mennonite Brethren, Brethren in Christ, Church of the Brethren, Old Order Mennonite, and Evangelical Mennonite. There are nearly twenty Mennonite groupings in North America alone.

What Makes a Church Mennonite?

Most Mennonite groups affirm three statements of faith—the Schleitheim Confession of Faith drafted in 1527, the Dordrecht Confession of Faith of 1632, and the more recently revised Mennonite Confession of Faith of 1963. While some groups adhere more strictly to certain standards of behavior, generally speaking, most Mennonites agree with the following summary of the mennonite confession of Faith of 1963:

- God eternally exists as Father, Son, and Holy Spirit.
- God has revealed himself in the Scriptures of the Old and New Testaments, the inspired Word of God, and supremely in his Son, the Lord Jesus Christ.

- God created all things by His Son; humanity was created in the divine image, with free will, moral character, and a spiritual nature.

- Humanity fell into sin, bringing depravity and death upon the race; that as sinner, man is self-centered and self-willed, unwilling and unable to break with sin.

- There is one Mediator between God and men, the Man Christ Jesus, who died to redeem us from sin and arose for our justification.

- Salvation is by grace through faith in Christ, a free gift bestowed by God on those who repent and believe.

- The Holy Spirit convicts of sin, effects the new birth, gives guidance in life, empowers for service, and enables perseverance in faith and holiness.

- The church is the body of Christ, the brotherhood of the redeemed, a disciplined people obedient to the Word of God, and a fellowship of love, intercession, and healing.

- Christ commissioned the church to go into all the world, making disciples of all the nations, and ministering to every human need.

- It is the will of God that there should be ministers to teach the Word, to serve as leaders, to administer the ordinances, to lead the church in the exercise of discipline, and to serve as pastors and teachers.

- Those who repent and believe should be baptized with water as a symbol of baptism with the Spirit, cleansing from sin, and commitment to Christ.

- The church should observe the communion of the Lord's Supper as a symbol of his broken body and shed blood, and of the fellowship of his church, until his return.

- The washing of the saints' feet as a symbol of brotherhood, cleansing, and service, and in giving the right hand of fellowship and the holy kiss as symbols of Christian love.

- God has established unique roles for man and woman, symbolized by man's bared head in praying and prophesying, and by woman's veiled head.

- Christian marriage is intended by God to be the union of one man and one woman for life, and that Christians shall marry only in the Lord.

- Christians are not to be conformed to the world, but should seek to conform to Christ in every area of life.

- Christians are to be open and transparent in life, ever speaking the truth, and employing no oaths.

- It is the will of God for Christians to refrain from force and violence in human relations and to show Christian love to all men.

- The state is ordained of God to maintain order in society, and that Christians should honor rulers, be subject to authorities, witness to the state, and pray for governments.

- At death the unsaved enter into everlasting punishment and the saved into conscious bliss with Christ, who is coming again, and will raise the dead, sit in judgment, and bring in God's everlasting kingdom.

Mennonite Church USA

The Mennonite Church USA grew out of the original group that landed in Germantown, Pennsylvania, in 1683. The concept and the experience of community is highly valued among Mennonites. Some go so far as to share housing and resources, but most connect to one

Just the **FACTS**

Mennonite Church USA

Kind of Church:	Radical Protestant
Worship Style:	Free-Form
Trinity Affinity:	Son
Clout Continuum:	1st Place: Scripture
	2nd Place: Personal experience
	3rd Place: Tradition
Founded in USA:	1725
Members in USA:	92,002
Churches in USA:	935
Headquarters:	P.O. Box 1245
	Elkhart IN 46515-1245
Phone:	574-294-7523
Web site:	www.mennonites.org

another as a church family. Brent Alderfer and Vern Rempel wrote in *The Mennonite,* March 2, 1999, "If we haul our flesh and bones out and down to the meeting, we are doing the work of community. We are combating isolation—the urge to privacy. We let ourselves look each other in the eye, smell the smell, shake the hand, give the hug, experience the body language. Community doesn't happen by remote control."

In 1995 a new Confession of Faith in a Mennonite Perspective was adopted. A summary from their web site includes:

We believe that God exists and that God became flesh through Jesus Christ who is the Savior of the world. We believe in the Holy Spirit and that all Scripture is inspired by God through the Holy Spirit.

We believe that God created the world and that God created human beings in God's image. We believe that humanity has sinned but that through Jesus, God offers salvation and a new way of life.

We believe that the church is the assembly of those who have accepted salvation through faith in Jesus and that the church's mission is to proclaim the kingdom of God and to make disciples.

We believe that baptism of believers with water is a sign of cleansing from sin and a pledge to walk in Jesus' way. We believe that the Lord's Supper (Communion) is a sign by which the church remembers the new covenant which Jesus established by his death. We believe that in washing the feet of his disciples Jesus calls us to serve one another in love as he did. We practice discipline in the church as a sign of God's offer of transforming grace.

We believe that ministry is a continuation of the work of Christ. We believe that the church of Jesus Christ is one body with many members and that Jesus calls us to discipleship, to take up our cross and follow him.

We believe that to be a disciple of Jesus is to know life in the Spirit. We believe that God intends human life to begin in families and to be blessed through families. Even more, God desires all people to become part of the church, God's family. We are called to chastity and to loving faithfulness in marriage.

The Amish

The Amish and Mennonites trace their roots to the Anabaptist movement. However, in 1693, Jacob Ammann, a Swiss Anabaptist leader, felt a stricter separation from the world was in order. Those who followed Ammann became known as the Amish, noted for specific practices that distinguish them from the larger society. These include untrimmed beards, using hooks and eyes in place of fancier buttons, relying on horse and buggy transportation, plain and distinctive dress, and no electricity in their homes.

We are committed to telling the truth, to avoid the swearing of oaths, to live in faithful stewardship of all that God has given us. We believe that peace is the will of God and that led by the Holy Spirit, we follow Christ in the way of peace, doing justice, bringing reconciliation, and practicing nonresistance, even in the face of violence and warfare.

We believe that the church is God's holy nation. We place our hope in the reign of God and its fulfillment in the day when Christ will come again.

While progressive in their stance toward violence, the Mennonites have set few records regarding leadership roles for women. Even though in 1911 the First Mennonite Church in Philadelphia ordained a woman named Ann J. Alleback, it took until the 1995 Confession of Faith in a Mennonite Perspective to state that "The church calls, trains, and appoints gifted men and women to a variety of leadership ministries on its behalf. These may include such offices as pastor, deacon, and elder as well as evangelists, missionaries, teachers, conference ministers, and overseers." Essentially, each congregation has the freedom to include women in all roles of leadership. Some extend ordination to women, while others don't. At this point less than 5 percent of the clergy are women.

There are at least two web sites that can give you more information about the Mennonite Church and other peace-focused groups: www.mennonites.org and www.thirdway.com.

What to Expect When You Visit

Worship styles vary widely among Mennonite churches, but all share in the idea that God is the "audience" of the congregation rather than the people in the pews being an audience for a spiritual performance. The community as a whole, rather than the preacher or selected authority figures, discern God's message. You may find that after the sermon the congregation is invited to comment, ask questions, or disagree with the pastor. It's common for people to share stories from their lives illustrating God's work in their lives. Many services will include time for silence and reflection.

You will find a broad spectrum of musical styles in Mennonite churches as well. Originally, four-part singing was the norm for Mennonite worship without use of musical instruments. Today, more congregations are using instruments in their worship. Congregations draw their hymns from a variety of traditions and locations around the world, offering a wider variety than might be found in more uniformly organized denominations.

Most Mennonite churches share the Lord's Supper only twice a year. In most, Communion is open to all Christians, regardless of denominational affiliation. However, if you visit a more conservative congregation, and certainly if you're visiting an Amish gathering, check with a member before participating.

Still Pacifists After All These Years

Mennonites take seriously Jesus' teachings about loving your enemies and turning the other cheek. Consequently, most members of the Mennonite church will not serve as soldiers. Some serve in noncombatant positions in war. Others do not participate at all, declaring themselves conscientious objectors. There are even some Mennonites who take a stand during peace times by figuring out how much of their taxes go to the military and withholding that percentage.

The more conservative the congregation, the more conservative the dress. In Amish congregations, men should wear a jacket but no tie. Oddly enough, the more casual the congregation, the more acceptable it is to wear a tie. Women are advised to wear dresses of darker colors that cover their arms with hems below the knees. Also, open-toe shoes and jewelry is not acceptable. Members of denominations, such as the Mennonite Church USA, dress much like other traditional churches—a coat and tie for men and a dress or skirt for women. You may even find congregations that dress much more casually than this, but before you get too trendy, you might want to call ahead to make sure you won't be noticeably (and offensively) dressed.

More Mennonite Churches

Beachy Amish Mennonite Churches
www.mhsc.ca (unofficial)

Conservative Mennonite Conference
www.cmcrosedale.org

Evangelical Mennonite Church
www.brookside.org

General Conference of Mennonite Brethren Churches
www.mbconf.org

Missionary Church
www.mcusa.org

Further Info

- Marlene Kropf, Kenneth James Nafziger, and John L. Bell, *Singing: A Mennonite Voice* (Herald, 2001)

- Mary Swartley, Rhoda Keener, and Anne Stuckey, eds., *She Has Done a Good Thing: Mennonite Women Leaders Tell Their Stories* (Herald, 1999)

- Harry Loewen, Steven Nolt, Carol Duerkson, and Elwood Yoder, *Through Fire and Water: An Overview of Mennonite History* (Herald, 1996)

fifteen

The **Salvation**
Army

Early one morning in 1878, William Booth, a former Methodist minister, was writing an annual report for the Christian Mission, a charitable organization he had founded in London's East End in 1865. Sadly, William didn't have a lot to show for the thirteen years he'd worked among the "poor and wretched." He was regularly harassed by the homeless and orphaned children living on the streets, who threw rocks and fireworks through the windows of the warehouse while he preached. His wife, Catherine, wrote that Booth would "stumble home night after night haggard with fatigue, often his clothes were torn and bloody bandages swathed his head where a stone had struck."

As is true of many church founders, Booth's original vision was to work within an existing church structure. He'd had some converts from his preaching, but he had trouble getting them involved in organized church life. The poor and homeless of Victorian London, often shabbily dressed and foul-smelling, felt out of place in urban churches primarily made up of middle- and upper-class churchgoers. They didn't fit in and wouldn't go back, so Booth provided them with their own worship services. But growth was slow and the report he was writing was far from encouraging.

Booth asked his son, Bramwell, and a good friend, George Scott Railton, to review what he'd written. One of his lines read, "The Christian Mission is a volunteer army." At the time, part-time soldiers in Queen Victoria's military were called "Volunteers," a term that generated a great deal of ridicule. His son pointed this out and further criticized the term, saying he felt compelled by God to be in ministry.

In reaction to his son's critique, William crossed out the word "Volunteer" and wrote "Salvation," a change that would soon put this struggling mission on the map and all over the globe. The military symbolism captured the hearts and imagination of his congregants. Having declared war on sin, military terms replaced traditional church jargon. "Church halls became corps; giving in the offering was called 'firing a cartridge'. Flags, badges, brass bands and uniforms were added together with a military style rank system for its staff. Orig-

Strike Up the Band

In the early days, bands of brass musicians drew crowds to hear the message of God's love. Since then, the Salvation Army has produced some of the most accomplished and acclaimed musicians and arrangers in the world. These include composers William Himes, James Curnow, and Stephen Bulla. Bulla presently serves as the principle arranger for the "President's Own" United State Marine Corps Band in Washington, D.C.

inally, each individual pulled together his or her own uniform. In time, the uniforms were standardized and have been re-designed a few times. According to the years of service, position level of responsibility in the organization, trimmings worn on the uniform indicated rank."

The movement spread like wildfire throughout England, Scotland, and Wales. In 1880, George Scott Railton set up the first stronghold in the United States. Today the Salvation Army is "nationally recognized for being on the cutting-edge in creating and modeling innovative social service programs that make a difference in people's lives. The Salvation Army covers a broad spectrum and varies in each community based on local needs and resources."

What Makes a Church part of the Salvation Army?

The Salvation Army is both a church and a social service provider—defining itself as "an evangelical branch of the universal Christian Church. . . . Its mission is both spiritual and practical, encompassing the preaching of the gospel of Jesus Christ and alleviating human suffering and distress without discrimination."

Doctrinal beliefs are similar to other denominations following in the Wesleyan tradition. While other churches may draft statements of faith, the Salvation Army outlines its beliefs in the "Articles of War." Their web sites states:

> We believe that the Scriptures of the Old and New Testaments were given by inspiration of God, and that they only constitute the Divine rule of Christian faith and practice.
>
> We believe that there is only one God, who is infinitely perfect, the Creator, Preserver, and Governor of all things, and who is the only proper object of religious worship.

We believe that there are three persons in the Godhead—the Father, the Son and the Holy Ghost—undivided in essence and co-equal in power and glory.

We believe that in the person of Jesus Christ the Divine and human natures are united, so that He is truly and properly God and truly and properly man.

We believe that our first parents were created in a state of innocency, but by their disobedience they lost their purity and happiness, and that in consequence of their fall all men have become sinners, totally depraved, and as such are justly exposed to the wrath of God.

We believe that the Lord Jesus Christ has by His suffering and death made an atonement for the whole world so that whosoever will may be saved.

All Dressed Up

While donning a uniform in our day and age may seem a bit unappealing, for lower- and working-class urban dwellers in the late 1800s, getting to wear uniforms was a draw. Even though their uniforms were homemade, they no longer felt embarrassed about their dress. After two years of "an odd assortment of clothing and headgear," the Salvation Army navy blue serge uniform was standardized for both men and women. "Men wore a high neck tunic with a stiff collar over a scarlet jersey. Their headgear was a military cap with a red band, on which the words 'The Salvation Army' had been worked in gold letters. Women wore long navy skirts, close-fitting high neck tunics with white lace-edge collars. The large black straw bonnet was Catherine Booth's idea. Cheap, durable, protective and solidly unworldly, the bonnet with its red band and huge ribbon bow became a well-known symbol of The Great Salvation War." Today, most women wear a felt bowler-type hat and the high-collar tunics are being replaced by an open-neck jacket.

We believe that repentance towards God, faith in our Lord Jesus Christ, and regeneration by the Holy Spirit, are necessary to salvation.

We believe that we are justified by grace through faith in our Lord Jesus Christ and that he that believeth hath the witness in himself.

We believe that continuance in a state of salvation depends upon continued obedient faith in Christ.

We believe that it is the privilege of all believers to be wholly sanctified, and that their whole spirit and soul and body may be preserved blameless unto the coming of our Lord Jesus Christ.

We believe in the immortality of the soul; in the resurrection of the body; in the general judgment at the end of the world; in the eternal happiness of the righteous; and in the endless punishment of the wicked.

Putting these spiritual beliefs into practice focuses Salvationists on service to others. The Salvation Army would make John Wesley proud by the way this denomination holds onto core message of the gospel and translates Christian faith into worldwide ministry to those often overlooked and in great need. They believe that to address a person's holistic needs, spiritual piety is insufficient, asserting that "each person is a seamless fabric of the physical, emotional, mental and spiritual." The Salvation Army often works cooperatively with other churches, social service agencies, and the government to maximize efforts in "meeting people's needs, helping this life change occur and improving communities while preserving people's dignity."

The Salvation Army

The Salvation Army is structured somewhat like other denominations—but with a military twist. The denomination is lead by a General, with corps (or churches) commanded by an officer (pastor) who may range in rank from lieutenant to major. Corps are grouped into

Just the **FACTS**

The Salvation Army

Kind of Church:	Protestant/Wesleyan
Worship Style:	Free-Form
Trinity Affinity:	Son
Clout Continuum:	1st Place: Scripture
	2nd Place: Personal experience
	3rd Place: Tradition
Founded in USA:	1865
Members in USA:	472,871
Churches in USA:	15,486
Headquarters:	P.O. Box 269
	Alexandria VA 22313
Phone:	703-684-5500
Web site:	www.salvationarmyusa.org

divisions, which in turn are under the command of divisional commanders. To join the denomination, one doesn't become a member, but a soldier, and is required to sign the Articles of War (their statement of beliefs). Soldiers are expected to give voluntary service, while officers are commissioned to full-time service, much like clergy in other denominations.

In addition to maintaining over fourteen thousand corps in the United States, the Salvation Army provides an array of social, medical, educational, and other services. You might find the military imagery a bit off-putting, but you can't beat the services the Salvation Army provides. These include:

- Residential and nonresidential alcohol and drug treatment programs;

- Community recreation programs such as drop-in centers, clubs, social activities, gym programs, day camps, seasonal camping, and field trips;

- Residential prerelease and parole programs to help offenders transition back into society, as well as community service restitution, probation supervision, pastoral visitation, seasonal visitation, and gifts and services to offenders' families;

- Counseling services that include individual, family, and group therapy, crisis intervention, homemaker/chore services, activities of adult daily living skills, employment assistance, family preservation, guidance, and referrals to other community service agencies or organizations;

- Day care programs for children and senior adults including clubs, social activities, drop-in centers and seasonal camping programs for adults, seniors, developmentally and physically disabled adults, and the homeless;

The Salvation Army's ABC's of Salvation

Admit your need—
"For all have sinned and fall short of the glory of God" (Romans 3:23).
Believe in Christ—
"Believe in the Lord Jesus, and you will be saved" (Acts 16:31).
Commit yourself to Christ—
"Yet to all who received Him . . . He gave the right to become children of God" (John 1:12).
Being truly sorry for your sins, and through the power of Christ forsaking them, go forth to live for Christ. He will give forgiveness, power, victory, purpose, the Holy Spirit, and life eternal!

- Domestic violence services including crisis intervention, counseling, emergency shelters, and transitional housing for families;
- Emergency assistance such as providing temporary lodging due to fire, flood, or eviction, utility bill assistance, and clothing, household items, and food to people in need;
- General health screening, assessment, referral, and access to medical treatment;
- Emergency shelters for men, women, children, or families;
- Child and adolescent residential treatment programs for children who are unable to live at home for a variety of reasons;
- Permanent housing for senior citizens in Salvation Army facilities;
- Moderate to long-term housing and supportive services such as case management, skills for living, and counseling;
- Worship centers that provide pastoral care, counseling, and opportunities for spiritual regeneration and worship.

What to Expect When You Visit

In addition to the uniforms and military talk, the Salvation Army is distinguished from other Christian churches by excluding the sacraments from their worship. Salvationists see the sacraments as an outward sign of an inward experience, and it is the inward experience that is the most important thing. Salvationists are not prohibited from being baptized or receiving communion in the services of other churches, rather it is believed the sacraments are not essential to becoming a Christian or living a holy life of service. This stance is due, in part, to avoid the controversy and schisms arguing over the sacraments has caused in the church history. An aspect of this controversy relates to the ordination of women. The Salvation Army supports women taking an equal part in ministry with the men. The denomination sidestepped any controversy over women administering the sacraments by eliminating the sacraments instead of the women.

As for what to wear, I'd recommend you put on whatever feels comfortable. The Salvation Army does not discriminate against anyone, most certainly not because of one's fashion statement. You'll be welcome no matter what you wear.

More Salvation Army Affiliations

American Rescue Workers
  www.arwus.com
Volunteers of America, Inc.
  www.voa.org

Further Info

- Roy Hattersley, *Blood and Fire: William and Catherine Booth and the Salvation Army* (Doubleday, 2000)

- R. David Rightmire, *Sacraments and the Salvation Army* (Scarecrow, 1990)

Part 3

A Few Items to Help Make Sense of It All

sixteen

Different Ways to Look at Denominations

Churches in Alphabetical Order with Web Sites

African Methodist Episcopal Church . . . . . .www.amecnet.org

African Methodist Episcopal Zion . . . . .www.amezion.org
Church

American Baptist Churches . . . . .www.abc-usa.org
in the U.S.A.

Assemblies of God .www.ag.org

Christian Church (Disciples of Christ) . . . . .www.disciples.org

Christian Methodist Episcopal Church . . . .www.c-m-e.org

Christian Reformed Church in North . . . . .www.crcna.org
  America

Church of the Nazarene . . . . .www.nazarene.org

Churches of Christ . . . . .no web site

Conservative Congregational Christian . . .www.ccccusa.org
  Conference

Cumberland Presbyterian Church . . . . .www.cumberland.org

Episcopal Church .www.episcopalchurch.org

Evangelical Lutheran Church . . . . .www.elca.org
  in America

Greek Orthodox Archdiocese . . . . .www.goarch.org
  of North America

International Church of the . . . . .www.foursquare.org
  Foursquare Gospel

Lutheran Church-Missouri Synod . . . . .www.lcms.org

Mennonite Church, USA . . . . .www.mennonites.org

Moravian Church in America . . . . .www.moravian.org

National Association of . . . . .www.naacc.org
  Congregational Christians Churches

National Association of Free . . . . .www.nafwb.org
  Will Baptists

National Baptist Convention of America . . .www.nbcamerica.org

National Baptist Convention, USA . . . . .www.nationalbaptist.com

Orthodox Church in America . . . . .www.oca.org
  (Russian Orthodox)

Presbyterian Church in America . . . . .www.pcanet.org

Presbyterian Church, USA . . . . .www.pcusa.org

Progressive National Baptist Convention . .www.pnbc.org

Protestant Reformed Church . . . . .www.prca.org (unofficial)
  in America

Reformed Church in America . . . . .www.rca.org

Roman Catholic Church . . . . .www.uscccb.org *and*

. . . . .www.vatican.va

Salvation Army . . . . .www.sarmy.org

Southern Baptist Convention . . . . .www.sbc.net

United Church of Christ . . . . .www.ucc.org

United Methodist Church . . . . .www.umc.org

VineyardUSA . . . . .www. voa.org

Wesleyan Church .www.wesleyan.org

Churches in Order of Size in the U.S.A.

Roman Catholic Church 61,200,000

Southern Baptist Convention 15,900,000

National Baptist Convention, USA .8,500,000

United Methodist Church 8,333,770

Evangelical Lutheran Church in America 5,125,919
   (includes Caribbean)

National Baptist Convention of America 3,500,000

Lutheran Church-Missouri Synod 2,582,440

Assemblies of God 2,577,560

Presbyterian USA 2,525,330

African Methodist Episcopal Church 2,500,000

Progressive National Baptist Convention 2,500,000

Episcopal Church 2,333,000

Churches of Christ 2,000,000

Greek Orthodox Archdiocese of North America 1,500,000

American Baptist Churches in the U.S.A. 1,436,909

United Church of Christ 1,401,682

African Methodist Episcopal Zion Church 1,276,662

Orthodox Church in America (Russian Orthodox) 1,000,000

Christian Church (Disciples of Christ) 823,018
   (includes Canada)

Christian Methodist Episcopal Church 784,114

Church of the Nazarene 643,568

Salvation Army 472,871

Presbyterian Church in America 303,176

Christian Reformed Church in North America 300,000

Reformed Church in America 300,000
   (includes Canada)

International Church of the Foursquare Gospel 269,349

National Association of Free Will Baptist 206,000

VineyardUSA 150,433

Wesleyan Church 121,000

Mennonite Church, USA 92,002

Cumberland Presbyterian Church 86,049

National Association of Congregational 70,000
   Christian Churches

Conservative Congregational Christian Conference 66,262

Moravian Church in America 50,000
   (includes Canada)

Protestant Reformed Churches in America 6,730

Churches in Order of Founding Date in the U.S.A.

Roman Catholic Church 1565

Reformed Church in America 1628

Mennonite Church 1725

Moravian Church 1735

Episcopal Church 1789

Orthodox Church in America 1794/1970

Cumberland Presbyterian Church 1810

American Baptist Churches in the U.S.A. 1814/1845

Southern Baptist Convention 1814/1845

African Methodist Episcopal Church 1814

African Methodist Episcopal Zion Church 1821

Christian Church (Disciples of Christ) 1832

Wesleyan Church 1843

Lutheran Church-Missouri Synod 1847

Christian Reformed Church in North America 1857

Greek Orthodox Archdiocese of North America 1864/1922

Salvation Army 1865

Christian Methodist Episcopal Church 1870

National Baptist Convention, USA 1895/1915

Churches of Christ 1906

Church of the Nazarene 1908

Assemblies of God 1914

International Church of the Foursquare Gospel 1923

Protestant Reformed Church in America 1926

Conservative Congregational Christian Conference 1948

National Association of Congregational
   Christian Churches 1955

United Church of Christ 1957

Progressive National Baptist Convention 1961

United Methodist Church 1968

Presbyterian Church in America .1973

VineyardUSA 1977

Presbyterian Church, USA 1983

Evangelical Lutheran Church in America 1988

Churches that Do and Don't Ordain Women

Denominations that ordain women include:

American Baptist

Assemblies of God

Christian Church (Disciples of Christ)

Church of the Nazarene

Episcopal

Evangelical Lutheran

International Church of the Foursquare Gospel

Free Methodist Church

Moravian Church

Presbyterian Church USA

Salvation Army

United Church of Christ

United Methodist Church

Wesleyan Church

In addition, the Mennonite Church and the Christian Reformed Church leave the decision up to local congregations.

Denominations that do not ordain women include:

Southern Baptist

Roman Catholic

Lutheran Church–Missouri Synod

Orthodox

Denominational Timeline Charts

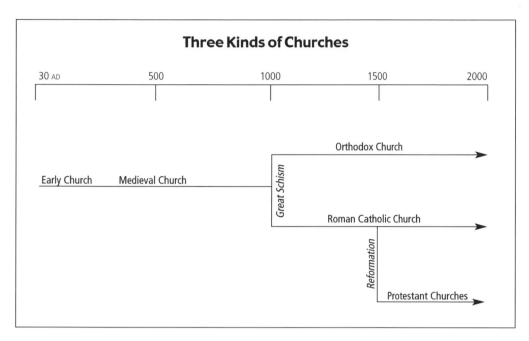

Three Kinds of Churches

30 AD — 500 — 1000 — 1500 — 2000

Early Church   Medieval Church

Great Schism

Orthodox Church

Roman Catholic Church

Reformation

Protestant Churches

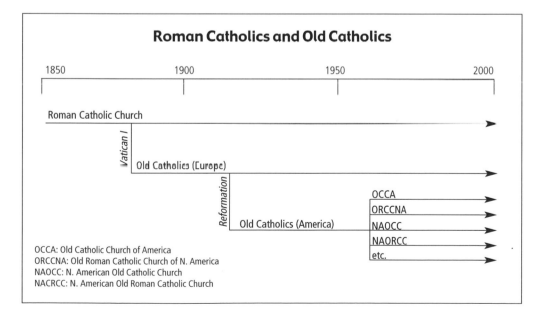

Roman Catholics and Old Catholics

1850 — 1900 — 1950 — 2000

Roman Catholic Church

Vatican I

Old Catholics (Europe)

Reformation

Old Catholics (America)

OCCA
ORCCNA
NAOCC
NAORCC
etc.

OCCA: Old Catholic Church of America
ORCCNA: Old Roman Catholic Church of N. America
NAOCC: N. American Old Catholic Church
NACRCC: N. American Old Roman Catholic Church

A Few Items to Help Make More Sense of It All

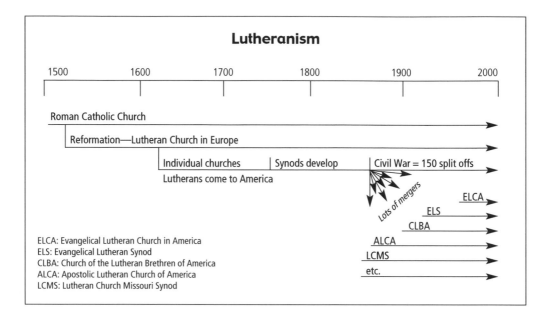

Lutheranism

1500 — 1600 — 1700 — 1800 — 1900 — 2000

Roman Catholic Church

Reformation—Lutheran Church in Europe

Individual churches | Synods develop | Civil War = 150 split offs

Lutherans come to America

Lots of mergers

ELCA
ELS
CLBA
ALCA
LCMS
etc.

ELCA: Evangelical Lutheran Church in America
ELS: Evangelical Lutheran Synod
CLBA: Church of the Lutheran Brethren of America
ALCA: Apostolic Lutheran Church of America
LCMS: Lutheran Church Missouri Synod

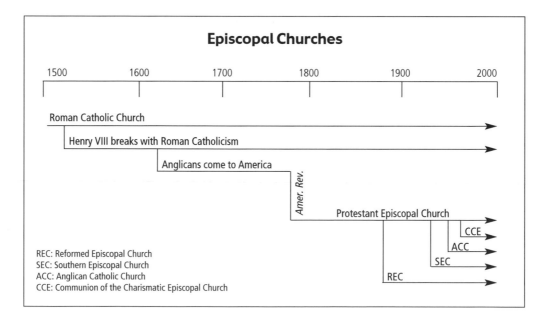

Episcopal Churches

1500 — 1600 — 1700 — 1800 — 1900 — 2000

Roman Catholic Church

Henry VIII breaks with Roman Catholicism

Anglicans come to America

Amer. Rev.

Protestant Episcopal Church

CCE
ACC
SEC
REC

REC: Reformed Episcopal Church
SEC: Southern Episcopal Church
ACC: Anglican Catholic Church
CCE: Communion of the Charismatic Episcopal Church

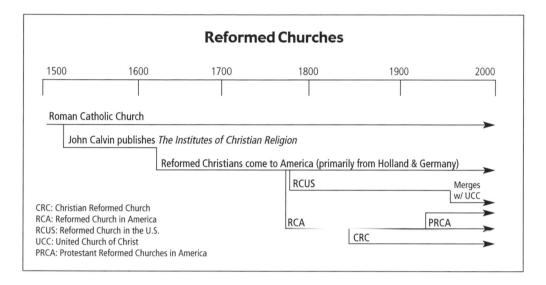

Reformed Churches

1500   1600   1700   1800   1900   2000

Roman Catholic Church

John Calvin publishes *The Institutes of Christian Religion*

Reformed Christians come to America (primarily from Holland & Germany)

RCUS

Merges w/ UCC

CRC: Christian Reformed Church
RCA: Reformed Church in America
RCUS: Reformed Church in the U.S.
UCC: United Church of Christ
PRCA: Protestant Reformed Churches in America

RCA

PRCA

CRC

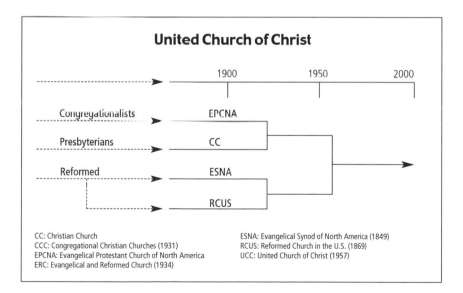

United Church of Christ

1900   1950   2000

Congregationalists   EPCNA

Presbyterians   CC

Reformed   ESNA

RCUS

CC: Christian Church
CCC: Congregational Christian Churches (1931)
EPCNA: Evangelical Protestant Church of North America
ERC: Evangelical and Reformed Church (1934)

ESNA: Evangelical Synod of North America (1849)
RCUS: Reformed Church in the U.S. (1869)
UCC: United Church of Christ (1957)

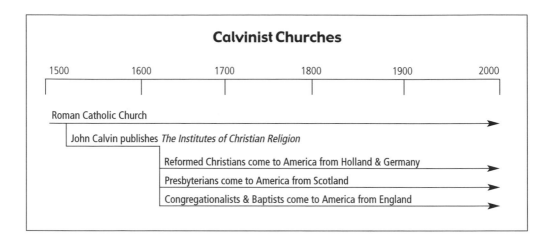

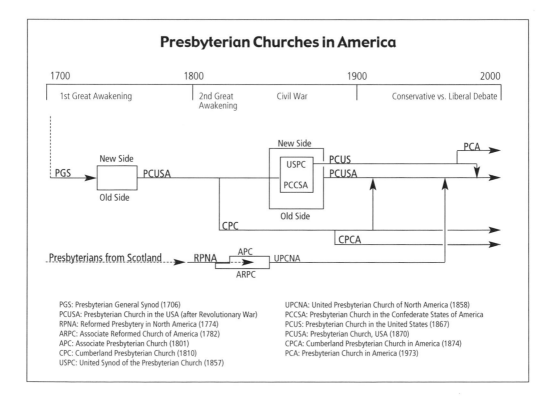

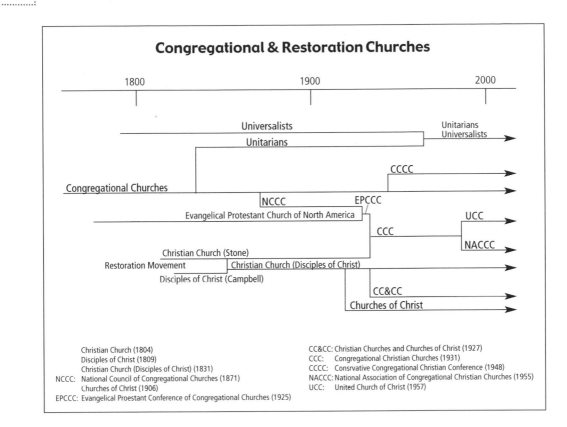

Congregational & Restoration Churches

1800 — 1900 — 2000

Universalists
Unitarians
— Unitarians
Universalists

CCCC

Congregational Churches

NCCC — EPCCC
Evangelical Protestant Church of North America

UCC

CCC

NACCC

Christian Church (Stone)
Restoration Movement — Christian Church (Disciples of Christ)
Disciples of Christ (Campbell)

CC&CC

Churches of Christ

Christian Church (1804)
Disciples of Christ (1809)
Christian Church (Disciples of Christ) (1831)
NCCC: National Council of Congregational Churches (1871)
Churches of Christ (1906)
EPCCC: Evangelical Proestant Conference of Congregational Churches (1925)

CC&CC: Christian Churches and Churches of Christ (1927)
CCC: Congregational Christian Churches (1931)
CCCC: Consrvative Congregational Christian Conference (1948)
NACCC: National Association of Congregational Christian Churches (1955)
UCC: United Church of Christ (1957)

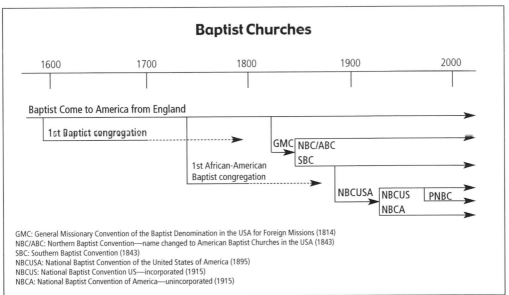

Baptist Churches

1600 — 1700 — 1800 — 1900 — 2000

Baptist Come to America from England

1st Baptist congregation

GMC NBC/ABC
SBC

1st African-American
Baptist congregation

NBCUSA NBCUS PNBC
NBCA

GMC: General Missionary Convention of the Baptist Denomination in the USA for Foreign Missions (1814)
NBC/ABC: Northern Baptist Convention—name changed to American Baptist Churches in the USA (1843)
SBC: Southern Baptist Convention (1843)
NBCUSA: National Baptist Convention of the United States of America (1895)
NBCUS: National Baptist Convention US—incorporated (1915)
NBCA: National Baptist Convention of America—unincorporated (1915)

Methodist & Holiness Churches

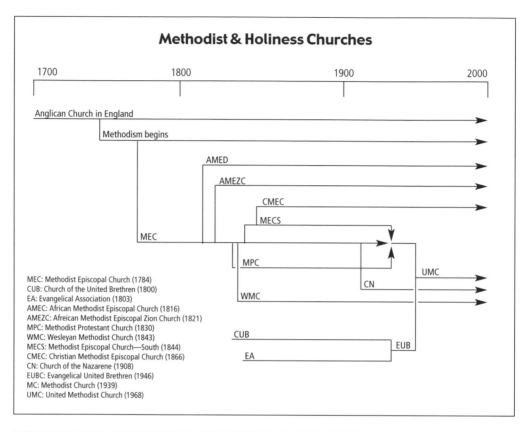

MEC: Methodist Episcopal Church (1784)
CUB: Church of the United Brethren (1800)
EA: Evangelical Association (1803)
AMEC: African Methodist Episcopal Church (1816)
AMEZC: Afreican Methodist Episcopal Zion Church (1821)
MPC: Methodist Protestant Church (1830)
WMC: Wesleyan Methodist Church (1843)
MECS: Methodist Episcopal Church—South (1844)
CMEC: Christian Methodist Episcopal Church (1866)
CN: Church of the Nazarene (1908)
EUBC: Evangelical United Brethren (1946)
MC: Methodist Church (1939)
UMC: United Methodist Church (1968)

Pentecostal and Charismatic Churches

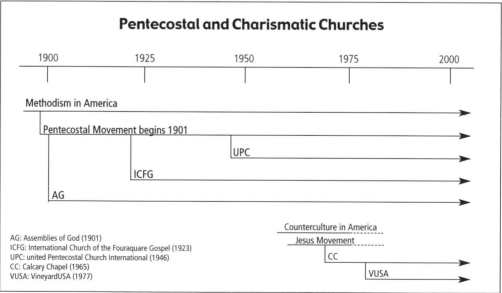

AG: Assemblies of God (1901)
ICFG: International Church of the Fouraquare Gospel (1923)
UPC: united Pentecostal Church International (1946)
CC: Calcary Chapel (1965)
VUSA: VineyardUSA (1977)

seventeen

Creeds

Creeds, creeds, and more creeds—we Christians are prolific. I'm including three creeds in their entirety because they're affirmed by most denominations, and they're short enough not to turn this into a book the size of New Jersey.

Apostles' Creed

The Apostles' Creed may be the most universally accepted statement of faith. The earliest version, called the Interrogatory Creed of Hippolytus, is dated around 215. The first copy of the form used today is found in the writings of Caesarius of Arles who died in 542. According to legend, the apostles each wrote a statement of the creed ten days after Jesus ascended into heaven. Even though this story is not accepted as accurate, the doctrines reflect statements made in the apostolic era. The focus was on the humanity of Jesus, including his material body, to denounce overspiritualizing Jesus. There are a few versions, but they vary slightly. I'm citing a version that is commonly used today.

The Apostles' Creed

I believe in God, the Father almighty,
creator of heaven and earth.
I believe in Jesus Christ, God's only Son, our Lord,
who was conceived by the Holy Spirit,
born of the Virgin Mary,
suffered under Pontius Pilate,
was crucified, died, and was buried;
he descended to the dead.
On the third day he rose again;
he ascended into heaven,
he is seated at the right hand of the Father,
and he will come again to judge the living and the dead.
I believe in the Holy Spirit,
the holy catholic Church,
the communion of saints,
the forgiveness of sins,
the resurrection of the body,
and the life everlasting. Amen.

The Nicene Creed

Having a hard time grasping the nature of Christ being both human and divine, Arius (founder of Arianism) argued that Jesus was created of a different substance than God the Father. In opposition was the idea of the Trinity—one God in three distinct persons, with Christ uncreated and on par with God the Father. The Council of Nicea convened in 325 to settle this dispute. The creed was revised by the Council of Constantinople in 381 and accepted in its present form at the Council of Chalcedon in 451. The filioque phrase, "and the Son" in relation to the Holy Spirit, was not added until 589, an addition the Orthodox Church has rejected. With that exception, the Nicene Creed is accepted by nearly every Christian denomination (translation from the Christian Reformed Church Synod of 1988).

> We believe in one God,
>> the Father almighty,
>> maker of heaven and earth,
>> of all things visible and invisible.
>
> And in one Lord Jesus Christ,
>> the only Son of God,
>> begotten from the Father before all ages,
>>> God from God,
>>> Light from Light,
>>> true God from true God,
>> begotten, not made;
>> of the same essence as the Father.
>> Through him all things were made.
>> For us and for our salvation
>> he came down from heaven;
>> he became incarnate by the Holy Spirit and the virgin Mary,
>> and was made human.
>> He was crucified for us under Pontius Pilate;
>> he suffered and was buried.
>> The third day he rose again, according to the Scriptures.
>> He ascended to heaven
>> and is seated at the right hand of the Father.
>> He will come again with glory

to judge the living and the dead.

His kingdom will never end.

And we believe in the Holy Spirit,

the Lord, the giver of life.

He proceeds from the Father [and the Son,]•

and with the Father and the Son is worshiped and glorified.

He spoke through the prophets.

We believe in one holy catholic and apostolic church.

We affirm one baptism for the forgiveness of sins.

We look forward to the resurrection of the dead,

and to life in the world to come. Amen.

•the "filioque" phrase added in 589

Athanasian Creed

No one knows for sure who wrote this creed, but until the seventeenth century its authorship was attributed to St. Athanasius, Bishop of Alexandria (A.D. 293–373). Most likely someone in southern France was the author between 415 and 542. Some of the phrases are direct quotes from St. Augustine's *On the Trinity* and St. Vincent's *Notebooks* (so much for copyright laws).

It's a bit tedious, but you have to give the writer credit for trying to be very clear. The Eastern Orthodox Church does not affirm this creed, but Roman Catholics and many Protestant denominations do. I've used the translation adopted by the Christian Reformed Church Synod of 1988, but have altered the spacing so it doesn't take up so much room.

Whoever desires to be saved should above all hold to the catholic faith. Anyone who does not keep it whole and unbroken will doubtless perish eternally.

Now this is the catholic faith: That we worship one God in trinity and the trinity in unity, neither blending their persons nor dividing their essence. For the person of the Father is a distinct person, the person of the Son is another, and that of the Holy Spirit still another. But the divinity of the Father, Son, and Holy Spirit is one, their glory equal, their majesty coeternal.

What quality the Father has, the Son has, and the Holy Spirit has. The Father is uncreated, the Son is uncreated, the Holy Spirit is uncreated. The Father is immeasurable, the Son is immeasurable, the Holy Spirit is immeasurable. The Father is eternal, the Son is eternal, the Holy Spirit is eternal. And yet there are not three eternal beings; there is but one eternal being. So too there are not three uncreated or immeasurable beings; there is but one uncreated and immeasurable being. Similarly, the Father is almighty, the Son is almighty, the Holy Spirit is almighty. Yet there are not three almighty beings; there is but one almighty being. Thus the Father is God, the Son is God, the Holy Spirit is God. Yet there are not three gods; there is but one God. Thus the Father is Lord, the Son is Lord, the Holy Spirit is Lord. Yet there are not three lords; there is but one Lord.

Just as Christian truth compels us to confess each person individually as both God and Lord, so catholic religion forbids us to say that there are three gods or lords. The Father was neither made nor created nor begotten from anyone. The Son was neither made nor created; he was begotten from the Father alone. The Holy Spirit was neither made nor created nor begotten; he proceeds from the Father and the Son. Accordingly there is one Father, not three fathers; there is one Son, not three sons; there is one Holy Spirit, not three holy spirits.

Nothing in this trinity is before or after, nothing is greater or smaller; in their entirety the three persons are coeternal and coequal with each other. So in everything, as was said earlier, we must worship their trinity in their unity and their unity in their trinity. Anyone then who desires to be saved should think thus about the trinity. But it is necessary for eternal salvation that one also believe in the incarnation of our Lord Jesus Christ faithfully.

Now this is the true faith: That we believe and confess that our Lord Jesus Christ, God's Son, is both God and human, equally. He is God from the essence of the Father, begotten before time; and he is human from the essence of his mother, born in time; completely God, completely human, with a rational soul and human flesh; equal to the Father as regards divinity, less than the Father as regards humanity.

Although he is God and human, yet Christ is not two, but one. He is one, however, not by his divinity being turned into flesh, but by God's taking humanity to himself. He is one, certainly not by the blending of his essence, but by the unity of his person. For just as one human is both rational soul and flesh, so too the one Christ is both God and human.

He suffered for our salvation; he descended to hell; he arose from the dead; he ascended to heaven; he is seated at the Father's right hand; from there he will come to judge the living and the dead. At his coming all people will arise bodily and give an accounting of their own deeds. Those who have done good will enter eternal life, and those who have done evil will enter eternal fire. This is the catholic faith: one cannot be saved without believing it firmly and faithfully.

eighteen

Timeline

In the beginning

God created the heavens and the earth.

4ish

Jesus, a descendant of King David, is born (4 years before himself? Go figure); Israel is a reluctant part of the Roman Empire with Caesar Augustus as Emperor.

26ish

Beginning around the age of thirty, Jesus preaches his message for three years—turns water into wine, heals the sick, and claims to be the Son of God, all of which rile those in religious and political power.

30ish

With support from the Jewish religious leaders, Pontius Pilate orders Roman soldiers to crucify Jesus. Three days later Jesus is resurrected, obviously causing a big stir. Jesus spends a short while with his followers and then ascends into heaven.

30–100ish

Believers meet in local temples, but when friction with traditional Jews develops, they move to private homes (A.D. 75). The general public doesn't like Jesus' followers any more than they liked him, and Christians are persecuted. Nevertheless, the faith spreads rapidly, with groups of believers, called churches, forming across the known world. Lots of letters are written and sent back and forth among groups of believers. Some of these letters (see A.D. 393) are later added to Jewish Scriptures and become what we now call the Bible.

32

Peter serves as bishop of the church in Rome. Roman Catholics consider him to be the first pope.

67

Linus begins his service as pope.

76

Anacletus begins his service as pope.

79

Mount Vesuvius erupts, destroying Pompeii. This doesn't have anything to do with church history. I just thought it was interesting.

88–311

Lots of Popes come and go.

300ish

Armenians adopt Christianity as their state religion.

313

Edict of Milan: After becoming Emperor of Rome, Constantine makes Christianity the established faith of the Empire.

314

Sylvester begins his service as pope.

325

First Ecumenical Council, comprised of 300 bishops, is held in Nicea under Emperor Contantine. The council denounces Arianism (Jesus was human, not divine) by writing the first portion of the Nicene Creed, which many churches still support today.

330

Emperor Constantine moves the center of the Roman Empire to Byzantium and renames the city Constantinople.

336

Marcus begins his service as pope.

337

Georgia converts to Christianity under the missionary efforts of Nina; Julius I begins his service as pope; Emperor Constantine dies.

341

After converting to Arian Christianity, a Goth named Ulfilas becomes consecrated as a bishop in Constantinople and returns to the Visigoths as a missionary. He translates the Bible into Goth, and the Visigoths convert to Arianism.

352

Liberius begins his service as pope.

366

Damasus I begins his service as pope.

376

Two hundred thousand Visigoths flee from the Huns and are given safe haven within the Roman Empire by Emperor Valens.

378

After being mistreated within the Roman Empire, the Visigoths revolt and slay Emperor Valens; Theodosius becomes emperor.

381

Second Ecumenical Council, comprised of 150 bishops, is held in Constantinople under Emperor Theodosius with Patriarch of Constantinople, St. Gregory of Nazianzus, presiding. The council condemns the Macedonian movement that claims God is comprised of two persons—the Father and the Son, while the Holy Spirit is a power of God. The filioque clause ("and the Son") is added to the Nicene Creed to address this controversy.

382

Emperor Theodosius I makes peace with the Visigoths (who are Arian Christians) and tries to unite them with Christians who support the Nicene Creed.

384

Siricius begins his service as pope.

393

The Synod of Hippo agrees upon a list of inspired writings now referred to as the New Testament. Later in the Middle Ages at the Nineteenth Ecumenical Council of 1545–1549 the Roman Catholic Church includes additional books, called the Apocrypha, in its Scriptures.

395

Roman Emperor Theodosius dies; the Roman Empire is separated into eastern and western sections by Arcadius and Honorius, sons of Emperor Theodosius I; historians refer to the western portion as the Roman Empire and the eastern portion as the Byzantine Empire. The Visigoths elect Alaric as their king.

396

King Alaric leads the Visigoths in an invasion of the Balkan Peninsula.

399

Anastasius begins his service as pope.

401

Innocent begins his service as pope.

408

Byzantine Emperor Arcadius dies and his seven-year-old son, Theodosius II, succeeds him. During his reign, the empire starts to pay annual subsidies to the Huns to keep them from invading.

410

Rome is plundered by the Visigoths under King Alaric's command; King Alaric dies soon after the battle.

417

Zosimus begins his service as pope.

418

Boniface begins his service as pope.

422

Celestine I begins his service as pope.

431

Third Ecumenical Council, consisting of 200+ bishops, is held in Ephesus under Emperor Theodosius II with St. Cyril of Alexandria presiding. The council takes a stand against the Nestorians (the belief that Mary gave birth to a human) by declaring Jesus to be both God and man in one person and Mary the *theotokos* or God bearer.

432

Sixtus III begins his service as pope.

434

Attila is crowned king of the Huns.

440

Hilarius begins his service as pope.

441

Attila the Hun's invades of the Byzantine Empire a second time.

443

Byzantine Emperor Theodosius II agrees to double the annual subsidy paid to the Huns.

447

Attila the Hun's second invasion of the Byzantine Empire.

449

Attila the Hun and Byzantine Emperor Theodosius II make peace.

450

Theodosius II dies, Marcian becomes Byzantine Emperor and cuts off subsidy to Attila. Attila is busy conquering the west and doesn't retaliate.

451

Fourth Ecumenical Council, consisting of 150 bishops, is held in Chalcedon under Emperor Marcian with Pope Leo the Great. The council condemns the Monophysites (Jesus' humanity dissolved into his divine so was solely divine) and reiterates that Jesus is complete God and complete man. Five major Christian centers are established: Rome, Constantinople, Alexandria, Antioch, and Jerusalem.

453

Attila the Hun dies.

457

Byzantine Emperor Marian dies; Leo becomes emperor of the Byzantine Empire.

467–468

Byzantine Emperor Leo appoints Antemius as the emperor in the west. The east and west combined efforts to defeat the Vandals but are defeated.

468

Simplicius begins his service as pope.

474

Byzantine Emperor Leo dies; since Leo has no sons, he is succeeded by his daughter's infant son, Leo II. Leo II is murdered, most likely by his father, Zeno, who takes the throne.

475

Byzantine Emperor Zeno is tossed out by Basilicus, who takes over as emperor.

476

The Middle Ages begin in Europe, marked by the overthrow of Romulus Augustus, the last Roman Emperor, by Germanic general Odacer. Small feudal states develop throughout Europe.

477

Former Emperor Zeno returns to Constantinople with an army and tosses out Byzantine Emperor Basilicus.

483

Felix III begins his service as pope.

491

Byzantine Emperor Zeno dies; his wife appoints Anastasius as Byzantine Emperor.

492

Gelasius begins his service as pope.

496

Anastasius II begins his service as pope.

498

Symmachus begins his service as pope.

514

Hormisdas begins his service as pope.

518

Justin succeeds Anastasius as emperor of the Byzantine empire.

523

John I begins his service as pope.

526

Felix IV begins his service as pope.

527

Justinian, Justin's nephew, becomes Emperor of the Byzantine empire.

530

Boniface II begins his service as pope.

532

The Nika rebellion in Constantinople between Orthodox and Monophysites results in the destruction of most of the city. Byzantine Emperor Justinian crushes those who oppose him.

533

John II begins his service as pope.

534

Theodoric, ruler of Italy, dies leaving his daughter in charge as regent until her son comes of age; Theodoric's nephew, Theodahad, murders her and takes charge of Italy.

535

Byzantine Emperor Justinian invades Sicily and is welcomed with open arms (they aren't fond of their own ruler, Theodahad); Agapetus begins his service as pope.

536

The Goths remove Theodahad as ruler of Italy; Theodahad is murdered; Witiges, a Goth, becomes ruler; Byzantine forces fight the Goths and capture Rome; Silverius begins his service as pope.

537

The church Hagia Sophia is completed in Constantinople under Emperor Justinian; Vigilius begins his service as pope.

542

The Goths recapture Italy from the Byzantines.

553

Fifth Ecumenical Council, comprised of 165 bishops, is held in Constantinople under Byzantine Emperor Justinian. The council confirms the two natures of Jesus as divine and human and condemn the divergent beliefs of selected bishops. Byzantines destroy the Goths, drive out the Franks and restore Italy to the Byzantine (ancient Roman) Empire.

556

Pelagius I begins his service as pope.

561

John III begins his service as pope.

565

Byzantine Emperor Justinian dies; Justin II becomes emperor.

570

Mohammed, founder of Islam, is born in Mecca.

575

Benedict I begins his service as pope.

578

Byzantine Emperor Justin II dies, succeeded by Tiberius II.

579

Pelagius II begins his service as pope.

582

Byzantine Emperor Tiberius II dies, succeeded by Maurice I.

590

Gregory (the Great) begins his service as pope.

592

Lombards attack Rome.

602

Byzantine Emperor Maurice I alienates his military, who capture Constantinople, murder the emperor, and proclaim their leader, Phocas, the emperor of the Byzantine empire.

604

Sabinian begins his service as pope.

607

Boniface III begins his service as pope.

608

Boniface IV begins his service as pope.

610

Constantinople is captured by Heraclius the Younger of Africa, Byzantine

Emperor Phocas is killed, and Heraclius becomes emperor.

614

Persians capture Jerusalem and carry off what was believed to be the "true cross" on which Jesus was crucified.

615

Deusdedit (Adeodatus I) begins his service as pope.

617

Persians threaten to capture the Byzantine Empire; Byzantine Emperor Heraclius, with heroic support of the citizens of Constantinople, fights back.

619

Boniface V begins his service as pope.

625

Honorius I begins his service as pope; Constantinople successfully defends itself from Persian invaders.

639

The southern territories of the Byzantine Empire (Syria, the Holy Land, Egypt, and Jordan) are captured by the Saracens Muslims.

640

Severinus begins his service as pope, followed immediately by John IV.

641

Byzantine Emperor Heraclius dies, succeeded by his sons, Heraclius Constantius (who died almost immediately) and Heracleonas.

642

Byzantine Emperor Heracleonas dies, succeeded by his nephew, Contans II; Theodore I begins his service as pope.

649

St. Martin I begins his service as pope.

655

Eugene I begins his service as pope.

657

Vitalian begins his service as pope.

668

Byzantine Emperor Contans II is murdered, probably by an internal conspiracy, and is succeeded by Constantine IV.

670

Constantinople successfully defends itself against Muslims waging jihad against the city.

672

Adeodatus II begins his service as pope.

676

Donus begins his service as pope.

678

Agatho begins his service as pope.

680

Sixth Ecumenical Council, consisting of 174 bishops, is held in Constantinople under Byzantine Emperor Constantine IV and Pope Agatho. The council bans the long-standing enemies of Orthodox Christians, the Monothelites (Jesus' divinity was in charge and his humanity did what it was told) and declares that Jesus' two natures acted in concert, mystically united in one person.

682

Leo II begins his service as pope.

684

Benedict II begins his service as pope.

685

Byzantine Emperor Constantine IV dies, succeeded by Justinian II; John V begins his service as pope.

686

Conon begins his service as pope.

687

Sergius begins his service as pope.

695

Byzantine Emperor Justinian II is disfigured, deposed, and imprisoned by Leontius, one of his generals; Leontius becomes emperor.

698

Byzantine Emperor Leontius is, in turn, disfigured, deposed, and imprisoned by his military; Tiberuis III becomes Emperor.

705

Former Byzantine Emperor Justinian II escapes from prison, seizes the palace, tortures former Byzantine Emperor Leontius and Byzantine Emperor Tiberius III, and has them executed; John VII begins his service as pope.

708

Sisinnius begins his service as pope.

711

Byzantine Emperor Justinian II is killed and is replaced by Philippicus, one of his generals.

713

Byzantine Emperor Philippicus is ousted by Anastasius II.

715

Byzantine Emperor Anastasius II is replaced by Theodosius III; Gregory II begins his service as pope.

716

Byzantine Emperor Theodosius abdicates the throne to his general, Leo III.

717–718

The Muslims again attack Constantinople and are defeated.

726

Iconoclastic Controversy is launched by Byzantine Emperor Leo III who orders all icons destroyed. Thousands of people die protecting religious works of art. Pope Gregory in Rome opposes him.

731

Gregory III begins his service as pope.

740

The concept of a papal state was introduced giving the church "permission" to rule territory independently.

741

Zachary begins his service as pope.

752

Stephen II begins his service as pope, followed immediately by Stephen III.

754

Byzantine Emperor Leo III dies, succeed by his son, Constantine V, who continues his father's campaign against icons by hand-picking 338 bishops for the Council of Hieria. Calling itself the Seventh Ecumenical Council, the group rejects the use of icons in worship and violators are harshly punished.

757

Paul I begins his service as pope.

762–775

"Decade of Blood:" Thousands of people who protect icons from destruction are exiled, publicly humiliated, tortured, or killed in the Byzantine Empire; Byzantine Emperor Constantine V dies, succeeded by his son, Leo IV.

767

Stephen IV begins his service as pope.

772

Adrian I begins his service as pope.

775

Byzantine Emperor Constantine V dies, succeeded by his son, Leo IV. Leo is an iconoclast but not as aggressive as his father.

780

Byzantine Emperor Leo IV dies; his wife, Irene, rules as regent for their son, Constance VI, who is ten when his father dies. Irene had secretly been pro-icon and, once in power, reverses direction.

787

The legitimate Seventh Ecumenical Council, comprised of 367 bishops, is held in Nicea under Byzantine Empress Irene and Pope Adrian I. The use of icons in worship is reestablished, distinguishing between venerating icons and worshiping God.

790

Byzantine Emperor Constantine VI removes his mother, Irene, from power, but gives her freedom in the court.

795

Leo III begins his service as pope.

797

Former Empress Irene has her son, Byzantine Emperor Constantine VI, seized, his eyes gouged out, and then imprisoned in a monastery. For the first time, a woman claims the throne on her own behalf.

800

Charlemagne, King of the Franks, is crowned "Emperor of the West" by Pope Leo III of Rome. Charlemagne challenges the rule of the Emperors in Constantinople as rightful "descendents" of the Roman Empire by calling his kingdom the "Holy Roman Empire." This further aggravates tension between the eastern and western parts of the church.

802

Empress Irene is seized in the night, taken to a convent, and forced to take vows of a nun by Nicephorus who becomes emperor.

811

Byzantine Emperor Nicephorus dies and is succeeded by Michael Rhangable, his son-in-law.

812

Byzantine Emperor Michael Phangable recognizes Charlemagne as the emperor of the west.

813

Byzantine Emperor Michael Phangable is deposed by one of his soldiers, Leo V, the Armenian.

815

Byzantine Emperor Leo V once again abolishes icons.

816

Stephen V begins his service as pope.

817

Paschal I begins his service as pope.

820

Byzantine Emperor Leo V is assassinated, succeeded by another soldier, Michael II.

824

Eugene II begins his service as pope.

827

Valentine begins his service as pope soon followed by Gregory IV.

829

Byzantine Emperor Michael II dies and is succeeded by his son, Theophilus.

842

Byzantine Emperor Theophilus dies and is succeeded by his infant son Michael III. Until he comes of age the empire is run by a council run by his mother, Theodora.

843

Byzantine Empress Theodora restores the use of icons once and for all.

844

Serius II begins his service as pope.

847

Leo IV begins his service as pope.

855

Benedict III begins his service as pope.

856

Byzantine Emperor Michael III rules along side his mother and develops a drinking problem, earning himself the nickname "Michael the Drunkard."

858

Byzantine Emperor Michael III replaces the Orthodox patriarch Ignatius with Photius. The patriarch in Rome, Pope Benedict III, denounces both the Michael III and Photius; Nicholas (the Great) begins his service as pope.

867

Byzantine Emperor Michael III's drinking buddy, Basil the Macedonian, has him murdered and assumes the role of emperor, launching the Macedonian dynasty that rules Constantinople for nearly two centuries; Adrian II begins his service as pope.

869

Eighth Ecumenical Council, consisting of 102 bishops, three papal legates, and four patriarchs, is held in Constantinople under Byzantine Emperor Basil with Pope of Rome Hadrian II presiding. The Council condemns Photius, the Patriarch of Constantinople, for challenging clerical celibacy, the "filioque" addition to the Nicene Creed, and the crowning of Charlemagne as the Emperor of the Holy Roman Empire. The Orthodox Church does not recognize the authority of this and successive ecumenical councils. Concludes in 887.

872

John VIII begins his service as pope.

882

Marinus I begins his service as pope.

884

Adrian III begins his service as pope.

885

Stephen VI begins his service as pope.

886

Byzantine Emperor Basil dies and is succeeded by his son, Leo VI; in an effort for a male heir, Leo VI marries four times.

891

Formosus begins his service as pope.

896–911

In this twenty-year period, ten popes come and go, leaving Anastasius as pope.

912

Byzantine Emperor Leo VI dies and is succeeded by his brother Alexander.

913

Byzantine Emperor Alexander dies and is officially succeeded by his nephew, Constantine VIII (who is five), but the empire is ruled by Romanus, a respected soldier.

913–942

In this twenty-nine year period, eight popes come and go, leaving Marinus II as pope.

945

Bulgaria is declared a patriarchate by the church in Constantinople.

946

Agapetus II begins his service as pope.

954

Princess Olga of Kiev (Russia) is baptized an Orthodox Christian.

955

John XII begins his service as pope.

959

Byzantine Emperor Constantine VIII dies and is succeeded by his son, Romanus II.

963

Byzantine Emperor Romanus II dies while his two sons are still infants. His wife, Theophano acts as regent for Basil II and Constantine VIII. Nicephorus, a general, marries Theophano and moves into power; Leo VIII begins his service as pope.

964

Benedict V begins his service as pope.

965

John XIII begins his service as pope.

969

Theophano conspires with John Zimisces, a captain, who kills her husband, Byzantine Emperor Nicephorus, in his sleep. Zimisces then imprisons Theophano in a covent and co-rules with her sons.

972

After a couple of battles, Byzantine Emperor Zimisces makes peace with Russia; the future Emperor Otto II of Germany marries a Byzantine princess.

973

Benedict VI begins his service as pope.

974

Benedict VII begins his service as pope.

976

Byzantine Emperor Zimisces dies.

983

John XIV begins his service as pope.

985

John XV begins his service as pope.

988

Orthodox Christianity is adopted as the state religion by the Grand Prince Volodymyr of Kievan Rus (now Ukraine, Belorus and Russia).

996–1012

In this sixteen-year period, six popes come and go, leaving Benedict VIII as pope.

1014

Byzantines defeat the Bulgarians, taking 15,000 captives; Byzantine Emperor Basil II's cruelty earns him the nickname of Slayer of the Bulgars.

1024

John XIX begins his service as pope.

1025

Byzantine Emperor Basil II dies, succeeded by his brother, Constantine VIII.

1028

Byzantine Emperor Constantine VIII dies, succeeded by the four husbands of his daughter, Zoe.

1032

Benedict IX begins his service as pope.

1045–1049

In this four-year period, six popes come and go, leaving Leo IX as pope.

1054

The Great Schism: The church formally splits into the Orthodox Church (east) and the Roman Catholic Church (west) when the Patriarch of Constantinople and Pope Leo IX excommunicate each other.

1055

Victor II begins his service as pope.

1057

Stephen X begins his service as pope.

1958

Nicholas II begins his service as pope.

1061

Alexander II begins his service as pope.

1071

The Turks attack the Byzantine Empire and take most of Asia Minor.

1073

Gregory VII begins his service as pope.

1086

Victor III begins his service as pope.

1088

Urban II begins his service as pope.

1095

Council of Clermont: Pope Urban II of Rome declares that anyone who fights in the Crusade against the Muslims in occupied Jerusalem will receive full pardons of sin and criminal offenses. Approximately 60,000 men and women volunteer.

1096

Crusaders pillage across Europe, losing two-thirds in battle.

1099

With reinforcements, Jerusalem is captured by Crusaders starting the Latin Kingdom of Jerusalem; Paschal II begins his service as pope.

1118

Gelasius II begins his service as pope.

1119

Callistus II begins his service as pope.

1123

Ninth Ecumenical Council is held in Rome under Pope Callistus II, consisting of 900 bishops and abbots. The Council clarifies election of bishops and abbots and decides that ordained priests cannot marry.

1124

Honorius II begins his service as pope.

1130

Innocent II begins his service as pope.

1139

Tenth Ecumenical Council is held in Rome under Emperor Conrad and Pope Innocent II, consisting of approximately 1,000 prelates. The Council ends a church schism by voiding the decrees of Anacletus II, an antipope. The Neo-Manicheans (who denounced the Mass as "vain show," opposed marriage and baptism of children) are denounced along with the teachings of Arnold of Brescia.

1140

First Gothic structure is built in France by Saint-Denis.

1143

Celestine II begins his service as pope.

1144

Lucius II begins his service as pope.

1145

Second Crusade, led by Louis VII of France, tries to come to the aid of survivors from the First Crusade who are starving within the walls of Jerusalem. Most in the Second Crusade die in route; the remainder are killed in battle; Crusade ends 1149; Eugene III begins his service as pope.

1153

Anastasius IV begins his service as pope.

1154

Adrian IV begins his service as pope.

1159

Alexander III begins his service as pope.

1179

Eleventh Ecumenical Council, consisting of 301 bishops, is held in Rome under Emperor Ferderick I and Pope Alexander III. The council regulates the election of the pope, ruling that two-thirds majority vote by the College of Cardinals is required and the emperor is excluded from voting. The decrees of three antipopes are nullified. The council also condemns the Albigenses and the Waldenses.

1181

Lucius III begins his service as pope.

1185

Urban III begins his service as pope.

1187

Muslims recapture Jerusalem; Gregory VIII begins and ends his service as pope; Clement III begins his service as pope; Third Crusade: Richard I (The Lionhearted) leads a combined effort of German, French, and English Crusaders to recapture Jerusalem (ends 1192). The Muslims retain control.

1191

Celestine III begins his service as pope.

1198

Innocent III begins his service as pope.

1204

Fourth Crusade: Intending to continue to fight for Jerusalem, Crusaders get sidetracked by greed and attack Constantinople instead. Even though Constantinople is a "Christian" city, western Roman Catholic Crusaders plunder Orthodox churches, stealing enormous amounts of art and destroying libraries and sacred documents. This seals the animosity between the western and eastern portions of the church.

1215

English noblemen force King John to sign the Magna Carta; Twelfth Ecumenical Council is held in Rome under Pope Innocent III and is comprised of the Patriarchs of Constantinople and Jerusalem, 71 bishops, 412 bishops, and 800 abbots. The Council declares that "there is but one Universal Church of the faithful, outside of which no one at all is saved." Catholics are required to go to confession at least once a year and the term "transubstantiation" is formally used for the first time. The Fifth Crusade is approved.

1216

Honorius III begins his service as pope.

1217

Fifth Crusade: With grand hopes, Crusaders attack Muslims in Sicily, North Africa, Turkey, Palestine, Spain, and parts of France. The campaign hurts a lot of people but doesn't accomplish much (ends 1221).

1221

The Mongols conquer vast areas including Persia, parts of China, Armenia, Georgia, Hungary, eastern Tibet, and the cities of Baghdad, Moscow, and Kiev (through 1258).

1227

Gregory IX begins his service as pope.

1228

Sixth Crusade: Frederick II leads another attack on the Muslims (ends 1229).

1241

Celestine IV begins his service as pope.

1243

Innocent IV begins his service as pope.

1245

Thirteenth Ecumenical Council, King of France, and Pope Innocent IV, consisting of the Patriarchs of Constantinople, Antioch, and Venice plus 140 bishops is held in Lyons, France under Emperor Baldwin II, Louis VII, King of France, and Pope Innocent IV. Emperor Frederick II is excommunicated and deposed for trying to make the church a department of state. The Council also launches another crusade against the Saracens and Mongols under the command of King Louis VII.

1248

Seventh Crusade: Louis IX leads the campaign, in which he spends time as a captive of the Muslims (ends 1254).

1254

Alexander IV begins his service as pope.

1261

Late Byzantine era is marked by the recapture of the empire by Byzantine Emperor Michael Palaeologus; Urban IV begins his service as pope.

1265

Clement IV begins his service as pope.

1270

Eighth (and final) Crusade: Louis IX tries again to conquer the Muslims; Louis IX dies outside of Tunis.

1271

Blessed Gregory X begins his service as pope.

1271–1292

Marco Polo is out and about.

1272

Prince Edward (who becomes King Edward I of England) arranges a truce and puts an end to the Crusade era.

1274

Fourteenth Ecumenical Council, consisting of the Patriarchs of Antioch and Constantinople, 15 cardinals, 500 bishops, and more than 1,000 theologians and dignitaries. The council effects a temporary reunion of the Orthodox Church with Rome; recovering Palestine from the Turks is discussed.

1276–1294

In this eighteen-year period, nine popes come and go, leaving Boniface VIII as pope.

1302

Pope Boniface VIII declared that it is "absolutely necessary for the salvation of every human creature to be subject to the Roman Pontiff."

1303

Blessed Benedict XI begins his service as pope.

1305

Giotto, a Florentine artist, paints the first frescoes (paintings on damp plaster) in a Renaissance style; Clement V begins his service as pope.

1311–1312

Fifteenth Ecumenical Council, comprised of the Partriarchs of Antioch and Alexandria, 300 bishops (114 according to some authorities), is held in Vienne, France under Philip IV of France, Edward II of England, James II of Aragon, and Pope Clement V. The council deals with the crimes and errors of selected knights and condemns the Beghardsm/Beguines for teaching that a spiritual person can give free reign to all desires; Serbia is declared a patriarchate by the church in Constantinople.

1316

John XXII begins his service as pope.

1328

Scotland declares independence from England.

1334

Benedict XII begins his service as pope.

1338

Edward III, King of England, starts the Hundred Years' War as he attempts to conquer and rule France.

1342

Clement VI begins his service as pope.

1346

Serbia is declared a patriarchate by the Orthodox Church in Constantinople.

1348

The plague (Black Death) spreads into Europe from China.

1350

Beginning of the Renaissance.

1352

Innocent VI begins his service as pope.

1362

Blessed Urban V begins his service as pope.

1370

Gregory XI begins his service as pope.

1378

Urban VI begins his service as pope.

1389

Boniface IX begins his service as pope.

1406

Innocent VII begins his service as pope, soon followed by Gregory XII.

1414

Sixteenth Ecumenical Council is held in Constance, Germany under Roman Catholic Popes Gregory XII and Martin V (ends 1418). The legitimate pope, Gregory XII, along with antipopes Benedict XIII and John XXIII, abdicate for the sake of church unity. The council elects Martin V as pope, marking the end of the western schism. John Wycliffe and John Huss (who taught that Scripture is the sole rule of faith, the pope is not the head of the church, bishops have no authority) were condemned.

1417

Martin V begins his service as pope.

1427

Thomas á Kempis releases *The Imitation of Christ*.

1429

Joan of Arc leads the French to victory against English forces attacking Orleans as the Hundred Years' War continues. Charles VII takes the throne in France.

1431

Joan of Arc is burned at the stake; Eugene IV begins his service as pope; Seventeenth Ecumenical Council is first held in Switzerland under Pope Eugene IV. This Council is called to address the problems in Bohemia but squabble and move the meeting to Ferrara, Italy. Things don't go any better there, so the group takes off for Florence in 1439. For a short time a union is forged with the Orthodox Church

1440

Johann Gutenberg (c. 1398–1468) invents moveable type and revolutionizes printing.

1447

Anabaptists draft the Schleitheim Confession of Faith; Nicholas V begins his service as pope.

1448

The Orthodox Church in Russia becomes independent from the Patriarchate of Constantinople.

1453

The Ottoman Turks capture Constantinople, cutting the Orthodox Church from the western portion of Christendom; the church Hagia Sophia is turned into a Muslim mosque; to escape Turkish rule, many teachers and scholars go to Italy with books and artifacts from Constantinople; Muslims subjugate all Orthodox churches within the control to the Patriarchate in Constantinople; End of Hundred Years' War with France winning back territory from England.

1455

Wars of the Roses (ends 1485), a series of civil wars in England, devastate the population, culminating in the victory of Henry IV, who founds the Tudor dynasty. Medieval period in England ends; Callistus III begins his service as pope.

1458

Pius II begins his service as pope.

1464

Paul II begins his service as pope.

1466

Erasmus, Dutch scholar and leading humanist, is born.

1471

Sixtus IV begins his service as pope.

1478

The Spanish Inquisition persecutes Jews, Muslims, and Christian as heretics.

1483

Martin Luther is born.

1484

Innocent VIII begins his service as pope.

1492

Rodrigo Borgia begins his service as Pope Alexander VI; Christopher Columbus arrives in the Americas.

1497

Leonardo da Vinci completes his painting, *The Lord's Supper*.

1503

Pius III begins his service as pope, soon followed by Julius II.

1504

Michelangelo sculpts the statue of *David*.

1509

John Calvin is born in northern France; Henry VIII becomes King of England.

1511

Erasmus publishes *The Praise of Folly*, in which he criticizes the Roman Catholic Church.

1512

Eighteenth Ecumenical Council, comprised of 15 cardinals and approximately 80 archbishops and bishops, is held in Rome under Emperor Maxmilian and Popes Julius II and Leo X. The council makes disciplinary decisions and discuss a new crusade that is never executed due to problems caused by Martin Luther and the beginning of the Reformation.

1513

Leo X begins his service as pope.

1514

John Knox is born in Scotland. Some believe he was born in 1505.

1516

Thomas Moore publishes *Utopia*, in which he outlines society concerned with the health and happiness of all citizens.

1517

The Reformation is formally launched when Martin Luther nails 95 theses on the door of the church in Wittenberg, Germany.

1519

Zwingli, a Swiss Catholic priest, promotes more radical reforms than Luther; Charles, archduke of Austria and King of Spain is crowned Charles V, Holy Roman Emperor.

1521

Luther is brought before the Diet of Worms (doesn't that sound disgusting?) but he won't recant; Ignatius of Loyola is hit by a cannon ball.

1522

Adrian VI begins his service as pope.

1523

Zwingli presents his doctrines in 67 theses; Zurich church council bans all teaching that is not based on Scripture, thereby breaking with Rome; Clement VII begins his service as pope.

1524

Zwingli legalizes his "union" with the woman he has been living with.

1525

The first Anabaptist congregation is founded in Zurich, Switzerland, in opposition to Zwingli; Martin Luther marries Kathrine von Bora.

1527

Charles V invades Rome and captures Pope Clement VII.

1528

Protestant Patrick Hamilton is burned at the stake in Scotland by Roman Catholic Archbishop of St. Andrews.

1529

Luther and Zwingli try to iron out their differences, but fail; Luther writes "A Mighty Fortress Is Our God."

1531

Zwingli, acting as chaplain and standard-bearer for Swiss Protestant forces, is wounded in battle and then killed by Catholic forces.

1532-1534

John Calvin experiences a "sudden conversion."

1534

Henry VIII of England severs ties with Rome (Act of Supremacy of 1534) and establishes the Church of England; in an effort to reform the Roman Catholic Church, St. Ignatius Loyola founds the Society of Jesus (the Jesuits); first record of Anabaptist congregations established in Holland; Paul III begins his service as pope.

1535

Thomas Moore is beheaded for refusing to take an oath acknowledging King Henry VIII's authority over the pope.

1536

Calvin publishes his *Institutes of the Christian Religion* in an effort to persuade the king of France to support Protestantism. The king doesn't. Calvin hits the road; Menno Simons, a former Catholic priest, is baptized in an Anabaptist congregation. The movement is eventually renamed as the Mennonites.

1538

Calvin is thrown out of Geneva for being too pushy.

1541

Calvin takes permanent residence in Geneva and moves into leadership by declaring Geneva to be the "City of God."

1543

Copernicus's theory that the sun is the center of the solar system is published.

1545

Nineteenth Ecumenical Council, comprised of 5 cardinal legates of the Holy See, 3 patriarchs, 33 archbishops, 235 bishops, 7 abbots, 7 generals of monastic orders, and 160 doctors of divinity, is held in Trent, Italy, under Emperors Charles V and Ferdinand and Popes Paul III, Julius III, and Pius IV. The council condemns Luther and other Reformers, addresses needed reforms in the church, and adds the Apocrypha to Roman Catholic Scriptures. It is the longest of any council and issues the most dogmatic and reformative decisions.

1546

Luther dies of heart failure; Protestant George Wishart is burned at the stake in Scotland by Roman Catholic Cardinal Beaton; two months later, Cardinal Beaton is stabbed to death by Scottish Protestants who take over his castle.

1547

Henry VIII, King of England dies; his Protestant son, Edward, is crowned King; King Edward of England dies; Mary Tudor kills off a distant relative who competes for the throne and becomes Queen of England; Ivan IV (the Terrible) becomes Czar of Russia.

1549

Church of England's *Book of Common Prayer* is printed.

1550

Julius III begins his service as pope.

1553

Michael Servetus is burned at the stake by John Calvin for heresy; King Edward of England dies and Mary Tudor ascends to the throne of England; John Knox marries Marjorie Bowes.

1555

German Catholics and Lutherans are legally required to follow the religion of their rulers; Marcellus II begins his service as pope, soon followed by Paul IV.

1559

(Bloody) Mary Queen of England dies; her half-sister Queen Elizabeth I takes the throne and sets up a moderate form of Protestantism known as Anglicanism; Calvin publishes the final version of *The Institutes of Christian Religion*; Knox returns to Scotland after 13 years in exile; Pius IV begins his service as pope.

1560

Scottish Parliament ratifies Knox's *The Confession of Faith Professed and Believed by the Protestants within the Realm of Scotland*; Jacobus Arminius is born in Holland.

1561

Belgic Confessions is written by Dutch Reformed theologians.

1563

Heidelberg Catechism is written.

1564

John Calvin dies and, in keeping with his wishes, is buried in an unmarked grave; William Shakespeare is born in England.

1565

First Roman Catholic parish is established in St. Augustine, Florida

1566

Pius V begins his service as pope.

1567

DeBres is martyred by Phillip II of Spain for Reformed beliefs.

1568

Mary Queen of Scots flees to England where she is imprisoned by Queen Elizabeth; Mary's infant son, James VI, is crowned King of Scotland; Holland rebels against Spanish rule (a fight that continues for decades).

1570

Tridentine Mass begins to be used.

1572

John Knox dies; 8,000 Protestants are killed in Paris, France, in the Massacre of St. Bartholomew; Gregory XIII begins his service as pope.

1575

Lutherans and Orthodox begin a six-year correspondence to find common ground for cooperative affiliation, but Orthodox had more in common with Roman Catholics than Protestants.

1578

Presbyterian leader Andrew Melville publishes *The Second Book of Discipline* in

Scotland; Anglican Church brought to America by Sir Francis Drake.

1585

Sixtus V begins his service as pope.

1587

Mary Queen of Scots is beheaded by Elizabeth I for her role in a foiled assassination plot.

1588

The English defeat the Spanish Armada; Jacobus Arminius is ordained.

1589

The bishop of the Russian Orthodox Church is recognized as the Russian patriarch, fifth in honor.

1590

Urban VII begins his service as pope, soon followed by Gregory XIV.

1591

Innocent IX begins his service as pope.

1592

The Vulgate, or Roman Catholic Bible, is revised and published; Clement VIII begins his service as pope.

1598

Henry VI, King of France, declares toleration of Protestants.

1601

Shakespeare's *Hamlet* is performed for the first time at the Globe Theater, outside of London.

1602

Jacobus Arminius is given a professorship at Leyden University.

1603

Elizabeth I, Queen of England dies; with Elizabeth's prior approval, James VI of Scotland is crowned James I King of England (even though Elizabeth beheaded his mother a few years before). The kingdom of Great Britain comes into being: England, Scotland, and Wales.

1605

Leo XI begins his service as pope, soon followed by Paul V.

1609

Jacobus Arminius dies; John Smyth "rebaptizes" himself and his congregation.

1610

Followers of Arminius publish five articles called Arminian Articles of Remonstrance.

1611

The King James Authorized Version of the Bible is published in England; the first General Baptists Church is founded in England.

1614

The first Reformed Church in America is set up by Dutch immigrants in New York (then called New Amsterdam).

1616

Shakespeare dies.

1618

The Canons of the Synod of Dort are written in Holland to denounce Arminianism; Thirty Years' War starts in Germany and spreads throughout Europe.

1619

The first Lutheran service is held in America.

1620

English Puritans set sail in the Mayflower for the New World.

1621

Gregory XV begins his service as pope.

1623

Urban VIII begins his service as pope.

1628

Fifty Dutch immigrants gather to share communion—the Reformed Church in America traces its roots to this moment.

1629

Massachusetts Bay Colony is established.

1632

The Anabaptists and Mennonites draft the *Dordrecht Confession*; Arminians are included in "tolerated" category of Holland's government and no longer persecuted.

1633

Galileo is tried before the Inquisition in Rome.

1634

Roman Catholics found the state of Maryland

1638

The first Particular Baptist congregation is founded in England.

1639

The first Baptist congregation is founded in the New World.

1644

Innocent X begins his service as pope.

1647

Westminster Confession is written in England, becoming a standard for Presbyterian theology.

1648

The Congregational Church is founded in America through merging the Plymouth Pilgrims and the Massachusetts Bay Colony; Thirty Years' War ends in Germany.

1649

Charles I is beheaded by Protestant Parliament.

1655

Alexander VII begins his service as pope.

1658

Savoy Declaration of Faith is written.

1667

Clement IX begins his service as pope.

1670

Clement X begins his service as pope.

1677

The Particular Baptist Confession is written.

1678

General Baptist Orthodox Creed is written; Blessed Innocent XI begins his service as pope.

1683

William Penn offers the Mennonites asylum in Pennsylvania.

1689

Alexander VIII begins his service as pope.

1691

Innocent XII begins his service as pope.

1693

The Amish break away from the Mennonites under the leadership of Jacob Ammann, a Swiss Anabaptist.

1700

Clement XI begins his service as pope.

1706

First Presbyterian Association is formed in Philadelphia.

1720

The Presbyterians found Princeton University.

1721

Innocent XIII begins his service as pope.

1724

Benedict XIII begins his service as pope.

1725

The Mennonite Church is founded in America.

1729

John and Charles Wesley start the Holy Club in Oxford, England; *Westminster Confession and Catechisms* are formally adopted by the Presbyterian General Synod in America.

1730

Clement XII begins his service as pope.

1735

John and Charles Wesley go to the Georgia Colony as missionaries.

1736

Charles Wesley leaves Georgia.

1738

John Wesley returns to England from Georgia and experiences conversion as he feels his heart "strangely warmed" at a Moravian meeting.

1740

Benedict XIV begins his service as pope.

1743

John Wesley publishes rules for the Methodist societies.

1747

First German Reformed Synod is organized in Philadelphia.

1748

The first Lutheran Synod is established in America.

1758

Clement XIII begins his service as pope.

1769

Clement XIV begins his service as pope.

1773

The first Baptist church for slaves is founded on a Georgia plantation; Pope Clement XIV suppresses the Jesuit order.

1774

John Newton, author of "Amazing Grace," is ordained.

1775

Pius VI begins his service as pope.

1776

The American Revolution begins.

1779

"Amazing Grace" is published.

1784

John Wesley begins ordaining pastors for the United States; the Methodist Episcopal Church in America is founded.

1785

United Church of Christ is the first church to ordain an African-American pastor—Lemuel Haynes.

1788

Charles Wesley dies.

1789

The Episcopal Church is founded in America by splitting from the Church of England.

1792

The Reformed Protestant Dutch Church is founded in America.

1793

The Bethel Church for Negro Methodists is formed in Philadelphia.

1794

The first Russian Orthodox missionaries arrive in Alaska (then a part of Russia).

1795

The German Reformed Church is founded.

1800

The Church of the United Brethren Church is founded in the USA; Pius VII begins his service as pope.

1801

The Cane Ridge Revival takes place.

1803

The Evangelical Association is founded in the USA.

1808

The Christian Association is founded.

1810

Three Presbyterian churches meet in Dixon County, Tennessee, to form the Cumberland Presbyterian Church.

1814

The African Methodist Episcopal Church is founded in the USA (splits from the Methodist Episcopal Church); the General Missionary Convention of the Baptist Denomination in the United States of America for Foreign Missions (called The Triennial Convention) is founded; Pope Pius VI rescinds order suppressing Jesuit order.

1816

The African Methodist Episcopal Church is founded in the USA.

1821

The African Methodist Episcopal Zion Church is founded in the USA (splits from the Methodist Episcopal Church).

1823

Leo XII begins his service as pope.

1825

American Unitarian Association is formed primarily of Old Congregational Churches in New England.

1829

Pius VIII begins his service as pope.

1830

The Methodist Protestant Church is founded in the USA (splits from the Methodist Episcopal Church).

1831

Nat Turner leads slaves in a violent rebellion against slavery; Gregory XVI begins his service as pope.

1832

The Christian Church (Disciples of Christ) is formed in the USA by merging the Christian Church with Disciples of Christ.

1840

The first Bishop is assigned to Alaska's Russian Orthodox Church.

1843

The Wesleyan Methodist Connection is founded in the USA (splits from the Methodist Episcopal Church). Changes name in 1947 to the Wesleyan Church.

1845

The Southern Baptist Convention is founded in the USA (splits from the Triennial Convention); the Methodist Episcopal Church, South is founded in the USA (splits from the Methodist Episcopal Church).

1846

Pius IX begins his service as pope.

1847

The Lutheran Church-Missouri Synod is founded in the USA.

1848

Albetus Van Rag founds Holland, Michigan.

1850

Holland, Michigan, unites with the Dutch Reformed Church and becomes the Reformed Church in America.

1853

United Church of Christ is the first to ordain a woman—Antoinette Brown.

1857

The Christian Reformed Church splits from the Reformed Church in America; United Synod of the Presbyterian Church forms in the southern United States.

1861

Southern Presbyterian Church forms the Presbyterian Church in the Confederate States of America.

1864

First Greek Orthodox Church is founded in New Orleans, Louisiana.

1865

The Salvation Army (first called the Christian Mission) is founded in London, England.

1866

The Colored Methodist Episcopal Church is founded in the USA (amicably spiting from the Methodist Episcopal Church, South).

1869

Twentieth Ecumenical Council (Vatican I), comprised of 6 archbishop-princes, 49 cardinals, 11 patriarchs, 680 archbishops and bishops, 28 abbots, and 29 generals of orders, is held in Rome under Pope Pius IX. The council declares the pope to be infallible whenever he defines a doctrine concerning faith or morals; Colored Cumberland Presbyterian Church is founded; German Reformed Church drops "German" from name to become the Reformed Church in the United States.

1871

Swiss, German, Austrian, and Dutch Priests form the Old Catholic Church; the National Council of the Congregational Christian Churches is formed.

1872

The seat of authority of Russian Orthodox Church in America moves from Alaska to San Francisco.

1878

The Christian Mission in London changes its name to the Salvation Army; Leo XIII begins his service as pope.

1889

Gregorian Chant becomes official music of Roman Catholic Church; the Old Catholic Church writes the Declaration of Utrecht.

1895

The National Baptist Convention is formed; the Church of the Nazarene is formed by Joseph P. Widney and Phineas F. Bresee.

1896

The Salvation Army is founded in the USA.

1901

The beginning of Pentecostal Movement in the USA.

1903

Pius X begins his service as pope.

1905

The seat of authority of the Russian Orthodox Church in America moves from San Francisco to New York City.

1906

The Churches of Christ is founded in the USA.

1907

The Triennial Convention changes its name to the Northern Baptist Convention (America); most Cumberland Presbyterian churches return to the Presbyterian Church USA; the Association of Pentecostal Churches in America merges with the church of the Nazarene to form the Pentecostal Church of the Nazarene.

1908

The Pentecostal Church of the Nazarene is founded in the USA (splits from the Methodist Episcopal Church) and changes its name to the Church of the Nazarene in 1919; jurisdiction of U.S. Orthodox Churches moves from Constantinople to Greece; the first social creed is adopted by the Methodist Episcopal Church.

1911

Mennonite congregation ordains its first women clergy.

1914

Assemblies of God is founded in the USA (splits from the Holiness movement); Benedict XV begins his service as pope; The Old Catholic Church sets up Episcopacy in the United States.

1915

The National Baptist Convention of America splits from the National Baptist

Convention USA due to a dispute over who would control the publishing house.

1917

The Bolshevik Revolution in Russia; United Soviet Socialist Republic (USSR) is created, Christians in the USSR are imprisoned and killed; the Living Church is set up, controlled by the government.

1919

The Church of the Nazarene drops the term "Pentecostal" from its name.

1921

Famine hits Russia and Orthodox Church sells art to feed the starving.

1922

Pius XI begins his service as pope; the Greek Orthodox Archdiocese of North America is founded in the USA; jurisdiction of U.S. Orthodox Churches moves from Greece back to Constantinople before the U.S. is finally given its own jurisdiction.

1923

Foursquare Gospel Church is founded in the USA.

1925

The National Council of Congregational Churches merges with the Evangelical Protestant Conference of Congregational Churches; United Presbyterian Church in North America merges with the Presbyterian Church USA.

1926

The Protestant Reformed Churches in America split from the Christian Reformed Church.

1927

Stalin dismantles the Living Church, reinstates Orthodox Church, and releases clergy from prison camps.

1930

Constantinople is renamed Istanbul.

1931

Congregational Christian Churches is formed in the USA by merging the Congregational Churches with some of the Christian churches

1934

Evangelical and Reformed Church is formed in the USA by merging the Evangelical Synod with the Reformed Church.

1935

The National Association of Free Will Baptists is founded in the USA.

1939

Pius XII begins his service as pope; the Methodist Episcopal Church, the Methodist Episcopal Church South, and the Methodist Protestant Church combine to form the Methodist Church.

1943

Orthodox Church leaders meet with Stalin.

1946

The United Pentecostal Church International is founded in the USA; the Evangelical United Brethren Church is formed in the USA by merging the Church of the United Brethren Church with the Evangelical Association.

1947

The Wesleyan Methodist Connection changes its name to the Wesleyan Church.

1948

The Conservative Congregational Christian Conference is founded in the USA.

1950

The Northern Baptist Convention changes its name to the American Baptist Convention.

1954

The Colored Methodist Episcopal Church changes it name to the Christian Methodist Episcopal Church.

1955

The National Association of Congregational Christian Churches is founded in the USA.

1957

United Church of Christ is formed in the USA by merging Congregational Christian Churches with the Evangelical and Reformed Church.

1958

John XXIII begins his service as pope; Father Carmel Henry Carfova (leader of the Old Catholics in America) dies; Old Catholic Church splinters.

1959

The United Church of Christ adopts its own Statement of Faith; Unitarians merge with Universalists to form Unitarian Universalist Church.

1961

The Progressive Baptist Convention breaks away from the National Baptist Convention USA over level of involvement in Civil Rights movement.

1962

Twenty-first Ecumenical Council (Vatican II) is held in Rome under Popes John XXIII and Paul VI. The Council produces 16 documents emphasizing ecumenicalism Antisemetism is denounced; the Lutheran Church in America (LCA) is formed by merging German, Slovak, Icelandic, Swedish, and Danish congregations; the Southern Episcopal Church is formed.

1963

The American Lutheran Church is formed by merging German, Danish, and Norwegian congregations; Paul VI begins his service as pope.

1965

Calvary Chapel is founded in the USA; Reformed Presbyterian Church Evangelical Synod formed; Mennonites revise their Confession of Faith.

1967

The Confession of 1967 is ratified by the Presbyterian Church USA; the American Baptist Church establishes the General Board Committee on Christian unity.

1968

The United Methodist Church is formed in the USA by merging the Methodist Church and the Evangelical United Brethren Church.

1970

The Episcopal Church begins ordaining women as Deacons; Orthodox Church in America (formerly Russian Orthodox) is founded in the USA.

1972

The Reformed Church in America ordains first women deacons

1973

The United Church of Christ is the first to ordain an openly gay person to ministry— William Johnson; conservatives form the Presbyterian Church in America.

1976

The Association of Evangelical Lutheran Church is founded in the USA.

1977

Vineyard USA is founded in the United States; the Anglican Catholic Church is formed.

1978

John Paul I begins his service as pope, soon followed by John Paul II.

1979

The Reformed Church in America begins ordaining women.

1982

The Presbyterian Church in America merges with the Reformed Presbyterian Church, Evangelical Synod.

1983

The Presbyterian Church in the United States merges with Presbyterian Church USA.

1988

The Evangelical Lutheran Church in America is formed by merging the American Lutheran Church, the Lutheran Church in America, and Association of Evangelical Church; the Episcopal Church recognizes its first woman bishop.

1992

The Charismatic Episcopal Church is formed.

1993

The National Baptist Convention moves its headquarters to Nashville, Tennessee.

1996

The Christian Reformed Church begins ordaining women.

1999

His Eminence Archbishop Demetrios begins his service as Archbishop of the Greek Orthodox Archdiocese in America.

Glossary

Alb: A white tunic with sleeves that covers the body from neck to ankles.

Anointing the Sick: Usually someone who is sick has oil dabbed on his or her forehead while others pray for healing.

Apostles: Those who saw and spoke with Jesus after his resurrection—including but not limited to the twelve disciples.

Apostolic Succession: Some churches trace the commissioning of their clergy back to one of the original apostles. For these churches, only those who are in the line of succession are legitimate clergy.

Arminianism: There are five main tenets of Arminianism: (1) God elects us on the basis of foreseen faith or unbelief, (2) Christ died for everyone, although only believers are saved, (3) humanity is so depraved that divine grace is necessary for anyone to have faith in Christ or accomplish any good deed, (4) God's grace can be resisted, and (5) there's no certainty that all who are regenerated will persevere in the faith.

Baby Boomers: Generally speaking, people born between 1946 and 1964.

Baptism of the Holy Spirit: An additional spiritual experience from salvation through which a believer is empowering to live a holy life, to witness, have greater joy in spiritual service, and a heightened sense of one's mission to the world.

Believer's Baptism: The baptism of those who make a profession of faith.

Bible: Sixty-six books of the Hebrew Scriptures (the Old Testament) and Christian Scriptures (the New Testament) accepted as such by the Synod of Hippo.

Biblical Inerrancy: The view that when all the facts become known, they will demonstrate that the Bible in its original autographs and correctly interpreted is entirely true and never false in anything it affirms, whether that relates to doctrine, ethics or to the social, physical, or life sciences.

Bishop: A priest who has jurisdiction over a diocese in due submission to the larger church leadership.

Book of Common Prayer: The official service book of the Church of England that contains morning and evening prayers, the forms of administration of the sacraments and other public and private rites, the Psalter and the Ordinal (form for the consecration or ordination of bishops, priests, or deacons).

Born Again: A term used by a subset of Christians to refer to the salvation experience. They were once born physically and have now been "born again" spiritually.

Calvinism: A system of Christian interpretation initiated by John Calvin emphasizing the role of predestination in salvation. The five points of Calvinism were developed in response to the Arminian position—(1) *Total depravity:* all parts of a human being is touched by sin—body, soul, mind, and emotions, (2) *Unconditional election:* people do not deserve salvation and that God, out of free choice, gives grace. (3) *Limited atonement:* the grace that God gives is not intended for everyone. Christ did not bear the sins of every individual who ever lived, but instead only bore the sins of those who were elected or chosen for salvation (4) *Irresistible grace:* God's election cannot be resisted, and (5) *Perseverance of the saints:* once saved, always saved.

Camp Meeting: A religious service of several days' length held outdoors where attenders camped because most had traveled great distances.

Cassock: An undergown that is usually black.

Catechisms: Summaries of Christian doctrine for the instruction of those in a particular church.

Catholic: Often applied to the Roman Catholic Church when capitalized, the word simply means universal when lowercase, and refers to the entire Christian church.

Chalice: A cup, considered a sacred vessel, and a figure of speech synonymous with the blood of Christ.

Charismatic: From the Greek word *charisma*, which means "gift." In modern usage, a Charismatic is one who claims to have received from the Holy Spirit spiritual gifts such as speaking in tongues, healing, and miracles. Charismatic theology is similar to Pentecostalism but, in general, Charismatic individuals worship in non-Pentecostal churches.

Chasuble: A circular garment a bishop or priest may wear under the alb and stole.

Christian Perfection: Living as Christ would live.

Church: A body or organization of believers. Can be used to refer to a local congregation, a denomination or association, or the entire Christian community.

Confession: The verbal acknowledgement of personal sin—either privately to God or in the presence of others. In liturgical churches, confession is a sacrament and may involve a priest's absolution. Can be a sacrament or ordinance.

Confessional Lutheran: One who embraces the Lutheran Confessions as revealing God's word and plan for salvation.

Confirmation: The sacramental event in which those baptized as infants confirm their adult decision to continue in the church.

Conservative: Those who resist change and/or defend an established system of beliefs and practices. The content of conservatism depends on the context of the controversy. Generally speaking, Christian conservatives are more concerned with purity and truth than the unity of believers.

Contemporary Services: Often distinguished by music style, these services tend to avoid hymns and gravitate toward choruses. Usually less formal than traditional church services.

Control Freak: A person who attempts to supervise every detail of every situation.

Covenant: A mutual agreement between two or more persons or between a person and God.

Creed: A brief, authorized summary of the Christian doctrine that may be recited as an affirmation of faith.

Dalmatic: A deacon's chasuble that has sleeves.

Denomination: A religious organization uniting in a single legal and administrative body with a number of local congregations. Those at the top of a denomination "dominate" or have the final say over what happens in the local church.

Diocese: Geographical area containing a number parishes, missions, or congregations.

Ecclesiastical Calendar: A list of the feasts kept in any particular church, diocese, or country.

Eucharist: The sacrament of the Lord's Supper in which Jesus is present in the bread and wine.

Evangelical: A classification of Christians who focus on the practical expression of a redeemed life of piety based on inspiration from Bible study, prayer, and evangelizing others.

Fundamentalist Churches: A Protestant view that affirms the absolute authority of the Bible, holds that Jesus died and was bodily resurrected as a sacrifice for humanity's sins, denies the theory of evolution, and holds that alternative religious views within Christianity or in other religions are false.

Gen Xers: Generally speaking, people who were born between 1968 and 1979. Also referred to as postmodernists.

Genuflection: To bend the knee in worship.

Gift of Interpretation: The God-given ability to interpret what people are saying when they speak in tongues.

Good Friday: The English designation of the day in Holy Week marking the anniversary of the crucifixion of Jesus Christ.

Grace: The moving of the Holy Spirit upon a person that results in spiritual transformation.

Holiness: Separateness; anything or anyone that is separated from the common and dedicated to sacred use.

Holy Cards: Cards, usually with a picture of a saint, that are used as a memory prompter for specific prayers (that a good Catholic should know by heart).

Holy Water: Water that is blessed by a priest and consecrated to God. It symbolizes a believer's entry into life through the baptism of water; a person's need for clearing the conscience of sin, and for cleansing our mind of distractions that interfere with prayer. Holy water does not produce these effects, but is a visible, physical help to activate a person to prayer and worship.

Icon: A religious image typically painted on a small wooden panel and used in the devotions of Eastern Christians.

Infant Baptism: A baptism practiced from the second century on, by which infants receive salvation.

Jesus Movement: A movement that emerged from the North American counterculture of the 1960s that was developed as an experiential religious revival attracting teenagers and young adults to the historic tenets of Christianity. Also referred to as "Jesus Freaks," participants synthesized the hippie lifestyle with an allegiance to Jesus Christ.

John the Baptist: Jesus' cousin who prophesied that Jesus would appear, and encouraged his listeners to prepare. He baptized Jesus.

Justification: When a person believes in Christ and his redemptive work.

Last Rites (Extreme Unction): Consists essentially in the unction (anointing) by a priest of the body of the sick person, accompanied by a suitable form of words.

Lectionary: Any book containing biblical passages to be read aloud during worship services.

Liberal: Those who promote change and/or react against an established system of beliefs and practices. The content of liberalism depends on the context of the controversy. Generally speaking, Christian liberals are more concerned with the unity of believers than purity and truth.

Liturgy: A repertoire of ideas, phrases, observances, or rituals prescribed for public worship.

Lord's Supper: See Eucharist.

Mass: What Roman Catholics call their worship service.

Mitre: Headgear worn by bishops.

Monsignor: An ecclesiastical title reserved for bishops and archbishops, chiefly employed when speaking or writing to them.

Ordain: To commission, by the laying on of hands, a person with ministerial or priestly authority.

Ordinance: A symbolic expression of something that has already occurred between you and God.

Parish: A local church.

Pastors: Leaders of local congregations, usually ordained.

Pentecostal: Emphasizes the second experience of the "baptism in the Holy Spirit," and the gifts of the Spirit, especially speaking in tongues. Forerunner of the modern Charismatic renewal movement.

Priest: The minister of worship, and especially of the highest act of worship. In liturgical churches, this term refers to ordained clergy. In Protestant circles, all believers are considered members of the priesthood.

Priesthood of All Believers: Every Christian has direct access to God through Jesus Christ, our great High Priest, the sole mediator between God and human beings.

Puritan: Puritans had a deep conviction that spiritual conversion was central to Christianity. Spiritual rebirth separated the Puritan as one of the elect of God. The church may prepare a person for this experience, and, after it, it may provide guidance, but the heart of the experience, the reception of the grace of God, is beyond the church's control.

Rector: The priest who leads a parish in an Episcopal Church.

Resurrection of Jesus Christ: Three days after Jesus was crucified at Golgotha, he rose again and appeared to many of his disciples in Jerusalem.

Revivals: Predominantly North American Protestant phenomenon in which itinerant preachers exhorted people to accept forgiveness of sin through faith in Jesus Christ and to commit themselves to spiritual disciplines such as prayer, Bible reading, and church support.

Sacraments: Sacraments are outward signs of inward grace, instituted for our salvation and sanctification.

Sanctification: Sanctification is the process by which the Holy Spirit makes us more like Christ.

Sign of the Cross: A gesture of tracing two lines intersecting at right angles symbolizing the figure of Christ's cross.

Speaking in Tongues: When baptized by the Spirit, spiritual gifts are given to a believer. One of these gifts, speaking in tongues, allows a person to speak in a known language they have never learned or to speak in a "prayer language" that no one understands.

Spiritual Abuse: Spiritual abuse is any behavior on the part of a Christian or a church that damages your relationship with God. This can occur in many ways—a particular pastor or leader can misuse spiritual authority within the context of your personal relationship, a group of church members can become toxic, you can be taught to believe false things about yourself or God . . . the list is long.

Stole: A narrow band of colored fabric that deacons wear over one shoulder, and priests and bishops over both shoulders.

Sunday School: A mode of religious instruction, done on Sunday mornings before or after gathered worship.

Surplice: A gown that is white and gathered (the choir members often wear them over the cassock).

Systematic Theology: A branch of theology that tries to present a coherent, overarching schema of Christianity, and relate the faith to present-day settings.

Tradition: The motto for tradition is "because that's the way we've always done it!" Tradition is a pattern of thought, action, or behavior that is passed from one generation to the next.

Trinity Affinity: Relating more to one member of the Trinity than the other two.

Trinity: A central doctrine of the Christianity—that God is comprised of three persons, the Father, the Son, and the Holy Spirit. These three persons are truly distinct one from another and yet remain one God. (I don't get it, but I believe it . . .)

Verbally inspired: The belief that God spoke through the people who wrote the Bible so that their words did not come from themselves, but from God.

Vestments: Special outfits people wear in the services.

Vestry: The council who makes decisions for a parish.

Vicar: The priest who leads a mission.

Wesleyan: The theological and church tradition started by John Wesley in the 1700s that stressed justification by faith as the gateway to sanctification or "scriptural holiness."

Index